The Twin in the

The Twin in the Transference

SECOND EDITION

Vivienne Lewin

KARNAC

First published in 2004 by Whurr Publishers Ltd

Second edition published in 2014 by
Karnac Books Ltd
118 Finchley Road
London NW3 5HT

British Library Cataloguing in Publication Data

A C.I.P. for this book is available from the British Library

ISBN-13: 978-1-78220-143-4

Typeset by V Publishing Solutions Pvt Ltd., Chennai, India

Printed in Great Britain

www.karnacbooks.com

Contents

Acknowledgements

Many people have expressed an interest and have been helpful in my work on the subject of twins. I want to thank them for sustaining and stimulating me through the long process of preparing for and writing this book. I am particularly grateful to Matthew Lewin, Estelle Roith and Rick Morgan Jones who have spent much of their valuable time reading parts of my manuscript critically. I also want to thank the late Dorothy Daniell who has read some of the work. Christoff Hering and the late Eric Miller both helped me clarify my ideas. The late Elisabeth Bryan, Kathy Dallas and the Highgate and Crouch End Twins Club, Jackie Gerrard, the late Peggy Jay, Joanne Gordon, Joan Raphael-Leff, Jane Sarnoff, Professor Lewis Spitz and Marjorie Wallace have provided material and thoughtfulness.

I am grateful to all the patients who have generously given their permission for me to publish aspects of my work with them. I have made all accounts of my work unrecognizable to all except possibly the patient concerned in order to protect the confidentiality of their material.

I have drawn on the work of many published authors both for my general understanding and in referring to accounts of their analytic work. While I may raise critical questions about some of the work, it is always in the spirit of wishing to understand better this complex and fascinating subject. I have as far as possible quoted the sources from which I draw, but I am sure there are some which have become an integral part of my thinking and understanding, which I may have neglected to attribute. To those, I apologize for the omission, and offer my thanks to them for creating a framework for thinking.

About the Author

Vivienne Lewin is a psychoanalytic psychotherapist. She trained at the London Centre for Psychotherapy (now the British Psychotherapy Foundation) and was a training therapist and supervisor for the London Centre for Psychotherapy. She is a Fellow of the British Psychotherapy Foundation and other organisations. She has retired from clinical practice, but continues to supervise, teach, and write.

Foreword to the second edition

There are two possible reasons to buy this book. The first is the obvious one, that it is a profound resource for anyone whose clinical work has ever included work with a patient who is a twin or else with a parent or sibling of twins. The second reason is, I believe, the more important one. It is that Vivienne Lewin has demonstrated the relevance that experience and phantasies about twinship provide. In exploring twin phantasies, we are invited to explore and understand some of the depths of unconscious interaction in the clinical science and art that Freud heralded, in moving from the experience of being a body to the experience of becoming a person with a mind. Those who wish to delve into the complex psychosomatic and unconscious communications that underpin the daily clinical and social experience of split-off parts of the personality and projective identification as both violent riddance and attempt at communication will find this book a rich resource.

The Twin in the Transference demonstrates research in depth. The author has left no stone unturned in her search for narratives: clinical, theoretical, and mythological, in pursuit of producing what I believe is already the defining text on psychoanalytic work with twins. With her perceptive and critical appreciation of other writers' material and with her development of an original theoretical approach, positioned amongst the works of others, I believe that this book's academic standard is beyond clinical doctorate level.

She provides additional fascinating discussion of the ethics of intervening in a twin system in the way the analysis will affect the other twin; the neuroscience of attachment shaped by the insecurities of the twinship experience; the reproduction of the effects of twinship sexuality in real and phantasised incest and later choice of partner. Finally, she addresses the shaping and inhibiting of agonised and releasing grief in the experience of the death of one twin.

In her introduction, she declares her considerable indebtedness to the Kleinian and post-Kleinian traditions in its developments and, although not all of us carry the same orientation, she does illustrate the riches of working within that particular orientation. Particularly acute are the details of her own clinical work with twins. For the way patients' destructive narcissistic wounds are revealed in the subtleties of annihilating phantasies; revealed in her way of reading their material and in her own countertransference. She also deepens Kleinian theory by investigations into the universality of twinship phantasies within the longing for the retreat into fusion and control of the breast in the shape of the ever-present, never-to-be-relinquished twin transference and restricted identity.

Clinically, my view is that the book is well-worth buying for Chapter Six alone, with her description of work with a very entrenched, wounded twin expressing his addictive and destructive enmeshment through the impacts of besieging twin projective identifications fielded, considered, and interpreted by the analyst.

In addition to this piece of clinical practice and research, Vivienne Lewin has made an enormous contribution to professional psychoanalytic psychotherapy. In the years since we began our training together in 1978, within the London Centre for Psychotherapy, she has held key roles there over the years. She has been Chair and Vice-chair of Council, Chair of Training, as well as numerous other commitees, including the challenging work of ethical hearings.

More importantly, she has been one of the significant number of LCP members whose early training left them hungry for a deeper analysis and getting to grips more thoroughly with the need for containment through the use of countertransference, as well as more profound understanding of the traumatised, psychotic, destructive, narcissistic, and perverse violations to person-making that besiege the analyst at work.

Through years of psychoanalytic formation, she has not only put herself in a position to produce this groundbreaking book. Along with others, she has also provided a vision for the positioning of the LCP within the psychoanalytic community, where it carries a reputation as a training institution that produces humane, well-analysed, well-supervised members, competent to search for the holding environment of perceptively timed interpretation that will woo the patient out of destructive, addictive, and omnipotent narcissism into real relating. In consequence, the LCP has been able to pull itself up by its boot straps, from being a course that twenty-six years ago was probably on a par with current less-intensive training courses for psychodynamic counsellors, into the course in intensive psychoanalytic practice it is today. It has been through the leadership of colleagues like Vivienne Lewin that the LCP has been one of the key movers in the recent merger of the British Association of Psychotherapists, The Lincoln Clinic and Centre for Psychotherapy, and the LCP into the British Psychotherapy Federation, with its shared training, standards, and vision of intensive psychoanalytic work in psychotherapy.

At a personal level, it is agreat honour to write this foreword to the second edition that belongs so well in the Karnac list. For many years, Vivienne Lewin and I exchanged peer clinical supervison in a way that gave me personal and professional support and insight in dealing with the challenges that come from the deepening well of doing responsive psychoanalytic work. This experience also gave me insight into the ideas in this book as they were emerging. Those who read it will find, I have no doubt, a deepening of their own capacity to endure uncertainty and wait while the pattern of communication coheres into an experience that can be articulated for the sake of both analyst and patient.

Richard Morgan-Jones
Eastbourne

Preface to the second edition

I decided it was time to bring this book out as an e-book as well as having it in print, hence this new edition of *The Twin in the Transference*. Karnac have been most helpful in arranging this and I wish to express my appreciation of the warm reception I have received from Oliver Rathbone of Karnac.

The substance of the book has not been changed. People have continued to tell me about its usefulness and relevance to their work and thinking, and that it has contributed to their understanding of twin relationships. Although I have continued to research and work with the subject of twins and twin relationships, psychoanalytically I think that the book, as it stands, offers the essence of my understanding about twin relationships, and have decided not to amend it to include new developments or understandings. However, I do wish to mention, briefly, a few of these new ideas in the following pages.

This book explores both the unconscious phantasy of twin intimacy and an analysis of what is revealed in the transference/countertransference experience in clinical work. It addresses the actual experience of working with twin patients psychoanalytically and the complex task of trying to disentangle sensori-motor wired-in dynamics from psychic ones. We see something of this complexity in my brief mention of opposite-sex twins below.

Over the years since I started writing about twins and twin relationships, I have been asked a number of questions about twins—their relationships, their special place in our imagination, and their specific difficulties—issues that are mentioned in the book but which could perhaps do with a little further clarification. In some areas significant new research has thrown more light on the factors that affect twin development and relationships. This is especially so with new research in genetics[1] and epigenetics[2]. I will briefly address some of

---

[1] **Genetics** is the study of heredity and the variation of inherited characteristics, based on our understanding of the sequence of different genes and their impact on development.

[2] **Epigenetics** is the study of changes in the way genes are expressed, as a result of factors (chemical, hormonal, or environmental) rather than changes in the underlying DNA.

these issues below. I will also restate the central theme of this book, linking the nature of the internal twin relationship and our phantasies about twins.

The special qualities of twinship: why are twins so special?

I have been asked why I have focused on the difficulties twins encounter in their development towards maturity and in their relationships with their twin and with others, as they grow older, marry, and have children of their own. It is the developmental difficulties that have concerned me because that is what I have encountered in my work with twins. The nature of these relationships will come alive powerfully in the transference/countertransference relationship between the twin patient and the analyst, and it is here that they can be unravelled and understood, so that new development can take place.

There are specific positive aspects about being a twin, in addition to the particular qualities we project onto twins because of what twins represent to us psychically. Twins may experience an unparalleled closeness and understanding, though it is not necessarily so. Alternatively, they may be intimately connected in rivalry and hatred in an equally binding way. The extraordinary intimacy and closeness between twins represent the "special" factors in twin relationships that are highly prized by the twins, and the parents of twins, and envied by singletons, even though being a twin may create developmental difficulties for twins. We see the special ways twins are perceived in mythology (see Chapter Two) and cultural practices throughout the world, where twins may be regarded as god-like or, alternatively, evil.

The central theme of this book, and of my understanding about twins, focuses on the special, psychic factors that become a central developmental theme in twin relationships. The baby at the breast will have gloried in mother's unconscious attunement to, and understanding of, the physical and emotional needs of her baby. The infant experiences this as having an ideal twin of his- or herself (see Chapter One). This experience is intermittent and, in the gaps, a sense of having lost the ideal breast will ensue, generating a feeling of essential loneliness. The universal sense of longing for a twin is based on an experience that originates from this feeling of essential loneliness. Thus, the infant creates a phantasy twin from his or her good experience at the breast, hoping to alleviate the longing for perfect understanding that is a continuing factor in life—the longing for a twin self.

Our idealisation of the twin relationship is grounded in these concepts:

- each infant creates an unconscious phantasy of an identical twin self, a twin soul who will satisfy the universal longing to be truly known and understood, in an apparent resolution of ubiquitous essential loneliness;
- in twins, the twin self is perceived as being embodied in, or represented by, the other twin (Chapter Three);
- we idealise twins because we perceive them as having the depth of intimacy that we long for.

Phantasies of an ideal twin self are projected between twins, and into twins by others. This prompts our fascination with twins, as we project our own twin phantasies into them. But it may also interfere with the twins' needs to establish separate and individual identities rather than being seen only as twin selves. Many are the times I have heard a twin say, "we were always called 'the twins' rather than called by our names"; "we always received joint birthday cards, never individual ones", etc. Thus, as a result of the processes of internal twinning, parental and other projections, and confusions between and about the twins, twins have additional developmental obstacles to negotiate in their move towards maturity.

The unconscious nature of the twin relationship has deep roots in our earliest sensate and primitive experiences. The enduring nature of the internal twinning is created partly by primal biological and sensate resonances between the twins, both before and after birth. Research on brain development in early life indicates that the fact of being a twin will influence the nature of individual development in each infant according to both bio-rhythms between the twins and between mother and each twin, and affect-regulation by mother and the twin (Chapter Ten); as well as the relationship with mother and mother's relationship with each twin, and the relationship between the twins themselves (Chapter Two).

Clinical work with twins highlights the intensity of the internal twin relationship as it is lived out in the consulting room (Chapters Six and Seven). It elucidates processes that operate not only in twins, but also in all psychic development, processes linked with the centrality of projective identification as a form of communication from which unconscious phantasy can be explored and played with. The transference twin is a central concept in work with patients who are twins, one that is as important as the maternal or paternal transferences, and it is also a primary relationship. In order to understand a twin patient at depth, the quality and nature of the projected phantasied twin will need to be experienced, understood, and addressed by the analyst and the patient.

The aim of this projective identification may be, as with other projective identifications, to communicate something that cannot be otherwise easily expressed. Given the primitive nature of the deepest unconscious aspects of twin relationships, this is sometimes the only means by which the patient can express phantasies and experiences that are pre-verbal, protomental, sensate. It may also be an attempt by the patient to be rid of a troublesome unmanageable phantasy twin. And it may change from moment to moment. These primitive, preverbal, proto-mental phantasies and the experiences upon which they are based, will affect ordinary relationships throughout the lives of twins.

The concept of a phantasy twin is central to our fascination with, and idealisation of, twins, and to the excitement about twins, and the many magical qualities attributed to twins in mythology, and as seen in cultural practices in other countries. A close examination of the transference/countertransference relationships between patients and analysts may reveal not only the unconscious phantasies of twins in both their twinship and individual relationships. We also find out more about how the development of a sense of self, inter- and intra- the twinship, has been affected, at times transformed, by the expectations and the projections of others. The projected phantasies about twins and their relationships can be pervasive.

I wrote this book because I discovered a lacuna in my own understanding of patients with whom I was working, and I needed to explore and develop my understanding of twin relationships. In psychoanalytic practice, it is in the fearless exploration of previously untrodden territory, the search for what we repeatedly feel we have missed, that we find the "aha" moments, the revelations of newer and deeper kernels of personal truth that transform our understanding of the nature of who we are and how we become who we are. If we can risk facing our own uncertainties and gaps, new windows of understanding can open up.

Opposite-sex twins: won't it be different for opposite sex twins?

I have often been asked about the dynamics in relationships of opposite-sex twins, usually with the rider that it must be different from those of same-sex twins. It has been suggested that the twinship would be less entangled because the different sexes of the twins would offer less opportunity for primitive identification and more for individual development; that the dimension of developing sexuality of each twin will be different; or as has been suggested, that the opposite-sex twins will be no more alike than ordinary siblings.

In my experience the central dynamic of the relationship of opposite-sex twins is very similar to that of same-sex twins, either MZ[3] or DZ[4]. The early proto-mental relationship between the twins is just as powerful and indelible for opposite-sex twins as it is for any other twins, and the processes of individual development and separateness will likewise depend on many factors including psychic development, constitutional, parental, and other attitudes to the twin babies, and a deep understanding that each baby is an individual in its own right, as well as being a twin.

There may be some differences in the development of sexuality of the individual opposite-sex twin children, based on primitive and later identifications with the other twin and with the parents in the oedipal configuration. Glenn (1966) presents material from his own work and that of other analysts to support this view. I have not addressed these issues in this book.

---

[3] **MZ** stands for monozygotic twins, i.e., twins from one fertilised egg, so having near identical genetic make-up.

[4] **DZ** stands for dizygotic twins, i.e., twins from two fertilised eggs, so having genes as different as other siblings.

Genetics and environment: the old nature–nurture debate

A great deal of research has been carried out based on the assumption that MZ twins are genetically identical. Genes are the blueprint from which our development takes instruction, but they are rarely the singular factor determining which way it goes, nor are they immutable. There have been many new developments in this field and our understanding of how genes work has increased enormously.

Jay Joseph (2004) addresses this in depth in his book *The Gene Illusion*, where he examines, amongst other things, the much-reported research on cases of MZ twins separated at birth and brought up in different environments. The research findings that he questions state that these twins, extraordinarily and uncannily, make the same life choices, have the same taste and lifestyle, even marry someone with the same name, simply because of their genetic similarity. Joseph examines these studies and concludes from his extensive research that genes *per se* cannot determine how "identical" twins develop, whether reared apart or together. He asserts that many factors were not taken properly into account in the "twins separated at birth" research, thus skewing the findings.

Tim Spector (2012), as he describes in his book *Identically Different*, has explored the factors that operate in the development of all foetuses, both twins and others, according to the activation and de-activation of their given genes. MZ twins have long been regarded as a unique test of genes in action because they come from a single fertilised egg, and start off with identical genomes (the complete set of genes or genetic material present in a cell or organism). MZ twins are literally clones.

Our development depends on the expression of our genes. Research has shown that identical genes can diverge in their expression during foetal development and in the course of a lifetime, as a result of "epigenetic" factors. Epigenetics is the new focus for how we become who we are. It offers an understanding of how our genes will be activated or de-activated, and altered from conception and through life by various chemical, hormonal, and environmental factors, and will affect how we develop and who we become. Most genes act as multiples working together, and there are different versions of genes that become activated or de-activated.

Epigenetic factors will create differences between twins with consequent changes in their developmental patterns. "Epigenomes" are basically chemical switches that activate or de-activate the genes, which then lay the template for the formation of proteins—the building blocks for development of all kinds. Factors, including hormones, chemicals, or the quality of nutrition, will activate or de-activate genes, creating differences even in monozygotic twins.

For twins, the intrauterine environmental differences for each twin will depend on many factors, including the type of placental implantation—a shared placenta or individual placentas; this may affect levels of nourishment, which in turn has consequences for the level of growth affected in each twin and may lead to selective intra-uterine growth restriction where nourishment to one twin is restricted.

As a result of the action of epigenetic factors, the categorisation of twins as "identical" and "fraternal" falls apart, creating a much greater ambiguity in our classification of types of twins, and what we might understand about their genetic similarities and differences, and their development.

Thus, factors like health, personality, taste, and appearance, all depend on both nature and nurture, with epigenetics as the link between the two. Nutrition, space, exposure to hormones, small alterations in epigenetic profile, and minute differences in genome—all these factors create subtle but important differences in each twin. Genes alone do not create physical or mental attributes, or personality traits.

So, I return again to the psychic factors in twin development, both intra- and inter-psychic. If we can understand more about each individual twin person, we will enhance our understanding of early and later developmental processes in all of us, and enable each individual twin to move towards a more healthy sense of individual identity, and to value the twin relationship which is so central a part of their sense of self.

References

Glenn, J. (1966). Opposite-sex twins. *Journal of the American Psychoanalytic Association, 14*: 736–759.

Joseph, J. (2004). Genetic studies of twins reared apart: A critical review. In: *The Gene Illusion: Genetic Research in Psychiatry and Psychology Under the Microscope*, pp. 97–136. New York: Algora Publishing.

Spector, T. (2012). *Identically Different: Why You Can Change Your Genes*. London: Phoenix.

The Summer Garden*

... 'And the swan, as before, floats across centuries,
Admiring the beauty of its twin.

And sleeping there, like the dead, are hundreds of thousands of
footsteps
Of friends and enemies, enemies and friends.

And the procession of shades is endless,
From the granite vases to the door of the palace.

My white nights whisper there
About some grand and mysterious love.

And everything glows like jasper and mother-of-pearl,
But the source of the light is mysteriously veiled.'

* From "The Summer Garden" in *The Complete Poems of Anna Akbmatova*, first published in Great Britain in 1997 by Canongate Books, Edinburgh. Reprinted with permission.

Introduction
Why study twins?

Twins both fascinate and disturb us, and we tend to attribute special qualities to their relationship. In this book, I will explore what lies behind this special interest.

Our fascination with twins is linked with the universal urge towards twinning. The phantasy of having a twin is ubiquitous and is based on developmental factors linked with essential loneliness, a longing to be known, and the creation of a sense of self within a primary object relationship. The specialness with which we regard twins stems in part from our narcissistic wish to be totally understood and merged with an object, as well as from a sense of the uncanniness of the double. I believe that an examination of both the general nature of twinning and of twinning processes as experienced by and exacerbated in actual twins may lead to a greater understanding of developmental processes in both singletons and twins.

Twins excite all sorts of feelings and responses in others and are a source of considerable interest both scientifically and in everyday life. There are many books about twins. There are those written by a twin either to celebrate twinship, or to commemorate or compensate for the loss of a twin, either pre- or postnatally, at any and all ages. Parents of twins write about their experience of bringing up twins, both the pleasures and difficulties that they encounter. Scientists of all descriptions have studied twins for decades in the hope of learning the secrets of inheritability and the progress of both individual development and diseases. Children's books explore the many facets and functions of a phantasy twin through the twinships of the children in the story.

In one sense, I am writing this book as an outsider – I am not a twin, nor am I immediately related to one. However, in my analytic experience as a transference twin, I am an insider with an outsider's perspective. As a psychoanalytic psychotherapist, I have worked individually with a number of adult patients who have a twin, and through this route I have discovered the impact of the twin relationship on the analytic transference relationship. As a result, I have become particularly interested in twinning processes in both twins and singletons. The analysis of the transference twin seems to have been largely neglected in the psychoanalytic literature. This book is about the creation of the twin in the transference and its implications for psychoanalytic work.

While the parents provide a developmental framework for each infant, relationships with siblings offer an opportunity to negotiate and manage peer social relationships. In fact, the existence of siblings propels us into having to confront issues that are not encountered in the parent–child relationship (Mitchell, 2000). The tensions in sibling relationships and between children and their parents are more intense in twins because of the absence of an age gap between the twins. While the twinship lacks the developmental advantages offered by the age difference between non-twin siblings, the twin relationship does provide an opportunity for unparalleled companionship and for an understanding without words reminiscent of the earliest relationship with mother.

The existence of a twin may even ameliorate developmental difficulties in situations of maternal unavailability or neglect. However, a sound 'friendship' is not necessarily a feature of the twin relationship. Many factors will affect how the twin relationship develops, and the extent to which each twin within the relationship develops a companionable rather than a narcissistic relationship with the other twin. Siblings and others may envy the closeness of twins, and the twins may use the twinship to create a barrier between themselves and the parents. I will trace some of these factors through this book.

The book is based on the premise that no two people are identical, not even monozygotic twins. To believe that they are identical is a defence against difference and separateness, whatever the genetic make-up of the twins. There are, to a greater or lesser extent, genetic, psychological and behavioural differences between twins, as well as similarities. However, each twin has to struggle with his/her own processes of development to carve out a personal sense of identity. For each twin, this individuality will overlap to varying degrees with that of the other twin, and this may lead to aspects of a shared identity.

There are two central hypotheses that I plan to explore in this book:

1. Twins are fundamentally affected in their emotional development by the fact of being a twin.

I am taking as a base the Kleinian view that the phantasies of the breast and of the parental couple are innate and are central to the development of each individual. Where then do the other twin and siblings fit in? I believe that the indelible twin relationship is linked with the infant's earliest experiences with both mother and twin, including during the prenatal period. The central internal structure that gives us a sense of identity would be developed through the infant's relationships primarily with its mother and, later, its father, and its acceptance of an oedipal parental couple of a different generation. For twins, this internal structure would be more complicated.

The presence of the other twin leads to a situation in which mother and twins create a triad (prior to the oedipal triad), rather than the dyadic relationship that exists for singletons. As a result, for twins there would be three pair relationships: mother–twin 1, mother–twin 2, and twin 1–twin 2. The initial developmental process, say for twin 1, would be shaped both by the relationship with mother and by the relationship with twin 2. The relationship with twin 2 could theoretically be on a continuum between sibling rivalry and merging, and would include twin 1's perception of the twin 2–mother relationship. It is through this complex structure that each twin will develop a sense of identity.

If the twin bond is strong, it will interfere with each infant's relationship with mother. In addition, mother would be less available to each twin than she would be to a single baby. Whenever she relates to one twin, the other would be at least partially excluded. Placing father in the picture would create six pairs, and four triads, thus complicating the picture further. When mother and father are engaged as a pair, the twins would be excluded, and if awake, they would probably be an interacting pair. If the twins are together, even asleep, it is likely that they would still be aware of each other. Awake or asleep, each twin is contributing to the formative experience of the other twin. Thus each twin has to engage with the processes of, and tensions between, separateness and relatedness to both the other twin and to mother, and later to father.

Separation from the other twin would be more problematic than separation from mother as the twinship offers a narcissistic refuge. At times when frustration may feel difficult to tolerate, twins would, to varying degrees, seek gratification from each other, thus filling the gap and avoiding the space that is necessary for the development of symbolic thought. The rather concrete nature of aspects of twin relationships may be linked with this area of lack of symbolization. There may be a confusion of ego-boundaries between twins and a relative and variable lack of a separate sense of identity. For twins the twinning is not only an external phenomenon. The other twin would be a potent and active internal object, and would be a source of transference manifestations. The emergence of a transference twin in psychoanalytic work would lead to an intense and tenacious relationship between analyst and patient, echoing the internal twinship. This internal twinship is inescapable and lasts for the lifetime of each twin, even after the death of one twin.

The intense sense of closeness between twins is felt by twins to be a special and unique aspect of being a twin. The twin relationship may profoundly affect the resolution of both the early and later oedipal conflicts, thus having a lasting impact on the structure of the inner world of the individual twin. With the acceptance of mother and father as a couple that are not of the generational sameness as the twin couple, development towards the depressive position can proceed. Where such development is hampered, and where there is in any case an additional binding internal relationship with the twin, problems are likely to ensue. The twinship may be used as a 'psychic retreat' (Steiner, 1993).

The nature of the infant's affectional bond with the mother has been shown to affect the development of brain structures connected with emotional relationships (Schore, 1994). I propose that differential brain development ensues as a result of being a twin. With the inescapable presence of the other twin, persistent psychobiological patterns will be created between the twins and in each twin in relation to mother. These psychobiological patterns would affect all their relationships, especially the close relationships such as that of husband and wife, and children.

The internal twinship is a representation of the relationship with an actual twin, alive or dead. The internal twin object is inextricably linked with the 'self', as are parental and other sibling imagos. However, the chronological closeness of the twin pair leads to the development of a unique bond with a consequent internal object relationship that is of a different order from other object relationships. Separation from the internal twin may therefore be experienced as a threat to the integrity of the self at a primal level. Analysis of the twin transference would threaten the unity of the internal twin pair and may be resisted by the patient, even when desirous of separateness from the actual twin.

2. Twinship is generally sidelined and treated as largely irrelevant in current psychoanalytic practice.

Despite Freud's (1900) recognition of the importance and permanence of sibling relationships in our internal world, twins and siblings have been neglected in psychoanalysis. As a result, the presence of the twin in the transference is largely ignored, or is paid insufficient attention by many analysts. I propose that there may be two possible explanations for this lack of proper attention to the transference twin:

a) It may be that analysts underplay the significance of the twin relationship because they are in collusion with the (twin) patient who feels driven to maintain and to defend the twinship against any interference in it, even when overtly seeking to separate from the twin. Separation from the twin may be experienced as extremely threatening, even catastrophic, as it exposes the patient to a loss of known boundaries, with the consequent fear of dropping into a void or 'nameless dread' (Bion, 1962b). This may result in a narcissistic collusion between analyst and patient, echoing the narcissistic twinship, and designed to maintain the 'special' relationship between them and to cover up the painful and difficult developmental matters that are being avoided by the patient. As I hope to demonstrate, the tendency of some analysts to justify this enactment supports the view that there is a cover-up of a state that is too painful to recognize.

b) It may also be that the analyst's recognition of the central importance of the twin relationship and hence of the transference twin, would lead to an experience of the analyst feeling threatened with a loss of parental authority and power. To 'actualise' (Sandler, 1976) the transference twin involves the analyst in becoming, at least momentarily, a rivalrous clinging sibling rather than a more distant and powerful parental figure with enhanced capacities for understanding. Together with the twin patient's anxieties about separateness and difference, recognition of the twinning and the creation of 'sameness' between the analytic pair may cause the analyst considerable discomfort.

There is another perplexing issue that seems to occur almost without comment or question by either professionals or the wider public. I have heard of instances, most commonly amongst monozygotic twins, in which the twins are regarded, and regard themselves, as interchangeable as mothers. Thus we hear of a woman suing for the custody of her twin sister's child after the death of the twin (Segal, 2001) on the basis that they are assumed to be genetically identical and therefore interchangeable. This notion ignores the fact of difference in genetically similar (not identical) twins and suggests that we are no more than a product of our genes. It is genetic determinism gone mad.

Somewhat more frequently one hears of a mother giving her new infant to her twin sister who has lost a child. Perhaps the rivalry in the twin mothers is appeased in this way, but the 'gift' is made in the face of the fact that the infant is the child of one, not both mothers. Surprisingly it seems to raise little comment. The delusional belief in the idea that twins are interchangeable, notably as mothers, is based on a lack of differentiation in both the twin pair and in the public eye. The twin mothers are seen as having achieved the perfect, universally longed for state of at-oneness with another. It is as if twinship has been elevated to a magical sphere where reality is ignored and the 'rules' regarding relationships are unique.

Nomenclature

For the sake of brevity and convenience, I will throughout this book refer to twins as MZ (monozygotic - single-egg twins), DZ (dizygotic - two-egg twins) and DZo (dizygotic, opposite-sex twins). I use the term 'identical' or 'non-identical' twin only in relation to the underlying dynamic processes that are active at any particular moment, and not to describe the genetic status of the twins. While there are certain to be differences in the development of each of these types of twins as a result of their zygocity, I have found that the emotional processes explored in analytic work do not particularly reflect this difference. Twinning processes go on in each type of twinship and are reflected in the transference relationships with the analyst and in many other relationships.

This book is essentially an analysis of the transference twin and its origins. I will therefore use the term 'analysis' when referring to both published descriptions of a traditional psychoanalysis by a psychoanalyst, and also to the work of both psychoanalytic psychotherapists and psychoanalysts who are analysing the twin transference. Thus, I use the term 'analyst' throughout this book in a generic sense for any practitioner who works psycho-analytically. This nomenclature addresses the main focus of the book and avoids the clumsiness of having to distinguish between 'psychoanalyst' and 'psychoanalytic psychotherapist'. My aim is to understand the processes involved in the twin relationship from a psychoanalytic point of view, whatever the training of the practitioner.

In Section 1, I will outline developmental processes in relation to twinning and twins. Section 2 examines analytic work with twins and the associated transference phenomena, and Section 3 explores the enduring nature of the twinship.

SECTION 1
TWINS AND TWINNING

This section deals with the nature and the development of our internal world and the developmental significance of the twin relationship for twins.

The twinning processes between the infant and the breast in the earliest relationship with mother are intimately connected with the twinning processes between twins. Whereas for a single infant, twinning with the breast diminishes with the development of a clearer sense of self, for twins the intimacy of the twinship based on the closeness of the age-identical pair leads instead to a continuation of twinning processes. As a result, each twin faces a more difficult task in differentiating itself from its twin than does an infant from its mother-breast.

Many single children create a phantasy of an imaginary twin based on twinning processes, but this too usually diminishes with greater individual development. However, for twins, the other twin is a constant actual presence rather than an imaginary one. As a result, the process of relinquishing the intense bond with the internal twin is more difficult for actual twins than it is for a single child to 'give up' an imaginary twin. Both imaginary and actual twinships may be used as an aid to development in situations where experiences are felt to be overwhelming. However, the mutual gratification provided by the actual twin relationship also offers opportunities for the twins to use the twinship as a refuge from development. While imaginary twins may also be used in this way, this is a less frequent occurrence and the bond is less potent.

For twins, the merging of the breast-twin and the actual twin creates a permanent internal twinship, with the result that some of the more narcissistic elements of the twin relationship become intractable. This is the internal structure that twins may use as a 'psychic retreat' (Steiner, 1993).

We all negotiate developmental opportunities and obstacles as we grow and mature. What additional or different developmental tasks do twins face? And how does this affect them? In Chapter 1, I will trace the development of a sense of self, and suggest where twins might face particular difficulties. In Chapter 2, I will explore selected mythological and legendary stories that elucidate the unconscious processes that are particularly relevant to the development of twins. In Chapters 3 and 4, I will look more specifically at the development of twins.

Chapter 1
Twinning: the creation of a phantasy twin

Twins have to negotiate the same processes of emotional development as do singletons, but they also have to deal with the fact of being a twin. The presence of a twin both reflects and complicates common developmental phantasies of having a twin. In this chapter, I will briefly describe the processes of emotional development with reference to those aspects that have particular relevance for twins and for the creation of a phantasy twin. My focus will be mainly on Kleinian and post-Kleinian conceptualizations of development.

Loneliness and longing

It is not uncommon to hear someone wondering if they have lost a twin before birth, convinced that this would explain a persistent feeling of sadness, an unsatisfied longing, a sense of incompleteness. While this may have been true for some (the 'vanishing twin' syndrome, Ainsworth, 2001; Lewis and Bryan, 1988), for many it is more likely to be based on a longing for a phantasy twin. This longing for a twin has its origin in the infant's earliest experience in relation to its mother. The close preverbal contact between the unconscious of the mother and that of the infant provides the most complete experience of being understood. However, this contact is inconstant and the inevitable and irretrievable loss of, and an unsatisfied longing for, an understanding without words leads to a sense of internal loneliness. Klein (1963) suggests that this ubiquitous internal loneliness is the 'yearning for an unattainable perfect internal state' (p. 300). A phantasy twin provides the illusion of attaining this perfect state.

In Klein's view, the ego exists and operates from birth onwards, although in the early days it lacks cohesion and would be dominated by splitting mechanisms. Good and bad impulses are split and projected into the object creating the phantasy of a split mother – good and bad. This split engenders a sense of relative security as the good parts of the self and of the good object are preserved and protected from attack by the bad self and bad object. The urge to integrate operates along with the urge to split, and is achieved by the introjection of the good breast, based on the infant's experience with the mother. The 'good internal object' so created becomes the core of the developing ego. As an internal object created by the integration of the split good and bad mother, it is an object that is ambivalently related to, allowing for both doubt and uncertainty (Steiner, 2002).

For twin infants, not only is there a mother with whom each has a developmental relationship, but another baby is always present. If, as I believe, the infants relate not only to mother, but also to each other as primary objects especially in mother's absence, the sense of loneliness in each twin will be ameliorated by the presence of the other twin. It is as if the phantasy twin created to combat loneliness becomes embodied in the other twin. Mourning the loss of perfect understanding with mother may then be avoided by filling the gap with the other twin. The difficulty twins experience in separating from each other is the outcome of this primary bonding with the other twin, especially as they lack the dimension of a generational gap to add differentiation and separateness between them.

In the ordinary course of events, an infant's first contact with its mother is a passionate one, and one that leaves a lasting memory without words. However, the intensity of the contact is intermittent, as if too overwhelming to be maintained, and punctuated by both absence and disagreeable experiences including frustration, discomfort, pain, hunger and rage. When extreme, these unpleasurable experiences might lead to feelings of despair and a fear of disintegration or annihilation. Reuniting with a pleasurable mother brings cohesion again and ameliorates the familiar sense of internal loneliness. In a 'containing' presence (in the sense described by Bion, 1962a), the mother is felt by the infant to be part of itself; in her absence, it is as if that part of the self has been lost. In this state of mind the infant loses its sense of being at one with itself; in fact, of being whole. The sense of wholeness can at best only be fleetingly regained, and at each moment that this close contact is experienced, the infant is also aware that this closeness will again be lost.

The mother at the centre of the infant's world of contradictory and perplexing sensations and disturbance is thus a paradoxical figure, at once familiar yet unknown, bringing satisfaction and relief, but denying gratification; solely possessed but unavailable; a mother who holds the baby in her gaze, but then turns away. As Meltzer and Harris Williams (1988) note, she wears the Giaconda smile – the mother of the infant's phantasies is there and not there. Within this earliest relationship with the mother, born of these paradoxes, is the sense of longing for an available object that knows and gratifies but can never be possessed. The experience of a present/absent mother must be all the more intense and formally organized for an infant who is a twin, whose mother always has another baby in mind, another baby to attend to, an infant who never gains mother's full attention.

Infants are born with an innate preconception of the breast (Bion, 1962a; Money-Kyrle, 1968) and an expectation that there is a mother (Britton, 2002). The 'rooting' behaviour of infants when touched on the cheek is a clear indication of this. In an observation of an infant and its mother just seven hours after birth (Proner, 2000), the infant was noted to seek and respond to attention from its mother in what appears to be a directed way. Proner suggests that a protomental synchrony operates between mother and infant in these very early moments, prior to the use of projective identification (see Chapter 10).

The internalization of the 'containing' functions of mother (Bion, 1962a) through the early relationship between infant and mother, and the infant's identification with this function, results in the formation of what Bick (1968) describes as a 'psychic skin'. The 'psychic skin' functions to 'contain' parts of the self and gives rise to a phantasy of both internal and external space. The construction of a containing object in the internal space provides the apparatus necessary to process experience. Prior to the development of such an internal integrating object, 'the function of projective identification will necessarily continue unabated and all the confusions of identity attending it will be manifest' (Bick, 1968: 484). As will be discussed in Chapters 3 and 4, this has implications for development in twins where a sufficiently stable internal integrating object based on the internalization of the mother may be lacking. In addition, the internalization of the twin as a primary object leads to a lack of an adequately developed individual 'skin' between the twins and a confusion of identity between them. It is as if the emotional 'skin' forms around the twin pair rather than within the individual.

The anxieties associated with the early unintegrated state in an infant, prior to the establishment of a sense of self within a 'skin', may be experienced as catastrophic, a falling into space. Once an internal integrating object has been established, the anxieties are more limited and specific, whether of a persecutory or depressive nature. Klein (1963) notes the importance of the interaction of both external and internal factors in this process. The infant's experience affects the mother's response and vice versa. 'Internalisation of a good breast which can only result from a favourable interplay between internal and external elements, is a foundation for integration which I have mentioned as one of the most important factors in diminishing loneliness' (Klein, 1963: 312).

The introjection of the good (integrating) internal object and the development of a 'psychic skin' may be impaired either by a lack of adequate maternal containment or by the infant's phantasied attacks on the containing object. Inadequate development of such an emotional 'skin' may lead the individual to develop a 'second skin' (Bick, 1968), using secondary measures to try and establish a coherent sense of self with which to negotiate life. These measures might include 'adhesive identification' (Meltzer, 1975), or the development of omnipotent phantasies of a defensive nature, such as an imaginary twin (see below).

The use of 'adhesive identification' leads to a situation where there is no sense of internal space. As a result there can be no phantasy of getting inside an object by projective identification (Mitrani, 1994). This would be the case in autistic states where a sense of being equated and contiguous with the object would instead prevail and there can be no 'psychological birth'. In this state, awareness of physical separateness and the existence of an external world are experienced as catastrophic. For some twins who are deeply enmeshed in the twin relationship, the experience of separation poses just such a threat. Mitrani refers to these states as 'pseudo-object-relations' (Mitrani, 1994: 348) and differentiates them from normal or narcissistic object relations. Any experience of space would be obliterated with a consequent inhibition of human relatedness through the processes of identification. Anxieties in these states would be 'raw and unmitigated panic, equated with the fear of falling forever, of discontinuity of being, of nothingness, dissolution and evaporation – of being a "no-body" nowhere' (Mitrani, 1994: 363). Miss D's experiences (Chapter 8) illustrate a state of mind like this.

With the establishment of an adequate psychic 'skin', the infant begins to develop a sense of self. The wish to understand oneself is bound up with the previously mentioned longing to be understood by a good internal object (see p. 9), and it is this need that engenders the universal phantasy of having a twin. A longing for perfect understanding is based on a phantasy of a perfect 'good object', a twin of oneself. In reference to Bion's work (1967) on 'The Imaginary Twin', Klein (1963) suggests that the twin figure 'represents those un-understood and split off parts [of the self] which the individual is longing to regain, in the hope of achieving wholeness and complete understanding' (Klein, 1963: 302). The imaginary twin thus represents an idealized internal relationship. As the approach towards the depressive position is negotiated, the idealization of the imaginary twin diminishes. This reduction in idealization then leads to greater integration of the destructive impulses and the hated parts of the self. The lessening of omnipotence diminishes the hope of regaining the perfect relationship. The infant experiences considerable pain as a result of the realization that the good object can never approximate the perfection of the ideal object. However, the good internal object helps the infant to tolerate the pain of loss of the ideal object.

The experience of being understood is achieved through introjective and projective identification, provided that neither process is excessive. Bion (1962a) describes the process by which the 'raw' projections of the infant are transformed by a 'containing' mother into thoughts that form a narrative that can be understood. The 'beta-elements' used for projective identification may produce acting out or they may be evacuated. They can also be transformed into 'alpha-elements' suitable for thinking, using mother's 'alpha-function' (capacity for thinking). The infant introjects such 'alpha-functioning', but it may also attack this capacity as a result of its envy or hatred. These attacks result in a loss of contact with self and others, as in psychosis. In contrast, feeling understood leads to an experience of closeness to an object and 'at-oneness' with oneself.

Where the developing infant has experienced a sufficiently containing environment, the helpful introjected objects enable it to move from the paranoid-schizoid position towards the depressive position, and towards greater integration. The infant's tolerable experience of the absence of the object enables the construction of the first thought (Bion, 1962a). The development of symbol formation occurs within the depressive end of the cycle, where the internal integrating object helps the infant to manage the absence of mother by enabling the creation of symbols. This cannot happen until the infant feels able to tolerate the wait for mother, when it feels less persecuted by paranoid-schizoid anxieties. Britton (1998) notes that the movement between the paranoid-schizoid and depressive positions is not one-way. Each time we revisit either position, it will contain different elements from the last time. Further, in our psychic growth through the cycles of the various paranoid-schizoid and depressive positions, we may take refuge from reality in a 'psychic retreat' (Steiner, 1993) in either position.

Meltzer and Harris Williams propose a fundamentally different sequence of development in the infant where they write of the 'ordinary beautiful baby with his ordinary devoted beautiful mother' (1988: 28) as the primary condition of the infant as it emerges from the womb. They suggest that the depressive position occurs before the paranoid-schizoid position in the establishment of a good internal object. In their view, the paranoid-schizoid position is 'the consequence of ... [the infant's] closing down his perceptual apertures against the dazzle of the sunrise' (Meltzer and Harris Williams, 1988: 28). Thus the authors believe that development begins with the impact of a present object rather than an absent object. Symbol formation is then connected with the primary experience of being inside mother and being born; of being with the object, rather than stemming from symbolizing the absent object. The experience of the present object is linked with passion rather than persecution. Object relatedness exists from the beginning in a passionate involvement in the infant–mother relationship, and love and hate come in as a secondary step.

The infant's experience of being overwhelmed by the beauty of the world and of the thinking apparatus exposes it to the 'aesthetic conflict' (Meltzer and Harris Williams, 1988: 7). The infant's first experience of beauty is immediately confronted by not knowing, and is punctured by losses and distortions by the mind. The beautiful object is thus enticing and satisfying, but also tantalizing and tormenting. So here we have the ambivalence again. In this intimate relationship, there is a fear of being overwhelmed by passion, the passion of the infant and the passion of the object. The father intervenes to tame the passionate involvement between the mother–infant pair, and to create a boundary for safe development. While the mother is of over-whelming interest to the infant, she is also experienced by the infant as enigmatic (the Giaconda). The development of a good internal object that can mitigate the loneliness experienced at the loss of the beautiful object is dependent on a capacity to mourn; that is, to experience the beauty of the contact without the need to destroy it when frustrated. A phantasy twin may be used in an attempt to mitigate this loss.

Twinning as a narcissistic state

The creation of a phantasy twin is a narcissistic affair based on the processes of splitting and projective identification operating between parts of the self, or between the self and an external object. Bion (1967) suggests that the breast is the infant's first imaginary twin, omnipotently created. The twin-breast may represent either a feeding-breast or a 'toilet-breast' providing projective relief (Meltzer, 1966). The phantasied twin, a double, an alter ego, thus has several functions. It may be used in an attempt to gratify unfulfilled wishes, or it may be used defensively as a receptacle for unwanted aspects of the self. A phantasy twin may be created at different times in development. It is a normal part of infant development, and is also encountered commonly in children and at times in adults.

I will outline various aspects of narcissistic states of mind that form a background to understanding twin relationships, both actual and imagined.

The infant uses the mechanisms of splitting and projective identification to create a twin, that is, an object as self. Either the mother/breast or an actual twin may be used in this way. In older children, other objects, both animate and inanimate, may serve as imaginary twins in addition. The form that a narcissistic twin object relationship may take will vary, but it is essentially an internal state of mind that is projected into an external object relationship. In a situation where the external object engages in a similarly narcissistic way, the resultant relationship between the two protagonists will itself become a narcissistic system. This would occur between twins or other immature external objects, in contrast with a more mature containing relationship that mother is perhaps more able to provide.

The early infantile mechanisms of splitting the object and ego preserve the good internal object from attack by separating love and hate (Klein, 1946). In a narcissistic relationship both good and bad parts of the self may be projected into the object, and the narcissistic object is then loved or hated depending on whether it contains the good or bad parts of the self. However, if the projective process is carried out excessively, good parts of the personality are felt to be lost to the self and the ego is weakened and impoverished. Twins may be particularly prone to this difficulty not only in terms of how they perceive each other from moment to moment, but also as regards the view of people external to the twinship. It is commonly observed that one twin is perceived as the 'good' twin while the other is 'bad', as the twins embody the splits both between them and in the eyes of the observer.

Twinship is a narcissistic state of mind exemplifying a confusion of ego boundaries between the twins. Rosenfeld (1964) outlines the way in which the self and other may become omnipotently fused in a narcissistic relationship. He suggests that narcissism is a primitive object relationship in which identification takes place by omnipotent projective and introjective identification. The self becomes so identified with the incorporated object that all sense of a boundary between self and object, and of a separate identity, is denied - a feature commonly observed in twins. The anxiety that is associated with the awareness of separateness and an experience of dependence on the object is sidestepped. Frustration and envy of the good and valued breast is avoided by the blurring of the boundaries, and a rigid defence against any awareness of object relations is created. In this way twins may use the narcissistic twinship to avoid the awareness of a need for a mature object.

The overvaluation of the twinship, compared with other relationships, represents what Rosenfeld (1971a) describes as a libidinal narcissistic organization. Rosenfeld distinguishes between libidinal and destructive aspects of narcissism. He notes that Klein stresses the libidinal aspects of narcissism based on a relationship with a good internal or idealized object that in phantasy forms part of the loved body and the self. In libidinal narcissistic states, there is a withdrawal from external object relationships to an identification with an idealized loving internal object - for twins this would be the idealized twinship. The idealization of the self (or the twinship) is maintained by omnipotent introjective and projective identification with ideal objects and values. In this state of mind all that is valuable relating to external objects is felt to be part of the narcissistic individual or twinship. For twins the sense of being doubly powerful as a pair relies in part on their belief that they are in omnipotent control. It is important to note that libidinal narcissism is a defensive state of mind, an essential protector of a vulnerable self.

The twinship may not always be idealized in a 'loving' way, but the twins may instead be bound by destructive narcissistic forces. Rosenfeld (1971a) notes that in a destructive narcissistic organization, it is the omnipotent destructive aspects of the self that are idealized and directed against positive libidinal object relations and against any libidinal part of the self experiencing a need or desire for an object. This leads to severe defusion (unbinding) of the life and death instincts with the resultant increase in the severity of the death instinct that is no longer tempered by the life instinct. The destructive parts of the self may remain disguised and split off. This omnipotent way of existing is often experienced as a good friend or guru, despite its destructive intent. The internal destructive forces maintain the status quo using suggestions and propaganda. In a destructive narcissistic twinship, one twin is not only dominant, but keeps the other twin in thrall, bound submissively in a relationship destructive to them both. The tyranny of one twin over the other is achieved by threats and manipulation, at times in the form of emotional blackmail.

The libidinal and destructive narcissistic states of mind exist side by side and their primary purpose is to hide the awareness of envy and destructiveness that is stimulated by the need for an external object. In twins, a narcissistic twinship protects them from awareness of the need for a parent.

I think it is important to distinguish between a narcissistic state of mind, as experienced in the early infant-mother relationship and the creation of the breast as a phantasy twin, and on the other hand, the development of a narcissistic organization or twinship as described above. Rosenfeld (1987) explores the symbiotic nature of the relationship between mother and infant with particular reference to Margaret Mahler's work on symbiotic states. He describes the 'early infant-mother relationship as a phase of object relations in which the infant behaves and functions as though he and mother were an omnipotent system (a dual unity with one common boundary, a symbiotic membrane...)' (Rosenfeld, 1987: 183). Rosenfeld differentiates symbiotic processes from projective identification. Projective identification involves ego-splitting and projection of good and bad parts of the self, and is based on an essential prerequisite awareness of the separateness of 'self' and 'not-self'. In symbiotic states, in contrast, there is an undifferentiated narcissistic fusion of self and other (mother), creating a delusion of oneness as a defence against feelings of helplessness. In a symbiotic relationship the awareness of separateness has not yet developed, whereas in a narcissistic organization it is the awareness of something known that is avoided. The symbiotic state so described fits with what Proner (2000) has called protomental synchrony (see Chapter 10).

The difference between longing for a twin and feeling trapped in a narcissistic twinship may be explained by Rosenfeld's differentiation between 'symbiotic longing' (Rosenfeld, 1987: 167) and 'symbiotic entanglement' (p. 168). The patient in analysis experiences a basic wish for symbiotic symmetry with the analyst, a wish to create a mirror-like twin relationship in which the analyst experiences identical complementary feelings and experiences in order to provide perfect communication and understanding - like Klein's longing for perfect understanding in the infant-mother relationship. However, Rosenfeld suggests that when symbiotic phantasies have combined with projective identification, a symbiotic phantasy is projected into the analytic situation and the patient feels trapped and unable to find his own self again, while the analyst feels paralysed. He emphasizes the importance of addressing the exact nature of the symbiotic phantasy and not treating it solely as projective identification.

The experience of some twins in relation to each other in what I have called an enmeshed twinship, closely resembles Rosenfeld's description of symbiotic entanglement. The twins feel bound to each other and extremely anxious when apart. But they also feel trapped in the twinship and unable to escape from it, as if they have been sucked in by the other twin. I believe that the early symbiotic processes that have taken place between the twins, as well as between each twin and mother, have been compounded by omnipotent projective and introjective identification. What is then created is a symbiotic entrapment in the twinship, where each twin feels trapped in the relationship with the other twin and unable to find a separate identity.

As I describe in an earlier paper (Lewin, 2002), the Gibbons twins (Wallace, 1996) are an example of extreme entanglement. June and Jennifer Gibbons were MZ twins who kept themselves isolated from their parents and siblings, and from the external world. From childhood, they shared a secret language and spoke only to one another, and to a younger sister. They allowed no parental intervention in their twin relationship, and perhaps not much parental attention was available in this displaced and isolated family. At school the twins remained frozen in their silence. As teenagers, they became even more reclusive. They exhibited rather bizarre and delinquent behaviour and at 17 they were jailed for repeated arson and theft. In jail they were separated.

Wallace describes her first interview with June in prison:

> I could see June's eyes flickering and her mouth edging into something resembling a smile. But her words were torn whispers, her whole being was strung between a desperate need to speak and some destructive internal command which forbade her such freedom. She would start to tell me something, then suddenly gag as though an invisible presence had put its hands around her throat. Who or what could hold such power over a human being, to compel her to lifelong silence and immobility? What inner force gave her the strength to reject everything and everyone offering help or affection? What had happened to allow a potentially attractive young girl to waste her youth, not just behind the walls of a prison but behind her own private defences? (Wallace, 1996: 5).

Jennifer Gibbons expressed the hatred between the twins by saying: 'She should have died at birth. Cain killed Abel. No twin should ever forget that' (Wallace, 1996: 140).

June writes:

> Nobody suffers the way I do. Not with a sister. With a husband – yes. With a wife – yes. With a child – yes. But this sister of mine, a dark shadow, robbing me of sunlight is my one and only torment (Wallace, 1996: 167).

And finally, the mortal entanglement and ambivalence between the twins is graphically expressed in a poem by June Gibbons:

> Without my shadow would I die?
> Without my shadow would I gain life?
> Be free or left to die? (Wallace, 1996: 255).

What leads to the development of such crippling narcissistic states of mind as those encountered in the Gibbons twins? Britton (2000) notes that two factors are central to the development of narcissistic disorders: constitutional factors may lead to a failure of primary splitting in the paranoid-schizoid position, and this may be further enhanced by a lack of containment by the primary caregiver. Narcissistic love is centred on the elimination of difference and a force within the narcissistic organization is hostile to object relationships. Britton maintains that libidinal and destructive narcissism differ in their aims. Libidinal narcissism is a defence against adverse object relations and is motivated by a wish to preserve the capacity for love by making the love-object seem like self, thus defending love. Destructive narcissism is based on hostility to object relations and the wish to annihilate the separate identity of the love-object, the aim being destructive rather than defensive. While neither type is encountered in pure form, one type will be predominant.

The generational sameness of twins, their lack of maturity, and in MZ twins the particular similarities between them, create a situation in which splitting and projective identification may continue unabated without the interference of a mature container. This offers an ideal opportunity for the development of a narcissistic system both inter- and intra-psychically. Twin relationships contain a mixture of both libidinal (protective and loving) and destructive (hatred of separateness and a separate identity) narcissism, with a coexistence of both types. As will be seen in the case material in Section 2, twins are torn by opposing needs. On the one hand, they feel a need to protect the twinship from outside interference, as if they are in a narcissistic loving embrace that denies separateness and difference, with a hatred of external object relationships. On the other hand, they feel a need for separateness and individuality – but an object relationship with the other twin is viewed with hostility, with a resultant wish to destroy the clinging twin self. As the other twin is to a greater or lesser degree experienced as self, the hostility to external object relations and to any interference in the narcissistic system is enhanced. The twins feel a need to protect the closeness (libidinal aspects) of their relationship, while at the same time wanting to rid themselves of unwanted aspects using the other twin as a 'toilet breast' (Meltzer, 1966).

Britton (2000) stresses that a narcissistic state is not just a withdrawal from external objects to an internal one. 'It is a particular kind of internal object relationship in which the separate existence and particular qualities of the internal object are denied and an internal object relationship created by projective identification' (Britton, 2000: 3). An idealized internal twin may be created to avoid a hostile or ego-destructive superego, thus avoiding the ego's need for a loving relationship with the superego. Britton suggests that in the libidinal, defensive narcissistic organization, the main factor is a lack of containment by the parents, while in the destructive narcissistic organization, object hostility in the infant is the major factor. Twins must inevitably suffer less containment by mother as a factor of the twinship. Whatever constitutional factors they possess, their use of each other as primary objects will enhance the development of a narcissistic relationship between them based on a denial of difference. Thus the likelihood that twins will develop a narcissistic system inter- and intra-psychically is high.

I will draw on Rosenfeld's and Britton's ideas regarding thick- and thin-skinned narcissism further to explore the relationship between twins. Rosenfeld (1987) suggests that 'thick-skinned' narcissists have created a narcissistic structure so impervious that they become insensitive to deeper feelings. 'Thin-skinned' narcissists, on the other hand, are hypersensitive and easily hurt. I propose that for twins, there is a too-thin narcissistic skin between them that allows great permeability and the interchange of projective and introjective identifications, resulting in enmeshment and a lack of separateness. The twins are hypersensitive to each other and it is frequently observed that the quality of communication between twins seems of a different order than that with others. The sense of 'perfect understanding' between twins is cherished by them and they frequently speak a private language.

Twins preserve the empathic understanding between them by splitting off any aspects that threaten their unity. In this situation, a relationship with a parent is felt to be an intruder into the empathic twinship. While the 'skin' between the twins is thin, the 'skin' around the twin pair is thick, making them relatively impervious to the world of external object relations, and to parental intervention in the twinship. Britton (1998) notes that the objectivity of an observer in a triangular rather than a dyadic relationship is felt to threaten the mutual empathic understanding between the pair. The observer is regarded as a source of malignant misunderstanding, an intruder to be kept out by denial. The narcissistic twins exclude parental intervention and even the need for a parent, like 'Twin internal souls united by a narcissistic love that might make redundant the ego's need for that love from the super-ego ...' (Britton, 2000: 30). The exaggerated subjectivity of the thin-skinned narcissistic relationship between the twins is encapsulated by means of their thick-skinned narcissistic relationship against the objectivity of the external world. Difference is eradicated and the oedipal conflict is evaded, as a result of which the capacity for thinking is reduced. This encapsulated dyadic situation may be supported in analysis by transference–counter-transference enactment (see Chapters 7 and 8).

Phantasy twins and imaginary companions

I have discussed above the creation of an omnipotently controlled phantasy twin in a narcissistic frame of mind, in both a singleton and in actual twins. Phantasy twins may be both unconscious and conscious constructions, and as already noted, the purpose for which they are created may vary.

The nature and the duration of a phantasy twin are important factors in the development of a sense of self. One of the major functions of a phantasy twin is to create a self that is felt to be more acceptable while the unacceptable aspects belong to the created twin. Meltzer and Harris Williams suggest that such narcissistic forms of identification are both projective and adhesive, and 'produce an immediate and somewhat delusive alteration in the sense of identity' (1988: 14). Introjective processes, on the other hand, modify our internal objects, 'setting up gradients of aspiration for the growth of the self' (Meltzer and Harris Williams, 1988: 14). Integration of the split-off aspects of the self (the phantasy twin) allows for growth and development. In contrast, a lack of integration of the phantasy twin leads to an arrest in development.

Internal object relationships are phantasies about lived experiences. Meltzer and Harris Williams point out that early internal object relationships are based on somatic stimuli, while later ones are influenced by the development of the perceptual apparatus and symbolic thought, and are thus influenced by the external world of object relations. Both early and later types are omnipotent phantasies based on splitting and projective identification. The developmental stage during which these processes occur will thus affect the nature of the created phantasy twin. The phantasy twin that is created by the infant will relate to the more primitive aspects of part object relating linked with somatic stimuli and the close relationship with the mother. For an older child, the awareness of and relationship with the external world, and the perception of external objects, will influence the nature of the phantasy twin.

The motive for the creation of the phantasy will be affected by the nature of the current anxieties. A phantasy twin may be created to represent a missing object relationship in the hope of regaining lost aspects of the self, and this serves a developmental motive. The splitting of the self in order to avoid recognizing loneliness by creating an imaginary companion may be defensive, but it may also have an organizing function. However, the splitting off of hated aspects of the self, which are projected into the imaginary twin and disowned, may have a more deleterious effect on development if not later integrated with the self.

The phantasy twin/breast of infancy, created within a developmental sequence, is an unconscious phenomenon. The imaginary companions and phantasy twins of childhood are, in contrast, conscious creations, although the mechanisms by which they develop and the function they serve may be similar to those already discussed. In a child, a phantasy twin may be helpful in enabling the child to fill the gap when a love-object has withdrawn or is felt to be unavailable. In this situation it may be used as a transitional stage in development, until the child feels able to relinquish control and tolerate the feelings of loss. Alternatively the phantasy twin may be used as a refuge from the pain of the reality of a temporary or permanent loss, in a longer-term internal arrangement, sometimes persisting into adulthood. Thus the phantasy twin may be variously used to gratify a longing for an object, as a temporary mechanism dealing with an unbearable situation, to maintain omnipotent control of an object, or to avoid an external object relationship altogether.

I will explore some of the cases in the psychoanalytic literature where phantasy or imaginary twins and companions illustrate some of the various functions of twinning.

A phantasy twin that is used as a refuge impedes development. Coen and Bradlow (1982) note the importance of distinguishing between the temporary developmental use of a phantasy twin and that of a stable persistent paradigm of twinship that extends beyond childhood and becomes active in the transference relationship with the analyst. They describe a patient whose mother is a twin and the transgenerational twinning that occurs. I discuss their paper in Chapter 11, where I consider the effects of twinship on intimate relationships. The persistent twinship that Coen and Bradlow refer to is the conscious awareness of a twin as it was uncovered in analysis; the analytic material described below reveals unconscious twinning of a detrimental nature.

A persistent paradigm of a conscious phantasy twin in an adult has been described by Bach (1971). He reports on the analysis of a woman who had created a phantasy twin that remained an important figure not just in childhood, but throughout her adult life. The patient's mother had been depressed and emotionally unavailable when she was born, and kept her young daughter confined to the house much of the time, for her own narcissistic needs. The grandmother, who had moved in to care for the child, had died when the patient was four years old. The patient's phantasied twin was built on an identification with grandmother, to avoid the stifling narcissistic relationship that the child had had with mother. The patient used the imaginary twin in her relationships with both parents – to avoid closeness to mother, and to establish a second-hand link with father. As a child the patient engaged in a daily ritual with her father in which he would tell her of his day in the outside world, and she would tell him stories of her phantasy twin's imagined adventures during her day.

The phantasy twin created by this patient appears to have been a narcissistic object that both mediated and interfered with her relationships with her external objects. The patient had thus created a refuge, using the imaginary twin in order to avoid real external relationships with either her parents or later with possible partners in her life. The phantasy twin represented a 'persistent, stable paradigm of twinship' (Coen and Bradlow, 1982: 613) which, while protecting her, also hindered rather than served her developmental needs.

A phantasy twin may either be integrated into the ego or it may be maintained as a refuge to avoid the integration of hated aspects of the self. Bach (1971) suggests that where a phantasy twin serves a developmental function, it will later be forgotten. Where it is retained in adult life, this can be taken as an indication of an emotional lag; i.e. it has served as a refuge from development. In each of the cases studied by Bach, the phantasied twin 'represented some vital aspect of mastery or competence, a core element of the active or spontaneous self' (Bach, 1971: 169), and its integration into the ego was therefore essential. In a developmental refuge, the phantasy twin remains neither completely integrated into the ego nor relinquished. To abandon the twin would be experienced as losing an important part of the self, while to integrate the twin would be felt to be too conflictual and beyond the synthetic capacity of the individual at that time.

The creation of a destructive narcissistic twin may have a devastating effect on development. Grotstein describes the perverse use of an unconscious 'negative twin' (Grotstein, 1979: 136). He examines the difference between creative imagination and what he calls pathological or 'negative imagination' (p. 136), the latter being a phantasy in which the infant can 'imagine away' (p. 136) painful experiences. Using Klein's concept of the 'lavatory breast' into which bad feelings are projected out, he notes that the infant not only believes that it has created a transformed internal object (as noted by Meltzer and Harris Williams, 1988), but that it has also given birth to a twin, 'a negative self, whose content is all he wished to evade' (Grotstein, 1979: 156). The negative twin is almost completely split off from the lively 'creator twin' (Grotstein, 1979: 136). Grotstein describes this negative twin in similar terms to Rosenfeld's 'gang' in negative narcissism, bent on destruction, and trapping the vulnerable infant by blackmail.

Grotstein reports on pathological twinning in the analysis of three patients. The first is a man who created an alcoholic twin in order to preserve the feeling of being unborn and therefore not having to face the world. The second patient used a phantasy twin to deaden or attempt to erase painful traumatic experiences from her early life and current disturbing experiences. She brought her phantasy twin to analysis to be cured, to 'plug the holes in her imperfections' (Grotstein, 1979: 157), so as to re-empower the twin in its deadening and murderous activities. The third patient also sought to remain unborn and evade any progress by using a phantasy twin. She turned to her twin for help instead of her analyst, and used the twin to try to persuade her analyst out of role, thus making him useless. Grotstein notes, 'The "twin" is the product of an act of birth by the imagination pressed into the service of denial of Truth. The return of the evaded Truth is felt to be; like a cross to a vampire – it means its very death' (Grotstein, 1979: 158).

In psychotic splitting, as described by Grotstein above, the dissociation of parts of the self is maintained by omnipotent destructive mechanisms. Nachmani (1979) suggests that the phantasy twins created by psychotic splitting are of major importance in the pathology of the individual. He believes these patients to be unanalysable because they lack a capacity for symbolization, although Grotstein (above) seems to have had success in his work with such patients. Nachmani notes that the imaginary companion or twin of normal childhood is ego-syntonic and at the service of development. It may at times be an imaginative solution to loneliness, providing companionship and consolation (a view also expressed by Myers, 1976). However, a destructive, narcissistic psychotic twin generates an experience of 'dread, fear of control, harsh criticism, humiliation, and generally "not me"' (Nachmani, 1979: 447). The psychotic twin's main function is to denigrate and disparage a need for others and it is the source of negative therapeutic reaction for these patients. What is denied is not just a need for dependency, but that dependency needs have not been met. (Britton describes a similar situation in a patient, see page 23.)

In this world of omnipotent phantasy, needed others are avoided and links are dismantled and reassembled with the purpose of maintaining the neglect rather than of repair, as the original neglect is denied. This results in a psychotic loss of reality and integrity. The potential for resolution lies in the capacity for metaphor, for symbol formation, but where this is attacked by the denial of a reliable external reality, there is little room for progress. Nachmani speculates that an ego-syntonic imaginary twin in childhood reflects a history of good-enough maternal care, an infant that was loved, accepted and sufficiently cared for. In contrast, a degrading phantasy companion emerges from a substantial absence of such experiences.

At this extreme end of the scale, Rhode (1994: 64) writes of psychotic splitting and the terror engendered by an experience of the catastrophic nature of change:

> The psychic ovum splits, and, secure in the symmetry of their relationship, two identities, the self and its *alter ego* travel down the same birth passage and through the same passage in time, as bound as the self and its mirror reflection. But the two personalities within the rigidly mask-like structures are unstable and interchangeable and possibly in a state of mutual projective identification with each other.

Rhode describes the idealization and concretization of the created phantasy, and the extreme opposition of the split aspects of the psychotic self. One aspect carries all the life, the other psychosis and death. Any attempt to renounce omnipotence and engage with depressive anxieties leads to a renewed deathly attack, as if allowing oneself to experience any vulnerability is a concession to an enemy. These twins are united in a deadly embrace.

The role of an ego-destructive superego in the creation of a phantasy twin has been addressed by Britton (2000). He describes the analysis of two patients, both of whom had developed an ego-destructive superego in consequence of a lack of containment. One patient developed a narcissistic phantasy-twin relationship as an alliance against the murderous superego. But the murderousness was evident in the narcissistic internal phantasy-twin relationship, and was expressed in a dream. The destructive narcissistic relationship with the phantasy twin was also realized externally in a perverse sado-masochistic relationship. As noted above, Britton suggests that where destructive narcissism exists, it is probable that the infant's object hostility is the major factor resulting in the lack of containment that leads to the development of the narcissistic object relationship.

Another patient described by Britton (2000) created an ideal twin to evade a relationship with the superego in a situation where mother was not just absent, but was a negating presence. The patient created an imaginary companion in order to avoid expecting help from a destructive mother. As noted by Nachmani, not only was the patient's need denied, but the fact that the infant's dependency needs were not met was obliterated. In place of an internal maternal object, there was a void. The patient had limited her expectations of her mother by seeking a soulmate elsewhere. The twin soulmate was an ideal self, a primary love-object of an ideal mother such as the patient had never known. The idealized phantasy twin could then be used to play both parts in the relationship: as an ideal mother, and a loved child. In this way, via projective identification, the patient could experience vicariously the love she had never known. This patient represents a predominantly libidinal type of narcissism, and Britton postulates that a lack of containment, rather than the infant's hostility, is the primary factor in its formation.

The conscious phantasy twins and imaginary companions of childhood

The imaginary twins or companions of childhood are consciously used by children as an aid to or avoidance of difficulties encountered in relation to their primary and oedipal objects. It is common to hear children talking about these imaginary companions as if they were present, both knowing and not knowing of the phantasy nature of their companion.

The creation of an imaginary companion or phantasy twin is commonly regarded as a defence against oedipal anxieties (Burlingham, 1945; Arlow, 1960), or against the loss of a loved object as the result of the birth of a younger sibling (Nagera, 1969). Burlingham has studied twins, both phantasy and actual, extensively. She suggests (1945, 1952) that in children in the latency period, the imaginary twin provides constant attention and love, and an escape from loneliness and solitude. This twinning has more to do with companionship than with Klein's views on the origins of essential loneliness and, as a conscious phantasy, it is of a different order from the breast as twin. Burlingham suggests that the phantasy twin is conjured up to take the place of the lost love-object by providing an inseparable companion to mitigate the pain of the loss. The desired twin of the childhood daydream is always a child (Burlingham, 1946), and of the same sex (Myers, 1976). Toys and animals are also used as twinned objects.

Children might imagine a twin as an addition to themselves in order to overcome their sense of inferiority. A characteristic of an imaginary twin is that it provides an illusion of great strength and invincibility, the two combining to provide double strength. The phantasy twin is a narcissistic object, someone like self, created in the child's own image. The phantasy twin might therefore complement the child in what s/he feels s/he lacks, as if the twins were two halves of one person (which indeed they are!). The love of the phantasied twin is a cover for narcissistic love, in the guise of object love. The phantasy twin may also be used to resolve ambivalent feelings by assigning some conflictual feelings to the twin. The 'twins' might thus represent two sides of an emotional conflict and the phantasy twin can be used to express discord and unity within the self.

Nagera (1969) also addresses the issue of the use of a phantasy companion either for the purposes of development, or as a retreat from reality to avoid depressive anxieties. He notes that the phantasy twin is observed in children between the ages of two and a half and ten years, but that it is rarely a feature in children who are in analysis. (Perhaps these children use their analyst as a twin, to enable them to either contain or avoid their difficulties.) In adult analyses, memories of an imaginary companion are rarely recovered. In cases where the imaginary twin is remembered in adult analysis, the phantasy figure has continued to play an active role in the patient's life – a persistent internal twinship.

In child analysis, an animal or toy might be regarded as a 'companion' part of the child, expressing feelings that are felt to be unacceptable. This type of encounter in the analysis of a child is more transitory and of a different nature from the creation of a longer-term phantasy twin who remains a constant companion to the child. Nagera suggests that it is the emotional immaturity of the child that leads to the creation of imaginary companions. Imaginary companions may be used to master conflicts and anxieties related to splitting and projection, until the child has achieved better control of its impulses. They may be used as superego auxiliaries until a superego is better established, in an intermediate step between reliance on external parental controls and the internalization of these functions.

The appearance of imaginary twin may be linked with mother's temporary withdrawal from the child, as when a new baby arrives. The imaginary companion created by the child is a more reliable and faithful figure than the mother who has turned away towards the new baby. The child defensively withdraws from the unpleasant external world to a more satisfactory internal world (i.e. a narcissistic state), from a world of real objects to imaginary ones. The initial withdrawal is quickly followed by the return to external reality and object relatedness. 'Having found a new solution, the child brings his imaginary companion back into his real life and tries to have it integrated with and accepted by his object world' (Nagera, 1969: 195).

In summary, Nagera (1969: 194) notes:

> I have earlier stated that the imaginary companion phenomenon is a special type of fantasy (and fantasying) that has all the characteristics of daydreams. Like ordinary daydreams, the imaginary companion fantasy is an attempt at wish fulfilment of one sort or another, is ruled by the pleasure principle, can ignore the reality principle, and need not be reality adapted, yet the fantasying person remains fully aware of the unreality of the fantasies that are being indulged in. In other words, reality testing remains unimpaired.

It is evident that the creation of a phantasy twin, whether in the infant or older child, or the maintenance of a phantasy twin in an adult, is based on the same processes of splitting and projective identification. The purpose may be benign or the aim may be the avoidance of difficult or painful experiences by the destruction of links. Whether the individual is consciously aware of the twinning or not, it is necessary for the phantasy twin to be integrated with the ego, in order that development may proceed satisfactorily. Where such integration is not achieved, the phantasy twin remains as a narcissistic refuge that hinders emotional growth and the adequate establishment of a sense of self.

Chapter 2
Twins in myths and legends

The twins of myths and legends illuminate our understanding of the processes of twinning. I will explore several mythical or legendary stories to illustrate some important dynamic processes of twinning including splitting and the creation of a double, love and hate, and rivalry.

Myths of creation, of splitting and doubles

In the Platonic discourse on the nature of love, Aristophanes proposed that the original nature of man was not as we now know it. A being of double nature, with two heads, four arms and four legs was split to create two halves that became a man and a woman. The motivation for this split was that these double beings were terribly strong and so full of themselves that they tried to attack the gods. Zeus decided to humble their pride and mend their manners by cutting them in two. In this way their strength would be diminished and their numbers increased. As these beings made offerings to the gods, splitting them in two would make them more profitable to the gods, doubling their value. Zeus thus halved them, healed their wounds and humiliated them, creating two halves that each desired the other half. On coming together, the two halves embraced and were so eager to grow into one again, that they would have died of hunger rather than separate. If one half died, the other half sought another mate to whom to cling. Zeus rescued them from this difficulty by adjusting their genitalia so that they could breed by sowing their seed in one another in an embrace, rather than on the ground like grasshoppers. Our desire for one another was thus founded in a wish to regain our original nature, making one of two. Each one, when separated, is but a half and is always looking for the other half, like lost twin souls:

> And when one of them finds his other half, ... the pair are lost in an amazement of love and friendship and intimacy, and one will not be out of the other's sight ... even for a moment: these are they who pass their lives with one another; yet they could not explain what they desire of one another. For the intense yearning which each of them has towards the other does not appear to be the desire of intercourse, but of something else which the soul desires and cannot tell, and of

which she has only a dark and doubtful presentiment ... human nature was
originally one and we were a whole, and the desire and pursuit of the whole is
called love. (Plato's Symposium, 360 BCE: 722).

This longing and loneliness (discussed in Chapter 1) is something we all
recognize and it is highlighted in twins, as will be seen in the case material in
Sections 2 and 3.

The idea that twins are two halves of one being, and were created by
splitting, is relevant not only biologically to monozygotic twins where the
fertilized egg has actually split to create two foetuses. In addition, both mono-
and dizygotic twins commonly have a sense of shared identity. When alone,
twins often experience a feeling of incompleteness, of something essential
missing. They feel lonely, yearning for a lost part of the self. Where one twin
dies, the surviving twin's sense of longing and loss can be overwhelming, and
there are many accounts of endless waiting, yearning to be reunited with the
lost twin (see Chapter 12). Rivalry between twins may also be intense, and
complicates their sense of oneness. Twins who feel they are two parts of one
person would experience any expression of violence towards the other twin
as a violent act against the self. Consequently, twins often adopt
complementary roles in order to deal with their rivalry and to limit their
sometimes murderous wishes towards each other.

Myths as unconscious phantasies

Myths are the stories we create to express, and to understand and resolve,
unconscious processes and conflicts. They represent universal phantasies
and can be analysed like dreams. Unconscious aspects of the psyche are
projected onto legendary figures in stories about the birth and evolution of
mankind, the coming into being of the psychological self. Mythical figures
are thus representatives of our internal world, an historical memory of
universal phantasies and struggles. Twins and doubles feature prominently in
myths and legends and they offer insight into particular unconscious
processes, notably the universal tendency to splitting, and the phantasy of an
identical or complementary other that may be used either as an aid to
integration or to disavow aspects of the self.

Myths and fairy tales have been described as 'the products of ethnic
imagination' (Freud, 1913: 185); or dynamic tales that explain the past, the
present and the future (Lévi-Strauss, 1955). Bion (1962a) proposes that a
'myth' is for the group what a 'model' is for the individual. That is, like a
model, a myth is an abstraction or artefact that is composed of elements of
experience. It is created to explain and communicate the experience in order
to test the validity of the experience by comparing it with the observable
facts.

Myths are a narrative way of organizing and making sense of human
experience and are used to try to master the unknown. Priel (2002: 436)
suggests that

> myths are intimately associated with the concept of primal phantasies as organising structures of phantasy life ... providing a narrative version of the problems of mental growth and human knowledge, its dangers, and the relationships between the individual and the group with respect to the search for knowledge.

Myths are symbolic representations of our experience as we move psychically from the more concrete objects of the paranoid-schizoid position towards the depressive position. Symbols in the internal world are the product of the experience of object relationships and are a means of creating, recalling and restoring the original object – they represent, but they never become, the original object. As object relationships are the essence of myths, myths have great significance in enabling us to understand our unconscious processes; and Anzieu (1979) states boldly, 'Greek mythology contains almost all there is to know of the unconscious' (p. 31).

The origin of myths in our earliest experiences is taken up by Luzes (1990), who suggests that myths are the product of archaic unlived and unused elements that exist in all of us and hail from the period of lack of differentiation of self and other, the earliest mother–infant relationship. Some of these elements correspond to primal phantasies and give rise to internal tensions that demand discharge or reworking, thus creating myths. Luzes further suggests that phantasies of brother–sister incest (and hence twin incest in mythological figures) have at their core phantasies of having a twin or imaginary companion, and of possessing the attributes of both sexes (see Chapter 11).

Two myths in particular seem to occupy a ubiquitous place in psychoanalysis: the stories of Narcissus and of Oedipus. Each refers to specific aspects of individual developmental history, and the lack of successful resolution of internal conflicts associated with those stages. Narcissus represents the difficulties and ultimate failure in the dyadic stage, the lack of recognition of the good breast, and the withdrawal from object relatedness. This lack of internalization of a good breast has implications for future development and character formation – it will adversely affect the successful resolution of the oedipal conflict that represents the infant's relationship with both parents. The lack of recognition of the parental couple as the sexual couple from whom the infant is excluded, and the lack of establishment of triangulation in which a third position is established, will interfere with the development of the ability to think.

There are several myths in which splitting or the creation of a double is central, and in which the creation of mythical twins elucidates the processes involved in twinning. The creation of two from one, or two representing different aspects of one, as in the Plato story above, are common themes in mythology. Stories of the creation of mankind are centred on such splitting, the creation of man and woman, of a double, of twin-like first beings, or gods and goddesses. The relationship between them, the bonds or disturbances, is also the stuff of myths, and represents the internal figures in the struggle for intimacy, love, and the envy and jealousy within actual relationships.

The sense of the uncanniness of twins and their apparent sameness contains complex feelings that exist both between the twins and in the perception of others in relation to them. Girard (1988) suggests that a perceived lack of difference between people, exemplified by twins, leads to feelings of violence which have to be managed or suppressed in order to protect society. This protection involves rigid ritual practice of a rather obsessional and superstitious nature. In many societies twins, and sometimes the parents of twins, are killed or banished in order to protect the group from such violence. An alternative way of managing these feelings is through idealization of the twins, as is the custom among the Yoruba of Nigeria, where prayers and gifts relating to the twins keep the society safe (Ulrich, 1996).

In Western societies, twins are not overtly regarded as harbingers of violence and destruction, but tend rather to be idealized. The sense of the uncanny in relation to twins probably relates to the very primitive phantasies about twins and their 'sameness', or lack of difference. The violence must be managed between the twin pair as well as within the society. Engel (1975) describes how aggression between twins may be dealt with via the development of complementarity between them. In order for the inter-twin aggression to be moderated in this way, there has to have been a sufficiently containing mother who could hold both infants in mind (see Chapter 4). Where the mother has not been able to create a space in her mind for each child separately, the rivalry between the twins will more likely result in violent hatred towards each other. However, even when inter-twin aggression has been 'managed', it does not disappear, but remains beneath the surface waiting to erupt.

Adam, Eve and Lilith

In the traditional story of Adam and Eve, the God of Genesis is an omnipotent, omniscient god who created two beings bound together as one. As in the Plato story, we see the creation of man and woman by a splitting process, the creation of two complementary beings out of one. On the sixth day, God created man (*ish*, in Hebrew) in his own image, out of the dust of the earth (*adamah*), and breathed life into his nostrils. He then caused Adam to fall into a deep sleep, and while he was unconscious, God took one of Adam's ribs, closed the wound, and made the rib into a woman (*ishah*). Woman was thus an extension of man, created by a split:

> And Adam said, This is now bone of my bones, and flesh of my flesh ... Therefore shall a man leave his father and his mother and cleave unto his wife; and they shall be one flesh (Genesis, 2:23-4).

God called the woman Eve (Chavah, from *chai*, meaning life) because she was the mother of all humans. As in Plato's story, Adam and Eve are of one flesh and they cleave together. (The dual meaning of 'cleave' is discussed on pages 33 and 48.)

There is, however, another story that is not told in the Book of Genesis, but is referred to in Isaiah 34, and explained by Graves and Patai (1992) and on internet websites. In this story it was Lilith, not Eve, who was Adam's first mate. According to this legend, after God had created Adam out of dust, he created Lilith in the same way, except that he used filth and sediment instead of pure dust. There was discord between Lilith and Adam. With twin-like rivalry, Lilith refused to submit to the rather tyrannical demands of Adam, claiming that like him she was made of dust and therefore his equal. Adam tried to compel her obedience by force, and, in a rage, Lilith (whose name derives from 'female demon', or 'wind spirit') uttered the name of the Lord, and soared up into the air. She fled to the Red Sea, where she remained. Adam then complained to God about his loneliness, and God created Eve from Adam's rib. In this version of the story, Lilith was the first female double of the first man (Lash, 1993), and as such she represented his 'other half'.

Adam thus had two doubles or counterparts, with Eve representing a complementary, docile, ego-syntonic part and an extension of Adam, while Lilith was a deeper, more destructive shadow self that Adam could not integrate but tried to suppress and banish to a distant desolate place:

> Wildcats shall meet with hyenas,
> goat-demons shall call to each other;
> there too Lilith shall repose,
> and find a place to rest.
> There shall the owl nest
> and lay and hatch and brood in its shadow
> (Isaiah 34: 14).

Smith (2002) suggests that there is a further contrast between Eve and Lilith. Eve bore human babies, whereas Lilith bore only demons. Eve was impregnated by sex that was procreative in the normal partnered way, and Lilith tried to destroy the offspring so created. In contrast, 'Lilith becomes the repository and incubationary of the male sexual drive that cannot be satisfied by normal means. It is sex without love, without mutuality, for the sake only of pleasing one's ego', i.e. masturbation and nocturnal emissions. Smith suggests that had there been a greater integration of the Lilith part of the self, there would be less urge to destroy the products of the creative internal processes.

In the traditional Adam-Eve story, we see a benign splitting of one into two, to create a couple, a pair related to each other by their difference, the first man and the first woman, Adam and Eve. They represent complementary twinning in an idealized couple, the infant and its twin-breast in a perfect and trouble-free state of mind, the Garden of Eden. The destructive aspects later emerged in the form of the serpent, the tempter, the corrupter of pure good – envy, the destructive side of the self (perhaps representing the return of the repressed. However, it might also represent the ever-present menace of the banished Lilith part). The idealized state of mind of the Garden of Eden was thus shattered. The couple were expelled from paradise and had to face the real external world: the knowledge of good and evil, the recognition of the facts of life – the existence of the good breast, of the good creative intercourse, and of the inevitability of death (Money-Kyrle, 1971).

Referring to the Eden myth, Bion (1965) discusses the difficulties encountered by some patients in accepting certain facts that are felt to be significant. He suggests that the patient feels persecuted both by the *meaning* of the facts and by having to tolerate this sense of persecution. This intolerance of depressive anxieties hinders the movement in the PS↔D dynamic. The patient's fear of depression is born of the presence of a dominant and cruel superego representing an omniscient and harsh god who is opposed to knowledge. The difficulty in the development from the paranoid-schizoid position towards the depressive position is thus a conflict between omniscience and enquiry.

The quest for insight is an ambivalent one, coexisting with and opposed by resistance in the form of repression and denial, 'with injunctions to not know, with warnings to let sleeping dogs lie, etc.' (Blum, 1981: 538). Blum suggests that insight was the prerogative of the gods and therefore Adam and Eve were expelled from the Garden of Eden in terrible retribution for eating from the tree of knowledge. The recognition of truth, of the facts of life, brings with it awareness of oneself and of being observed, a third position where it is possible to step back and think (Britton, 1989). Addressing the issue of selfhood, Rycroft (1990) suggests that in the Judaeo-Christian tradition, it is only God who possesses selfhood. The word Jahweh or Jehova means I AM, and religious Jews will never say or write the word as only God can properly claim it. Rycroft suggests that 'human beings are creatures, creations of God, and therefore objects of his consciousness and not subjects of consciousness in their own right. It is He who is aware of them, and self-awareness, self-assertion, constitutes an act of defiance of his will' (Rycroft, 1990: 147). Thus, 'When Adam and Eve betrayed God and ate of the Tree of Knowledge, it was self-knowledge, self-awareness (not sexual knowledge) that they acquired' (Rycroft, 1990: 147). As a result of acquiring self-knowledge they felt guilt at their awareness of their nakedness.

In addition to the guilt that Adam and Eve experienced after their transgression, Goldman (1988) suggests that they also felt shamed, the experience of being exposed, of being seen, and of self-consciousness (as described by Rycroft, above, and the 'third position' as elucidated by Britton, 1989). They used the processes of splitting and projection to try to absolve themselves of blame – Adam blamed Eve, and Eve blamed the serpent. Splitting in order to avoid responsibility rather than to preserve a good object and understanding is a perverse solution (Steiner, 1985). It is an avoidance of a developmental move towards owning and integrating aspects of the self that are felt to be unacceptable. As Damasio (2000) says, 'Do not blame Eve for knowing; blame consciousness, and thank it too' (p. 4).

Goldman (1988) takes up an interesting point about the tension between splitting and dissociation to avoid a unity on the one hand, and differentiation to maintain a unity on the other. She suggests that this tension is represented in the dual meaning of the word 'cleave' – to 'cleave together', or to 'cleave apart'. The tension between cleaving together and cleaving apart is marked in twins as they both cling together as a unit and also wish to be separate individuals.

The Lilith legend adds further to our understanding of the psyche, with Lilith as the split-off and dissociated aspect of the self. Adam and Lilith were an incompatible twin-like pair who could neither reconcile their differences, nor function satisfactorily alone. Neither felt whole alone. Their separation created loneliness and longing in Adam and an unrestrained destructiveness in Lilith. Their relationship was based on a power struggle, and a mutual hatred of difference, and Lilith murdered the products of their relationship, the demon children, nightly. The Adam-Lilith relationship is like a paranoid-schizoid state of mind, split and destructive, with Lilith representing the disowned, projected, and hated aspects of the self. Money-Kyrle (1971) suggests that the fear of death is a paranoid anxiety that 'results from the recognition of the murderously competitive split-off part of the self which threatens the self (persecutory anxiety) or its loved objects (depressive anxiety)' (p. 443-4). The recognition of the inevitability of death, in contrast, is based on the repeated experience that no good pleasurable encounter lasts forever, as discussed in Chapter 1.

Lilith's refusal to return to Adam could be seen as an expression of opposition to integration of the destructive parts of the self. However, Lilith did come to an agreement with the three messengers from God who had asked her to return to Adam (Graves and Patai, 1992). She agreed that she would not kill any male babies who were protected by the sign of the messengers in the first eight days of their lives, before they were circumcised and had become members of the community. Perhaps in this compromise, we might recognize a borderline state of mind (Steiner, 1987). Lilith is like a destructive narcissistic organization in the psyche (Rosenfeld, 1971a), making a bargain with the needy Adam-self to offer limited protection, and relinquish a little of her omnipotent destructive activity, so as to retain her split-off state and her power. The pain of a fuller compromise and integration is thus avoided.

Thus there was an Adam-Eve pair and an Adam-Lilith pair, differentiating two aspects of a narcissistic state (Rosenfeld, 1971a). The Adam-Eve pair represented the libidinal aspect of narcissism based on self-idealization, maintained by the omnipotent introjective and projective identifications with good objects and their qualities. In the Adam-Lilith pair the omnipotent destructive parts were idealized, and aggression directed against a positive libidinal object relationship between them and against any experience of the need for an object. There was no space for a loving dependent object relationship in the dominance/submission struggle.

In reconciling the splits, we recognize that Lilith and Eve were also a pair. Lilith was Eve's dark side, and Eve and Lilith were a twin couple representing the life and death instincts in a defused or unbound state (Rosenfeld, 1971a). Lilith was banished and therefore troublesome until some neutralization of the death instinct had been achieved by partial fusion or binding with the life instinct (her agreement to the protection of some babies). Perhaps a borderline Adam-Lilith state of mind offers some protection from an unbound death instinct threatening annihilation of the self. In contrast, Eve was an idealized object that crumbled when insight (the knowledge of good and evil) was offered by what was perceived as a bad object (the serpent). However, on leaving the paradise of the narcissistic world, Eve's journey with Adam into the outside world became an ordinary life struggle, suggesting that the Adam-Eve couple represented a more mature self, more able to tolerate disillusionment and frustration, and work through difficulties, than was the Adam-Lilith self.

Lilith's ruthlessness, her predatory sexuality and cruelty, have been used to describe states of mind in psychoanalytic literature. Winnicott (1945) links the mythological Lilith with the primitive ruthless stage, the stage of pre-concern, in the infant's development. He suggests that a ruthless self is an integral part of the infant and shows itself mostly in play where the child enjoys a ruthless relation to its mother. The infant needs its mother because only she can be expected to tolerate its ruthless relation to her, even though it hurts her and wears her out. 'Without this play with her he can only hide a ruthless self and give it life in a state of dissociation' (Winnicott, 1945: 141). It is this ruthless dissociated figure that Winnicott linked with Lilith. Where the mother can tolerate the ruthlessness of her baby, it can be modulated and integrated into the self.

Wittels (1932) formulated the idea of a 'Lilith Neurosis' (p. 394), in which the female (homosexual) component in a man is projected onto his sexual object. Wittels bases this on the inherent bisexuality of humans and suggests it is a type of narcissistic object-choice. In a later paper (Wittels, 1934: 39) he describes his work with a patient as follows:

> She also began a number of love affairs which meant little to either herself or her husband. He simply was not jealous. Finally she became acquainted with a young man who fell desperately in love with her, and agreed that she was the most wonderful creature under the sun. He was afflicted with what I call the 'Lilith Neurosis'. She tortured him in the most refined fashion, which but served to increase his passion for her. During this time, when she entertained the idea of leaving her husband, and did not do so chiefly because she felt that that was what her husband was waiting for, a severe anxiety-hysteria broke out because of which she came to me for analysis.

It seems that the patient and her lover were engaged in a sadistic narcissistic relationship in which the patient enacted the cruel 'Lilith' projections of her lover. Her husband did not rise to her bait, and was not receptive to her intense need to split, creating a situation in which her anxiety broke through as she was forced to own the tormented part of herself.

The sexually predatory, sadistic aspects of the self are counterbalanced by the victims of Lilith's attentions, tormentor and tormented ever hand-in-hand. Lilith has been regarded not only as the benefactor of masturbation and erotic dreams, conceiving demons from these nightly emissions (as described on p.31); she is also held responsible for erotic dreams (Lorand, 1957). She may appear in male or female form, attacking those who sleep alone. This is, of course, a very convenient way of disowning erotic dreams, masturbatory phantasies and nocturnal emissions, whether seminal, or prolonged bed-wetting with its sexual origin (Freud, 1924). The 'sinful' parts of the self are split off and attributed to Lilith. Moulton (1977) describes an identification with a Lilith figure by a patient who 'felt guilty and greedy, sexually depraved, an insatiable monster, and likened herself to a succubus or a Lilith, who seduced men in their sleep and drained them of their strength' (p. 79).

Narcissus

The myths of the creation of man and woman represent a narcissistic state in which the other is perceived part of self, rather than true object relatedness. As described in Chapter 1, twins are frequently engaged in a relationship that has powerful narcissistic elements and in an extreme form the twinship may operate as a narcissistic unit. The theme of love and the object of this love form the focus in the story of Narcissus. In the myth, the consequence of turning away from love for an object towards love of the self is psychic death.

The myth of Narcissus has been extensively explored in psychoanalytic works. I will take up selected themes that are pertinent to twinning. There are two main versions of the myth (by Ovid and Pausanias) and many variations on the story of Narcissus. Ovid's version centres on the creation of a double as Narcissus sees his reflection in the water. As I will explore, Echo also represents a complementary, reflective twin of Narcissus. The theme of a twin is again taken up in Pausanias' version, in which Narcissus pined for a twin sister who had died.

In Ovid's well-known version, the seer, Teiresias proclaimed that Narcissus would live to a ripe old age provided that he never knew himself, and that he would survive only until the moment he saw himself. Thus the theme of self-knowledge and its dangers (as encountered by Adam and Eve) is taken up again. Narcissus was the child of the river nymph, Liriope, conceived when she was raped by River Cephisus (Miller, 1994). Narcissus was a young Thespian full of pride in his own beauty and he spurned all those who loved him. Echo fell in love with Narcissus, but as she had previously been doomed by the Goddess Hera to repeat only the last words of others' speech and never to utter her own thoughts, she was unable to initiate a conversation with Narcissus. She could not, therefore, express her love for him in a way in which she could become noticeable to him as 'a desiring other' (Fayek, 1981: 310). Narcissus ignored or rejected Echo, and she spent the rest of her lonely life in caves and glens, pining for her lost love, repeating the last syllables of words. She died of a broken heart and her bones turned to stone, only her voice remaining. Another rejected would-be lover of Narcissus, Ameinius, killed himself with a sword sent him by Narcissus, while calling on the gods to avenge his death. Artemis heard this plea and made Narcissus fall in love, but denied Narcissus love's consummation.

On his return from hunting, as Narcissus lay exhausted by a silvery stream, he saw his reflection in the water and fell in love with it. He tried to embrace and kiss the beautiful boy he so encountered, but on recognizing it as himself, he lay gazing into the pool enraptured. He did not know how to endure both possessing yet not possessing this love. The grief at not possessing was destroying him, yet he rejoiced in this torment, knowing that his other self would always remain true to him. Eventually, in despair, he plunged a dagger into his breast, saying 'Ah, youth, beloved in vain, farewell' (Graves, 1992: 288). His blood soaked the earth and from it sprang the white narcissus flower with its red corolla. Narcissus oil is distilled from the flower and is apparently a well-known *nar*cotic – 'a sleep inducing blossom exchanged for the dynamism of life' (Miller, 1994: 173).

Freud (1920, 1924) used the term 'Nirvana' to describe the destructive pull of the death instinct, linking pleasure and annihilation. The dual nature of Narcissus's absorption with himself, the pleasure and the pain, is described by Andreas-Salomé (1962: 8–9):

> It is somewhat to the discredit of the godfather of our term, Narcissus, hero of the mirror, if its use brings to the fore only the erotism of self-enjoyment. Bear in mind that the Narcissus of legend gazed, not at a man-made mirror, but at the mirror of Nature. Perhaps it was not just himself that he beheld in the mirror, but himself as if he were still All: would he not otherwise have fled from the image, instead of lingering before it? And does not melancholy dwell next to enchantment upon his face? Only the poet can make a whole picture of this unity of joy and sorrow, departure from self and absorption in self, devotion and self-assertion.

The significance of reflections, mirroring, doubles and 'the gaze' is integral to our understanding of our internal world and has become incorporated into the foundations of psychoanalytic thinking (psychoanalytic mirroring, identification, etc.). Rank (1971) examines the role of the double in mirrors, shadows and phantasied doubles, in man's relation to himself. Used pathologically, the double is a split-off, dissociated part of the self (like Lilith), 'an independent and visible cleavage of the ego' (Rank, 1971: 12). The paranoid nature of this state of mind leads to a belief that one's innermost thoughts are expressed by a voice outside oneself (an Echo). The double is associated with death and seeing one's double is a harbinger of death, as prophesied in the Narcissus myth. Rank suggests that the link between the double and death was the original version of the Narcissus myth, and that the idea of falling in love with the self was added later in order to exclude the idea of death, which is felt to be too painful to acknowledge. The inevitability of death is the third 'fact of life' that needs to be faced if development is to proceed (Money-Kyrle, 1971). As Rank suggests, the idea of death is denied by a duplication of the self that is then incorporated into a shadow or reflected image. When the narcissistic state is threatened, the wish for immortality appears in an attempt to counteract the fear of, and the knowledge of, the inevitability of death. The recognition of the inevitability of death is a threat to narcissism and it is feared that it will result in a complete annihilation of the ego.

The mirroring water has been the theme of much writing. Shengold (1974) regards the mirroring water in the Narcissus myth as symbolic of birth and the mother. He suggests that the myth of Narcissus represents the wish for unattainable satisfaction in the early stages of development. The first reflections of the infant in its mother's eyes promote the development of a sense of identity, but like the watery mirror of Narcissus, the depths of the reflection may also lead to 'symbiotic entrapment' (see Chapter 1 and below).

In the mother–infant interaction, the searching gaze plays an important part in the attachment between them (see Chapter 10). Rosenfeld (1983) describes the searching gaze in the desire for 'symbiotic oneness' (p. 263) in analysis and the way in which this can lead to 'symbiotic entanglement' (Rosenfeld, 1987: 168). Phantasies of 'symbiotic oneness' lead the patient to believe that the analyst not only satisfies all the patient's desires, but is also equally desirous of the patient, 'as if presenting a mirror image of the patient's needs and desires' (Rosenfeld, 1983: 263). 'After momentary satisfaction, the patient becomes intensely passive, and this increases his immobility and inability to think, so that the apparently very happy state changes into a persecutory one where he feels trapped and often tantalized by the object which he believes has seduced him, sucked him in and now makes no attempt to release him from the trap. The most disturbing aspect of this state is that he feels entirely in the power of the symbiotic twin-object, with no possibility of doing anything active' (Rosenfeld, 1983: 264) – a Narcissus trapped hypnotically at the analytic mirror.

The nature of Narcissus' watery contemplation reflects his defence against the horror of his origins. 'Conceived in his father's violence and his mother's trauma, Narcissus is the son of a water nymph and a river. What reflects in the water is not an objective image, but recognition of his defensive reactions to others, beginning with the impact of significant others on him' (Miller, 1994: 175). Thus by gazing into his image Narcissus is defending himself against any violent intrusion that would shatter his fragile state. The intrusion of self-knowledge would lead to the death of the narcissistic state.

Narcissus and Echo are linked by their lack of development of self and hence of a capacity for object relationships. They are complementary twin aspects of the self; sound and sight, female and male, each a reflection of the incomplete other eternally bound together. Anzieu (1979) notes the importance in object relationships of both visual and sound images of the self. Echo withdrew from the world into her sound image, and Narcissus withdrew into his visual image, with the result that both wasted away. 'If the mirror, whether of sound or vision, only reflects back the subject to himself – that is, his request, distress (Echo) or quest for ideal (Narcissus) – the result will be a defusion of instincts. The death instinct is freed and becomes economically predominant over the life instinct' (Anzieu, 1979: 32).

The lack of self-awareness and of object relatedness between Echo and Narcissus are deathly themes. Fayek (1981) notes the way in which Echo's love for Narcissus and his love for himself actually bring about their deaths. They both lack self-awareness or a sense of becoming present in one's own consciousness. As a result Narcissus could not recognize Echo as separate and engage in a loving relationship with her. Echo was an 'auditory image' of Narcissus and therefore could only reflect the void that was his 'state of existence' (Fayek, 1981: 309). Echo could not be brought into being as a loved object by Narcissus because of his own lack of a sense of self. Thus she is his counterpart in an absence of self, and her death symbolizes his.

Like Adam and Eve, Narcissus was supposed to have been shielded from death by a lack of self-awareness. Fayek suggests that Narcissus' image in the water did *not* reveal the secret that was kept from him, i.e. his awareness of himself, but rather that his reflection was a visual echo into which he vanished. His profound ignorance of himself as a being, an ignorance of his existence, was the deadly factor. 'The core of the narcissistic drama, as it is presented in the myth, is the dilemma of identity, i.e. becoming and emerging from oblivion to recognition' (Fayek, 1981: 310).

Narcissus and Echo failed to develop interpersonal relatedness (Miller, 1994) and were both trapped in their longing for an image or for an unattainable object of desire (Singer, 1978; Major, 1980). As Pines (1984) notes of Echo and Narcissus: 'the theme of reflection appears twice, in sound ... as echo, in vision as reflected image ... Each person represents an isolated individual who has no partner for response, for dialogue, for the mutual nourishment of attachment and love' (Pines, 1984: 32). The narcissistic mirror reflecting only sameness must be replaced by 'the mirroring that comes from the active contemplation, recognition and exchange between two centres of autonomy and of psychic life' (Pines, 1984: 33). Narcissus' idealization of himself leads to his emotional death because not only did he turn away from a real external object, he 'destroys the perception of the need of a real object and replaces that object with a projected part of the idealised self, and is trapped, unable to seek further' (Brenman, 1993: 628).

With adequate containment, the infant's relationship with its mother may lead to a sense of knowing oneself in relation to another and to the death of a narcissistic state of mind. However, unlike Narcissus' reflection, an external object is not always present and available. In the immature infant, relinquishing a narcissistic object leads to a fear of fragmentation or annihilation, the primitive anxieties of the paranoid-schizoid position. According to Ortmeyer (1970), there was a superstition prevalent in Greece that to dream of seeing one's reflection in water was an omen of death. The prophecy was that Narcissus would survive only until the time he saw himself, and Narcissus, on seeing his reflection, took himself as his love-object. It was then that he entered the deathly grip of a narcissistic state. Thus, Narcissus denied his need for and his dependency on others, choosing instead a constant object, his reflection, that would lead to his death, rather than life with an inconstant object (a mother with a Giaconda smile, see Chapter 1).

The deadly cut-off nature of a narcissistic state is maintained by internal splits in order to avoid knowing aspects of oneself, in the belief that one will not survive this knowledge (the 'not knowing oneself' of the prophecy). To know oneself means to recognize and integrate split-off parts of the self. Grotstein (1979) suggests that what Narcissus 'saw on the other side of the veil of water was his unconscious self, his symmetrical twin' (p. 164) – a dissociated aspect of himself. Perhaps it was this dissociation that resulted in the death of Narcissus (Mack, 1971).

Whether MD or DZ, twins offer a mirror image of each other and a perfect opportunity to cut off from unwanted aspects of the self and avoid integrating them within the individual self. (This has more to do with the chronological closeness of the twins than with genetic similarity.) The other twin is an object that, like Narcissus' reflection, is very much like self and is constantly present, but is also not really self. Hence the other twin can act as a vessel to hold all unwanted aspects of the self without fear of either total loss or of having to take unwanted projected elements back. The narcissistic twin unit is, like Narcissus and his image, trapped at the pool in a deathly entanglement.

The narcissistic longing for the perfect understanding of the early infant–mother relationship is only ameliorated when the lost perfect object can be relinquished and mourned. Narcissus' inability to relinquish his love for his image and to grieve for the loss of a perfect love that is always true is typical of the difficulty faced by idealizing twins. The narcotic quality of narcissism kept Narcissus at the stream until he could no longer bear the pain of not having what he longed for, and he killed himself rather than turn to external objects that would be less than perfect.

The idea that Narcissus' image was his twin self was suggested in a second version of the Narcissus story. Pausanias suggested that the idea of Narcissus looking into the water, not recognizing he was seeing his own reflection, falling in love with himself, and dying of love at the spring, is 'absolutely stupid' (Pausanias, 1979: 376). Narcissus was old enough to know a human form from a reflection. Pausanias told another story: Narcissus had a twin sister and they were exactly alike in appearance, hairstyle and clothes. They even hunted together. Narcissus was in love with his twin sister (his reflection of himself!). When she died (perhaps by drowning in the same pool), he used to visit the spring to gaze at his own reflection, knowing what it was, but finding consolation in his reflection as it so closely resembled his sister.

In this version, we again see the narcissistic love of one's own image, both in his love of his twin and of his own reflection, as well as the difficulty twins face in the event of the death of one of them. Narcissus' inability to relinquish and mourn the loss of his twin-self, and his sense of incompleteness without his twin, led to his own neglect and death. He gazed into the stream looking at his own reflection to remind him of his lost twin, to compensate himself for her loss. As in Ovid's version, Narcissus was unable to relinquish his self-love object. He was bound to his dead twin, seduced by a deathly force, rather than turning to life and mourning his loss. He turned away from external object relationships to an internal twinship.

In both versions Narcissus was unable to mourn his loss. Steiner (1990a) describes the difficulty encountered by narcissistic and borderline patients in dealing with object loss and mourning. Where the other is experienced as part of the self, it cannot be relinquished.

The recognition of an external object and one's relatedness to it opens the door to rivalry, amongst other things. The rivalry in mythical twins is well documented, and the degree of rivalry in twins is exacerbated by the twinship, both through the closeness of the twin relationship and in the competition for mother.

Rivalry in twins

Twins in mythology emphasize two possible lines of development in the twin relationship. On the one hand, the major factors are intense rivalry, violent, murderous hatred and jealousy, as in Jacob and Esau, and in Romulus and Remus. On the other hand, twins have been depicted as so tied to each other in an apparently loving bond as to be unable or unwilling to survive alone, like Castor and Polydeuces.

Jacob and Esau

In Genesis chapter 25 we read that after childless Isaac pleaded with the Lord, his wife Rebekah conceived. The children struggled together in her womb and she questioned the Lord about this. She was told:

> 'Two nations are in thy womb, and two manner of people shall be separated from thy bowels; and the one people shall be stronger than the other people; and the elder shall serve the younger.' And when her days to be delivered were fulfilled, behold, there were twins in her womb.

Thus, the rivalry between the twins started before birth and, as God foretold, would last throughout their lives. The twins were Esau, the firstborn, and Jacob. They represented conflicting dimensions of power and authority.

Jacob, the intelligent manipulator, sought power and was to become Israel (literally one who struggles with God), the leader of his tribe. Esau would be deposed by Jacob and become a non-Jewish imperial ruler who was a hunter, a man of the land and animals. Esau was favoured by his father and Jacob by his mother.

Jacob was born grasping at the heel (*yaakov*) of his brother, trying to get out first – thus he emerged as he was to spend the first half of his life, struggling for power and personal advantage. He was a quiet man, dwelling in tents, thoughtful, but scheming and deceitful. In contrast, Esau was impulsive and lacking in thoughtfulness. Jacob first took advantage of Esau's impulsiveness when Esau, claiming to be faint from hunger, asked Jacob for a bowl of lentils. Jacob gave it only on condition that Esau, the firstborn, sold him his birthright (ceding his right to the inheritance of goods and position). Esau reasoned that as he was starving, he would have no further use for his birthright. However, it may be that it was his lack of steadiness and thoughtfulness that led him to respond impulsively to his hunger and the smell of good food, rather than prepare his own. Perhaps Esau gave up his birthright so easily because he did not really value it (Elazar, 2002).

On a second occasion, Jacob again used his twin's weakness to his advantage when he conspired with his mother to deceive his father into blessing him instead of Esau. Jacob was smooth-skinned while Esau was hairy. When their father, Isaac, was dying and wished to bless his firstborn son Esau, Jacob wore a sheepskin on his arms (impersonating Esau) to mislead the nearly blind Isaac into thinking that he was Esau. He thus cheated Esau out of his father's blessing for a second time and claimed it for himself.

The themes of narcissism and deceit are interwoven in this story. The fact that Jacob and Esau were twins would have enhanced the difficulty each had in developing a mature sense of personal identity, particularly as the parental split in affection towards each had heightened the rivalry between them. They lived their lives as if still in utero, consumed with hostility towards each other. This unresolved conflictual state was the result of the lack of personal integration in each. The hated aspects of the self were split off and projected, and carried unquestioned by the other twin, who was then hated. While it is too concrete to interpret the sheepskin itself as a 'second skin' in the sense described by Bick (1968), Jacob's use of it to deceive Isaac might be so interpreted. Thus impersonation was used as a 'second skin' to compensate for a lack of an adequate sense of self. Biven (1982) suggests that Jacob's 'second skin' acted as a refuge from the direct contact with Isaac that would have exposed the truth of Jacob's deception.

Jacob's claim to, and his deception regarding, the birthright on two occasions raises various issues. The birthright is essentially the oedipal gift, the father acknowledging his son's manhood. It involves the son first having to acknowledge his father's position rather than wanting to supplant him, and father ceding power to his adult son in his own lifetime. For Jacob and Esau, the first encounter in relation to the birthright was a struggle between rival twins for father's gift, as if it was theirs to sell or take. They had each taken omnipotent possession of the birthright. Esau was the eldest and father's favourite, so he believed he was in the line of inheritance. As Jacob had been favoured by his mother, he also felt entitled to take father's place in the oedipal struggle.

On the second occasion, there is the issue of Jacob's apparent deception of Isaac. It has been suggested (Bandstra, 1999) that the deception was not really necessary and that Jacob and Isaac were willing partners in the deceit. God had already ordained that the younger twin would inherit the birthright. Thus, Jacob schemed to get what God had already granted him at birth. It may also be that Isaac was not deceived. Isaac told Jacob that although he had the arms of Esau, his voice was that of Jacob. Why should they both have engaged in this deception? Perhaps the deception stands for an evasion of the oedipal conflict in both father and son. Esau and Jacob used their twinship and their intense rivalry to avoid facing the resolution of the oedipal conflict. Perhaps Isaac, old and blind, entered into the deceit because in his enfeebled state, he no longer had the heart to sort it out.

Kohut (1957) suggests that there is no doubt that Isaac wished to bless Jacob, not Esau, and that Isaac wanted to be deceived. Mann (1956), in describing how the unconscious shapes life, links the 'charming mythological hocus-pocus' (p. 114) enacted by Jacob to get his father's blessing, with Osiris. Jacob used the deception to re-create himself, as did Osiris, the 'mangled, buried and arisen god' (Mann, 1956: 114). But, like Osiris who was reconstituted minus his phallus (see page 45), Jacob, in symbolically castrating his father (Friedman, 1955), did not gain the godly omnipotence he desired, but a rather more conflictual and limited power. Jacob fell from paradise, as did Adam, and he too had to flee and face the real world in exile. The message is loud and clear: the oedipal conflict cannot be resolved by deception, theft or castration.

Jacob left home to avoid Esau's wrath at being robbed of his inheritance, and went to the land of Laban, his mother's brother. The hatred between Esau and Jacob was such that they lived apart for many years and the descendants of Esau (Edom) were regarded as the persecutors of Jacob's people, the Jews (Israel). They were eventually reconciled and Jacob again manipulated the event, sending many gifts to appease Esau's rage. The actual meeting was tense but non-violent. Feldman (1956) suggests that Esau's weeping at this meeting contained both the tears of joy and also those of a bitter hatred. Only in reuniting the twin aspects of the self can the duality acquire greater cohesion and the warring end.

The issue of the rights of inheritance to the firstborn is particularly fraught in twins. Perhaps Jacob entered into the deceit to redress his perceived injustice and resentment at being the second-born and therefore not the heir to his father's inheritance. Jacob felt aggrieved firstly because he had to share his mother's womb and his parents with his twin, resulting in a narcissistic injury. In addition, the laws of inheritance compounded this by promising to Esau something that Jacob believed he had been deprived of. Meissner (1994a) suggests that it was only by corruption of the superego that Jacob could pursue his deceitful claims without conscience or regard for Esau. In his destructive narcissistic state, Jacob felt superior and entitled, and this would have allowed him to transgress without shame and to enter the deception with his father. In the twin dualities of narcissism, the feelings of superiority and embitterment would hide feelings of inferiority and worthlessness. The 'second skin' (impersonation) that Jacob used to deceive Isaac may also be seen as an attempt to hide the shame of the exposure of his inadequacies, his feeling not good enough, of not being his father's favoured son.

The rivalry between these twins was such that it seemed there was no possibility of resolving it other than by total separation. The parents had encouraged the split, and there seemed to be no brotherly love that might have ameliorated the differences between them to allow them to overcome their jealousy and envy of each other. Instead, they took advantage of their differences for personal gain, as Jacob either bribed his lazy brother or impersonated him in order to steal what was rightfully Esau's by virtue of his being firstborn. It was a twinship enmeshed in mutual hatred and enmity. Perhaps the long separation from each other allowed some personal growth so there could eventually be reconciliation, but it seemed it was on a very tentative and cautious basis.

Castor and Polydeuces

In contrast to Jacob and Esau, Castor and Polydeuces (or Pollux) were twins who were bound by a love that obliterated any rivalry between them. They were born to Leda after Zeus (king of the gods) had seduced her while disguised as a swan. Leda had also conceived by her husband, Tyndareus. She gave birth to four children: Castor and Clytaemnestra, who were the children of Tyndareus (a mortal), and Polydeuces and Helen who were Zeus' children. Thus Castor was mortal and Polydeuces a god, and Leda was consequently deified. (There have been differing views about which were Zeus' children and which Tyndareus'.)

Castor and Polydeuces were inseparable and became renowned for their athletic prowess, Castor as a breaker of horses and Polydeuces as a master boxer. During a battle, Castor was killed and Polydeuces prayed to Zeus that he should not outlive his beloved brother (Graves, 1992: 248). However, it had been fated that only one of Leda's sons was to die, and since Castor was a mere mortal, Polydeuces, as the son of Zeus, was carried up to heaven. However, Polydeuces refused to accept immortality unless Castor shared it with him. Zeus conceded and allowed them to remain together, living alternately in the heavens and in the netherworld. As a further reward for their brotherly love, he set their images among the stars as the Twins

(Gemini), the Dioscuri (sons of Zeus). They represented the ever-changing cycle from light to dark, and dark to light. Castor and Polydeuces were made the patrons of shipwrecked sailors and were granted the power to send favourable winds when an appropriate sacrifice had been made. They are generally seen as helpers, and saviours of men, and some form of twin gods is found in many polytheistic religions.

Thus Castor and Polydeuces were twins inseparable even in death – an enmeshed twinship based on narcissistic love rather than the hatred that bound Jacob and Esau. Castor and Polydeuces used this love and their close adherence to each other to avoid any rivalry between them and they minimized their differences in their adherent narcissistic unit. No other relationship had the same significance for them as their twinship and in becoming a constellation, the Gemini, they remained 'forever united in a timeless universe miles away from that of people populating the earth' (Piontelli, 1989: 413).

Their twinship is an idealized state and the love between them is a narcissistic love based on the elimination of difference rather than on object love. They occupy the same revered place as do Yoruba twins, and this idealization is used to avoid the danger posed by minimizing the difference between them (Girard, 1988). They operated as a unit and their violence was directed outwards rather than internally between the twin couple. While they were rather too good to be true in relation to each other, they frequently engaged in fierce and murderous battles in the outside world. Castor and Polydeuces worked together as a fearless team, thus creating a stronger unit than each alone – another characteristic of twinships.

The split into god and mortal again illustrates the duality of narcissism as it leads to both idealization and denigration. Like Jacob and Esau, Castor and Polydeuces represent parental splitting that is reflected in the children. But unlike Jacob and Esau, Castor and Polydeuces avoid the internal conflict between themselves and turn it outwards as they work as a fighting team. However, their eternal twinning represents an inability to undo the splitting and projective identification between them, and a denial of their need for integration of the individual self and the separateness of the two. They form a narcissistic unit enclosed in a psychic envelope.

The Dioscuri type of twin experience is often seen in twins when one twin dies and the surviving twin maintains the twinship rather than mourn the lost twin (see Chapter 12). Garma (1962) suggests that Castor and Polydeuces' relationship, where one twin goes on living while the other dies, represents phantasies of intra-uterine life. The twin who lives is the child that is born, the one that dies is the placenta (a theme developed by Rhode, 1994, with particular attention to the paranoid state of mind and ensuing fears of murderous revenge of the dead twin).

All of the themes described above – splitting, dissociation, hostile rivalry and narcissistic love – are encountered in the myth of Isis and Osiris, below.

Isis, Osiris and Set

The processes of splitting and magical repair are graphically expressed in the myth of Isis and Osiris. There are many complexities of this multi-layered and multi-faceted myth and its links with the 'psychodynamic reality of the evolving individual to his surrounding social, religious and political reality' (Whitehead, 1986: 77). I will take up some aspects of the myth.

Osiris was the firstborn son of Geb and Nut, and his sister Isis was born three days later, in a time when the days were not counted as part of the year (Larousse Encyclopedia of Mythology, 1959). Although Osiris and Isis were regarded as brother and sister rather than twins, they shared the womb, as did their other brothers, Set and Horus, and their sister Nephthys. It was sometimes thought that Osiris and Isis were so in love they had intercourse in the womb (Raphael-Leff, 1990).

Osiris was known for his gentleness and he embodied the spirit of vegetation that dies with the harvest, to be reborn when the grain sprouts. He civilized Egypt and travelled the world spreading the benefits of his rule. He married Isis, who was also renowned for her good works, and who governed well in Osiris' absence. Their (twin) brother, Set, was murderously jealous of Osiris' position in the world and his marriage to Isis, and he plotted to kill Osiris[1]. Set was regarded as the incarnation of the spirit of evil, the personification of the arid desert, of drought and darkness, in eternal opposition to the spirit of good, the fertile earth, life-bringing water and light in perpetual renewal, represented by Osiris. 'All that is creation and blessing comes from Osiris; all that is destruction and perversity arises from Set' (Larousse Encyclopedia of Mythology, 1959: 19).

Isis knew of Set's plots against Osiris, and protected Osiris from Set. But one day Set conspired with others to lure Osiris to a banquet and then fool him into lying in a richly ornamented carved casket. Set then sealed Osiris into the casket so that he died. Set threw the casket into the Nile from whence it floated into the sea, and across to Byblos. Isis was distraught, and tore her clothes and cut her hair in mourning. Eventually Isis got wind of the location of the casket and set out to reclaim Osiris' body and bury it as proscribed. She shed her tears on Osiris' body and hid it in the swamp. But Set found the body and cut it into fourteen pieces, throwing them far and wide. Isis patiently searched and found thirteen of the fragments; the fourteenth, Osiris' phallus, had been eaten by a Nile crab (forever accursed for this crime). Isis reconstituted the body of Osiris, using her magical powers to join the pieces together, but without his penis. She then performed the rites of embalmment (creating the first mummy – Raphael-Leff, 1990), and thus restored the murdered god Osiris to eternal life. Osiris' magical restoration had, however, left him emasculated. Horus, the child

---

[1] Money-Kyrle, 1945, suggests that incestuous intercourse, such as that between Osiris and Isis, was likely to be punished by castration.

born to Isis, was magically conceived after Osiris' death and reconstitution, and he later avenged his father.

With the magical restoration of Osiris, there could be no mourning for his loss. Instead, he, like Lilith, occupied a dissociated state in the world of the dead:

> Resurrected and from thenceforward secure from the threat of death, Osiris could have regained his throne and continued to reign over the living. But he preferred to depart from this earth and retire to the 'Elysian Fields' where he warmly welcomed the souls of the just and reigned over the dead (Larousse, 1959: 16).

Facing the truth of one's inner life and the inevitability of death is a painful process, and resorting to processes of splitting and dissociation is a defence against this. The split-off and dissociated Osiris was not like the destructive dissociated Lilith, but rather represented a devotion to the dead in an idealization of a deathlike state.

The themes of splitting and dissociation are central to the Osiris–Isis myth. Howell (1996) particularly links the Osiris myth with dissociative processes that result from trauma and betrayal, leading to fragmentation of the self as encapsulated in the Osiris–Isis–Set relationships. Dissociation is maintained by envy, hatred and hostility to integration and object relationships, as represented by Set. Whitehead (1986) suggests that Set personifies the split-off and projected negative and uncivilizing principles of the id-like impulses, particularly in relation to unmet oral needs. This links us again with the infant's earliest relationship with mother. When incorporative difficulties interfere with the establishment of a good internal object, the Set-baby clings sadistically to a grievance over things lost, needs never met, and the mother who can never be possessed. His envy destroys all goodness. Only through the process of grieving and forgiveness can a true burial of lost objects and integration take place (Roth, 1992).

The womb that the five siblings shared is like a psychic envelope around them all, with each representing a different aspect of the self. I have explored three of the sibling-self representatives. Isis and Osiris were forever bound in harmony like the Gemini, or like the inseparable male–female twin parts of the self as in the Platonic discourse. Isis was inconsolable at the death of Osiris, as a lone twin might be. She was unable to relinquish Osiris, as if she had lost a part of herself, and was therefore unable truly to mourn him. In her grief, Isis magically reconstructed Osiris, but he was an impotent figure, committed to a deathly world. A magically restored object blocks the processes of relinquishment and mourning. Set (like Lilith) represents the split-off and dissociated destructive self. The fragmentation of the self and lack of integration of the split-off parts results in a situation where there can be no sense of separateness from others, as the parts of the self that have been projected into the object cannot be reclaimed. As a result, the ego is impoverished, and the guilt and pain associated with loss is avoided (Steiner, 1990a).

Osiris and Set represent the extreme aspects of the life and death instincts in a defused state. Set hated Osiris' goodness, creativity and power, and his harmonious marriage to their sister Isis. He was the personification of envious aggression and destructiveness, attacking all good and life-giving processes. 'The struggle between the two brothers is the war between the desert and the fertile earth, between the drying wind and vegetation, aridity and fecundity, darkness and light' (Larousse, 1959: 17). In this narcissistic system, Set's destructive attack on the Osiris-self was catastrophic in terms of all the relationships in the drama and caused damage which could only later be repaired by the loving son, Horus.

In the myths and legends discussed above, the damaging or deadly results of splitting of the personality in hatred, and of the lack of recognition of difference and essential object relatedness, are evident. Twins in mythology and legend exemplify these processes.

Chapter 3
Cleaving together: developmental processes in twins

> It was from out the rind of one apple tasted, that the knowledge of good and evil,
> as Two Twins cleaving together, leaped forth into the world.
>
> (*Areopagitica*, Milton, 1644: 13)

To cleave:
1. to split, chop, break or come apart, especially along a line of cleavage.
2. to stick fast, adhere.

(Concise Oxford Dictionary)

The intra- and inter-psychic twinning processes described in Chapters 1 and 2 play a prominent and distinctive role in the development of actual twins. While pathological development in twins is not necessarily attributable to the twinship *per se* (Shorr, 1965), the relationship between twins does have a profound and enduring effect on the development of a sense of self in each twin. The presence of a twin, whether MZ or DZ, same or opposite sex, offers the opportunity for twinning phantasies to become concretized and this may become a permanent feature in the personalities of the twins. Both the intense closeness of twins and the sometimes vehement insistence on their separateness indicates the difficulties that they may face in establishing individuality.

As described in Chapter 1, a phantasy twin may be either a breast-twin or an imaginary companion. A phantasy twin differs greatly from an actual twin – unlike a phantasy twin, the actual twin is not omnipotently controlled and is not just an expression or extension of the individual's personality. Conflicts and rivalry between actual twins complicate the closeness that is so longed for in a phantasy twin. The phantasy of having a twin that emanates from both the twins themselves and in the perceptions of others does play a prominent role in reinforcing the actual twinship. Thus there will be intra- and inter-psychic factors within the twin relationship and factors external to the twinship linked with the perceptions of the twin pair by external objects. The external and internal factors interact to create an enduring twinship.

Burlingham (1952) suggests that the phantasies of outsiders might amplify the twin relationship more powerfully than factors arising within the twinship. However, I believe that the powerful internal twinning processes based on both the infant-breast and the twin-twin relationships predominate in the creation of an enduring internal twinship. As Burlingham notes, the ubiquitous phantasy of having a twin leads to a fascination with twins and spontaneous identification with the twin pair. However, the actual life of twins is not as romantic or impressive as its reflection in phantasy. There *are* many similarities between phantasy twins and actual twins - they may be almost inseparable, they may both act as a substitute for an absent parent, and they may provide perfect understanding at both conscious and unconscious levels. However, the main difference is that in an actual twinship, negative and aggressive feelings, rivalry and jealousy are generated and expressed, unlike the untroubled and unchanging relationship with the phantasy twin.

The phantasy twin of infancy remains buried at an unconscious level, to be reawakened by the sight of twins. In contrast, as described in Chapter 1, a conscious imaginary companion of childhood usually fades away. Where a phantasy twin persists consciously into adulthood in a singleton, this would be indicative of a more narcissistic level of functioning. In actual twins, the internal twinship does endure and would consist of both narcissistic and more mature object-related elements. While the twinship is not untroubled, unlike a phantasy twin relationship, twins do usually adapt to the conflicts between them and adjust to the personality of the other twin (Burlingham, 1952). As a result of the complex twinning processes between twins, the twinship forms their closest tie.

The development of each twin will be affected by the presence of the other twin. Each twin impinges on the other twin's relationship with the mother. In addition, the twins may to varying degrees turn to each other rather than to the mother or the parental couple as a developmental object. The mutuality and the projective and introjective identifications evident in the mother-infant and in the mother-father-infant relationships will also be experienced in the twin-twin relationship. However, a distinctive feature in the twin relationship is that, unlike the relationships with the parents, there is a lack of generational difference between the twins. This is significant developmentally, as neither twin has the maturity to process adequately the projections of the other twin.

Twins (and other multiples) find themselves in a particular position in regard to their relationship with mother. Unlike the situation with a singleton, with twins mother has to divide her attention between two infants. They are never alone with mother - even when the other baby is asleep, it is still in her mind. Davison (1992) and Piontelli (2002) have both observed mothers of twins feeding one while engaging in social activity with the other twin. The attention given to each baby is in short bursts as mother's attention oscillates from one twin to the other. Piontelli also observes that mother initially chooses to focus more on one twin than the other one, and that this is a long-lasting pattern. The reasons for the choice are unconscious and are based on a variety of factors which may include choosing the weaker and smaller twin, the more active one, or one with particular physical features. In an observation of premature twins in incubators, Cohen (2003) notes the difficulty the mother experienced in holding both infants in mind, especially when one twin was more vulnerable and needy than the other. The temptation for mother was to switch her attention to the healthier infant, who did not arouse such primitive anxieties in her.

The nature of mother's engagement with each twin may vary over time. Burlingham (1952) suggests that in the early stages the mother responds to each twin as she does a single infant. It is only later that she takes pleasure in them as a unit, and this affects their relationship. As compared with singletons, twins have two early emotional ties, the twinship and the relationship with mother (later mother and father). These relationships are simultaneous and influence each other and also act against each other. Twins have a double task: firstly, that of dealing with their conflicting feelings of love and hate within both the relationship with mother and with the twin; and they also have to find a balance between the two relationships. Even separation from the other twin and being alone with mother proves not to be as pleasurable as expected, as the wish for sole possession of mother is too strong and leads to a too-great awareness of the absent rival. The experience of separation from the twin may be of the same order as a separation from mother. Klotz, Balier and Javal (1962) observed that a four-year-old MZ twin girl reacted to separation from her twin due to hospitalization in a manner similar to separation from her mother.

The sharing of their primary carer/attachment figure will have enduring developmental consequences for twins (see Chapter 10). The development of the ego and ego boundaries takes place within the primary relationship with the mother and the oedipal parental couple. Heimann (1942: 8) describes the 'ego' as the

> sum-total of an individual's feelings, emotions, impulses, wishes, capacities, talents, thoughts and phantasies, in short, all those psychic forces and formations which a person (assuming that his consciousness reached so far as to embrace so much) would identify as his own and which would make him feel: 'That is I.'

This is the 'sense of self' that I refer to in this book. The constant presence of the other twin and mother's divided attention create a situation in which ego boundaries are likely to be less easily defined for each individual twin.

Mother's attention would also be divided when there is a toddler about. However, when there is more than one infant of the same age the experience is more intense. Piontelli (2002) suggests that each infant is highly attuned to the level of age-appropriate attention, especially from the primary caregiver. Observations indicate that the infant's jealousy and disturbance at not having mother's exclusive attention is more acute when the rival is of the same age, and more tolerable when the other child is of a different age and requiring a different sort of attention.

In singletons, the primary relationship with the developmental figure is vertical, while siblings play a significant secondary role. In twins, however, the horizontal relationship with the other twin is highly significant and in some situations may become the primary relationship. As a result, it is not uncommon to find twins who are locked into an enmeshed relationship with each other, in a rigid structure that results in the impairment of individual development of each twin. Even where there has been a greater degree of personality development in each twin, and a sense of separate identity in each, there is always a shadow of the other.

Sibling relationships are significant to a developing child (Coles, 2002; Mitchell, 2000). Mitchell notes that sibling relationships are the first social relationships a child encounters. She suggests a radical rethink on development, and proposes that the Oedipus complex arises when a child, 'faced with a sibling ... regresses to its wish for infantile unity with the mother; it then finds the father in the way' (Mitchell, 2000: 23). It is not the breast *per se* that is lost, but the breast is usurped by the sibling, as a result of which the child will regress, and it is these emotions that create the psychic organization of the nuclear or Oedipus complex. For twins, where a rivalrous sibling is always present, the implication of Mitchell's theory is that as well as lacking that experience of a unique relationship with mother, the twins will also face the oedipal conflict much earlier - as soon as they are aware of each other. It has been noted (Engel, 1975) that twins have difficulty engaging with the oedipal conflict and may use the twinship to avoid this painful experience. If Mitchell's theory is valid, the twins' immaturity at encountering the oedipal conflict too early may contribute to this difficulty.

Nature vs. nurture

Chapter 1 outlined the 'normal' course of development for an infant. I will now consider the additional factors that have a significant influence in twin development. First, it is necessary to say a few words about genetic factors. The nature/nurture debate has prompted countless studies of twins in the hope of discovering the true and unambiguous nature of personality, and of explaining human behaviour. Twins have been widely regarded as nature's experimental offering, based on the assumption that MZ twins have an identical genetic component so that any variation must then be due to the environmental factors. DZ twins, on the other hand, are no more alike genetically than other siblings, while sharing an environment as similar or dissimilar as that of MZ twins.

MZ twins are commonly called 'identical' twins and some regard them as genetically interchangeable. Thus, Nancy Segal (1999) writes: 'When identical twins marry and raise families, each twin becomes a "genetic parent" to their nephews and nieces (their twin's children). These nephews and nieces become their aunts' and uncles' "genetic" sons and daughters. This happens because identical twins are *clones*, making them biologically "interchangeable"' (Segal, 1999, 16). And later: 'Identical twin parents are equally related to their own children and their twin's children, but only share home environments with their own children' (p. 17). Segal does concede that the development of MZ twins is not identical and suggests that genetically based developmental plans are influenced by environmental factors early in life.

Gringras and Chen (2001), in a review of the scientific research on twins, challenge the assumption the MZ twins are physically and genetically identical. They note the differences found in monozygous twin pairs as a result of various factors including intrauterine effects and genetic mechanisms. They found that the number and morphology of chromosomes may vary, and that there may be mutations in the DNA and epigenetic modifications within the chromosomes. Genetic mirroring in MZ twins, which occurs in 25 per cent of cases, may produce differences more profound than the easily observed ones such as opposite hair whorls. Discordant handedness in mirrored MZ twins was found to be reflected in differential brain development (cerebral hemispheric lateralization). As will be explored in Chapter 10, the development of relational bonds affects brain development. Gringras and Chen also note that cerebral lateralization is an important factor in certain conditions, such as schizophrenia, dyslexia, autism and depression. They believe that it is incorrect to assume that being monozygous is synonymous with being identical. They believe the widely used term 'identical twins' should be replaced with the more accurate term 'monozygous twins' - a view which I fully endorse!

There are several reports of twins who were separated early in life and reared apart (Wright, 1997; Segal, 1999). Abrams (1986) writes an account of such a separation for supposedly clinical reasons. (This paper raises many issues, some of which I will discuss.) The stated reasons for separating the twins are:

> (1) the parenting of twins was burdensome, so that care giving was often compromised; (2) the children invariably faced specific developmental hazards that appeared directly attributable to the twinship; and (3) they also appeared more vulnerable to a wide variety of pathological disturbances (Abrams, 1986: 41).

The adoptive parents and children were not told of the existence of a twin. The author notes that previous studies of twins reared apart were all retrospective studies. This experiment, in contrast, involved detailed observations and testing of the twins and their adoptive families from the time of adoption until they were 19 years old. The researchers found that both twins had serious disorders and were '*equivalently* pathological' (Abrams, 1986: 52), and showed similarities in their developmental difficulties. However, the author concludes that environmental influences were also important and interacted with inherited factors - hardly surprising!

In a later study by Abrams and Neubauer (1994), the authors compare their findings with those of Hartmann's 'Psychiatric studies of twins' (1964). Using four pairs of twins, including the same set of twins as that in the 1986 study (given different names), they confirm their conclusion, 'the presence of a silent inherent blueprint that co-determines the unfolding of the human mind' (p. 50). Abrams and Neubauer compare their study and Hartmann's. They note that while Hartmann studied twins reared together, they followed those reared apart. In common with Hartmann, they found that there were developmental difficulties in all the twins studied. Of particular note is their finding that the oedipal conflict was not resolved in a meaningful way that could be internalized as a useful structure. Oedipal achievements were limited in all four pairs of twins studied by Abrams and Neubauer. The authors seem at a loss to understand this and wonder if it is an artifact or perhaps due to 'something about twin development that has not been definitively understood until now' (Abrams and Neubauer, 1994: 58). I believe that this is the result of the lack of establishment of a good internal integrating object that could have helped the infant deal with the oedipal conflict, and is directly connected with the twin relationship. (This will be discussed in the next section.)

In both Abrams and Neubauer's studies, background details are missing, so that other than the difficulty of caring for twins successfully, we have no idea of the reasons why the children were offered for adoption. In addition to the serious questions that these 'experiments' raise about the ethical aspects of this work, various crucial factors are not accounted for. These authors notably omit any mention of the fact of a twin relationship being disrupted and what effect this might have had on the development of the separated twins. There is no notion of the twins' awareness of each other before separation from each other (at two and a half months for Amy and Beth), or of the effects of separation from the mother (at six weeks for Amy and Beth). The focus is strongly on the hypothesis that there is a genetic blueprint that evolves differentially in response to the environmental factors, and that 'identical' twins will therefore not differ significantly in their development – an extension of the nature–nurture debate.

As anyone who has worked with twins will know, even MZ twins differ as much in their personalities as do any siblings. The idea that a genetic blueprint determines our personality does not hold up to scrutiny as it ignores crucial factors that affect the development of all individuals. While the genetic component may determine the parameters within which individual development takes place, environmental factors, both internal and external, familial and other, will differentially affect which developmental genes become activated. Personal individual factors will shape our responses to, and our manner of dealing with, the situations we encounter.

The development of twinship

The interaction of internal and external factors in a twin relationship referred to at the beginning of this chapter results in an indelible internal twinship that affects all relationships that a twin encounters. The processes in the development of this internal twinship are outlined below.

The developmental processes for twins are more complicated than those negotiated by singletons. Using Bion's (1959) fundamental themes of development at an intrapsychic level, that is the concepts of container and contained, it is useful to explore how they might apply to twins. As I described in Chapter 1, normal projective identification combined with introjective identification creates the foundation for the development of a good internal integrating object (Klein, 1963) or a capacity for thinking (Bion, 1962a), as the mother's breast/apparatus for thinking is introjected by the infant. The infant uses the process of projective identification into a personality mature enough to contain its feelings in order to investigate its own experiences. This establishes in the infant a capacity to deal with the external world in a reflective way.

However, this link with the breast may be denied either by the mother's lack of receptivity to the infant's intense emotions, or because the infant's hatred and envy of the mother's capacity lead it to attack the link with the breast. The introjected internal object is then felt to be intrinsically hostile, greedy and devouring. The infant experiences mother's peace of mind as hostile indifference. What is then installed in the infant is an internal object that exercises its function as a severe and ego-destructive superego. The infant becomes overwhelmed by intense emotions with which it cannot cope. The ego is weakened as the intensity of the emotions increases, and the linking function of the emotions (between infant and breast) is attacked. Where the link between the infant and breast is destroyed, curiosity, upon which all learning depends, will be severely disordered – with a consequent arrest of development (Bion, 1962a).

In interactions with a maternal container, the infant's projections are received and modified in a way that reduces anxiety and promotes understanding and meaning, so that the modified experience then introjected by the infant can be used to aid its development towards the depressive position. In Bion's terms, the apparatus for thinking is introjected by the infant. This lays the foundation for the next step, the relationship with the parental couple, which, if successfully negotiated, can create a space for thinking, a third position where benign observation of oneself and others becomes possible (Britton, 1989).

For twins the projective and introjective processes are complicated by the presence of the other twin. With mother's attention being divided between the two, it is likely that they will both experience a deficit of contact with her. They will also use each other as an alternative object in her absence. However, the other twin is not a mature object that is able to transform the raw projections into something more manageable, and the internalization of the good breast will be disrupted. Instead of a primary good maternal introject as a central organizing object, there will also be a primary twin introject based on more primitive and disturbing experiences. As a result of the mutual exchange between the twins, development will be affected as the unmodified and perhaps exacerbated emotions lead to a weakening of the ego. Anxiety is not reduced and the capacity for learning will be hampered.

Projective identifications between the twins may not be re-introjected, but may instead become lodged in the other twin in a concrete way, leading to a sharing of ego functions between the twins. The difficulty in establishing a sense of separateness and of achieving separation from the other twin becomes greater the more enmeshed the twins are, whether it is a result of either constitutional factors or parental neglect. While generational difference aids the process of separation in the mother–infant pair, the generational sameness of the twin–twin pair exacerbates the link between them.

Weaning, and mourning for the lost object, is central to the process of separation and the establishment of separateness (Quinodoz, 1993). Money-Kyrle (1968) describes the weaning process by tracing the path of cognitive development from innate preconceptions to symbolization. He refers to 'the delusion of primary narcissism' (Money-Kyrle, 1968: 695), i.e. in phantasy, the infant gets into the breast by total projective identification, as a result either of envy for the breast or a wish to escape persecutory experiences. Thus the infant would believe it is the breast. In contrast, the normal developmental path 'involves a humiliating recognition of one's littleness, followed by a grateful dependence which ends after weaning, in the internalisation of the lost good object' (Money-Kyrle, 1968: 695). Central to the process of weaning and devel-opment is the recognition of the three basic facts of life (Money-Kyrle, 1971). They are the recognition of the breast as a supremely good object, the recognition of the parent's intercourse as a supremely creative act, and the recognition of the inevitability of time and ultimately death. Money-Kyrle suggests that the main impediment to the recognition of the breast as a supremely good object is the fact that it cannot be enjoyed forever; that it has to be relinquished and mourned, leading to the internalization of the first good object. Relinquishing the good breast is linked with the acceptance of the inevitability of death.

The good internalized breast mitigates the jealousy that is aroused in relation to the creative parental intercourse and the baby's exclusion from it. Misconceptions about the parental intercourse are based on the infant's phantasy of intrusion into mother using projective identification. Such phantasies may occur where there has not been an adequate internalization of a good breast. The recognition of the breast as a supremely good object makes the acceptance of the creativity of the parental intercourse easier because the infant can use the internalized good object and has less need to resort to continued projective identification.

Where twins use each other as primary objects, there will be a limited internalization of the good maternal breast. As a result, the infant twin will suffer a lack of true understanding and a limited capacity for symbol formation. What will instead be established is a rather bizarre structure based on misconceptions and offering a distorted view of the external and internal world. In this situation, the misconceptions of the parental intercourse will be particularly marked because, unlike the mother–infant pair, the twin couple are a generationally horizontal pair who lack the necessary generational differentiation that is needed to resolve the oedipal conflict. The extensive use of projective identification between them may instead lead them to identify themselves as a couple on a par with the parental couple and this would arouse inter-twin incestuous phantasies (see Chapter 11).

According to Britton (1998), the sense of 'otherness' of an observing object is created when an internal object is incorporated but not assimilated. 'Otherness' can apply to both internal and external objects and is a source of difficulty for some patients because they feel their sense of subjectivity is threatened by the objectivity of the other. The 'otherness' may be experienced as hostile, linking with the idea of the hyper-subjectivity of Rosenfeld's (1987) thin-skinned narcissists who find analytic objectivity intolerable. 'Otherness' may be idealized, thus impoverishing the sense of self, or it may be experienced as an alien intruder dictating to the impoverished host.

As in a thick-skinned narcissistic state, where a narcissistic twinship has been established, any intervention by an 'other' external to the twinship will be experienced as an attack. The external 'other' is felt to be hostile and dangerous. The other twin, in contrast, lacks the quality of 'otherness', and may be experienced as an auxiliary or complementary part of the self, a part of the individual's subjectivity – as expressed by Fanthorpe (2000: 64):

...the strangeness
Of the other who is the same.

However, when unwanted aspects of the self have been split off and lodged in the other twin any contact between them may be experienced as a hostile invader.

A lack of maternal containment, as may be experienced by twins, leaves the infant with a 'fear of being overwhelmed by uncontained, untransformed psychic elements or of living in the aftermath of their annihilation' (Britton, 1998: 54) – or Bion's (1962a) concept of 'nameless dread'. The entanglement of twins in an enmeshed relationship both perpetuates the lack of containment and defends them against anxieties about uncontained experiences that are the result of a lack of maternal containment. The separation of enmeshed twins stirs terror in them as it exposes them to these unmodulated and perhaps bizarre experiences when a good internal object has not been sufficiently established and the twins lack the ability to deal with their fears.

An omnipotently created object like a phantasy twin, originating in infancy as a result of the experience of helplessness, is always present to fulfil the infant's desires. Such narcissistic structures are more likely to persist as a result of too early separation, or of a lack of holding by a containing mother

(Rosenfeld, 1987). With twins this is endemic, as each twin will be repeatedly separated from mother by the other twin, and as already explored, maternal containment of twins is so much more problematic. Feldman (1989) writes of the infant's awareness of the parental couple: 'even when the infant is a participant in a creative act, sharing an enviable experience [such as feeding at the breast], he is also identified with the excluded party, with the consequent pain, envy and jealousy' (p. 126). This applies equally to the twin at the breast in relation to the excluded twin.

Twin–twin interaction

At what age do twins become aware of each other and when do they begin to interact with each other in a 'knowing' way?

The nature and development of the twin relationship both pre- and postnatally has been studied by Piontelli (1989 and 2002). She has pioneered the ultrasound observation of twins in utero. In her later work (2002), she notes that while each twin is influenced by the behaviour and actions of the other twin in utero, proper social interchanges only begin some months after birth. She thus concurs with Stern, below, with Davison's account (1992) of an observation of twin infants (see next chapter), and with Leonard (1961). In Piontelli's view, twinship is a largely social and emotional construction, built up around the complex network of mutual and external influences between the twins and those caring for them. Similarities and dissimilarities between twins will be largely accounted for by this network rather than genetically predetermined. No two twins have the same start in life, as they will be affected by many intrauterine factors, including their position in the uterus. Thus both pre- and postnatal experiences are unique to each twin. Piontelli stresses that the early interchanges between twins in utero are based on sensing, not perceiving, despite the continuity of behaviour in each twin before and after birth.

At whatever stage the twins take note of each other and interact, they do share the unique experience of being twins and therefore of being always present for each other, whether in utero or in mother's mind. Piontelli (2002) observes that infants are acutely sensitive to individual attention directed at them, and focus on the face of a caregiver. At birth they are uninterested in other babies, including their twin. As noted (pp.50–51), she suggests that they are sensitive to attention being given to the other twin rather than to them and that they seem to be able to distinguish between handling and communication appropriate to their age. Thus they are less disturbed when mother's attention is paid to a younger or older sibling than to their twin. While twins vary in their modes of relating to each other at birth, some seeking contact, others avoiding it, Piontelli distinguishes between this behaviour and the complex patterns of social relating that develop later. Up to three months the twin infants are aware of, and compete with, each other for the attention of the caregiver, but the social, mutual signalling between them begins after this. Piontelli notes that while each twin is always part of the environment for the other, it is only later that this takes on a psychological/emotional dimension. She concludes that no twins are identical, and no twins have an identical environment, either intra- or extra-uterine.

Gifford et al. (1966) observed MZ twins 'discovering', taking note of and vocalizing to each other at three months. They also note that prenatal elements influence the development of the twins (as does Spitz, 1966). Gifford et al. (1966) note that there were differences in size and development in MZ twin girls both at birth and later. They suggest that the observed personality differences between the twins relate to the physical differences between them and originate from their differing experiences of the uterine environment.

The issue of generational sameness leading to an enmeshed twinship is noted by Leonard (1961). She explores the intensity of the inter-twin identification and the fact that it occurs with an individual at the same level of development, unlike that with a parent or siblings. Like Burlingham (1952), Leonard suggests that the libidinal tie between the twins begins at an early age and conflicts with, and has to adapt itself to, the parental relationship. Thus each twin will have the task of separating from the other twin as well as from the mother. Leonard proposes the existence of a 'psychological syncytium' (Leonard, 1961: 307), i.e. an undifferentiated state preceding an awareness of body boundaries in which the twins experience a sense of oneness, or a lack of perception of separateness. This leads gradually through the continued visual confrontation with a mirror image to a state of primary identification with the twin. The primary twin inter-identification persists throughout life, as does the identification with mother. There is confusion of identity and blurring of self-images between the twins. The persistent presence of the other twin and the lack of a sufficiently available mother will hinder the development of an object relationship with mother. The twinship may retard the development of language and impedes the formation of other object relationships.

Visual contact and attachment in mother–infant twin pairs

Eye contact between mother and infant is crucial in early development (see Chapter 10). Stern (1971) suggests that the infant's true eye contact with mother starts at six weeks. Infant gaze aversion and turning away of the head are thought to occur as early as two weeks. 'Visual contact and the facing position between mother and infant are cardinal attachment behaviors which not only are under mature voluntary control early, but are increasingly thought to play a dominant role in forming the early mother–infant tie' (Stern, 1971: 502). By three months, the infant–mother visual contact is subject to subtle instant-by-instant regulation.

In an observational study of a mother with her DZ twins from the age of three to fifteen months, Stern (1971) found that the infants directed almost no behaviour towards each other, so that it was as if there were two mother–infant dyads. The twins differed markedly in their abilities to either hold mother's gaze or to terminate it by turning away. It was noted that the twin who was less able to turn away from mother and to cease responding to her, later had greater difficulty in separating from mother and in gaining his independence from her. We see in this a clear example of both constitutional (infant capacities) and environmental (mother's divided attention) factors at work.

The sense of individuality develops within the close relationship with mother. Contrary to the views of some psychoanalysts, most notably Margaret Mahler, Stern (1985) states that there is no early symbiotic stage where there is confusion between self and other. He maintains that infants have a sense of individuality and of self from birth, developing through the stages of a sense of an emergent self from birth or even before birth, a coming into being; a sense of a core self at 2-3 months, with a sense of having a body and history and that others do too; a sense of a subjective self at 7-9 months, where there is a sense of understanding of the existence of mental states in self and others; and a sense of a verbal self at 15 months in which the internal world of memory and experience may be verbally stored and there is a verbal ability to convey and share experience.

Patterns of subjectively experienced elements, rather than specific experiences at a particular time, form the infants' perceptions of inner and outer experiences. The pattern of interpersonal relatedness is enduring and is the basis of character structure. The infant is a social creature who uses whatever capacities are available to enhance its relatedness to the caregiver and to aid its attempts towards integration. The pattern of interpersonal relatedness between twins is a significant factor in their development and will become an enduring relationship between them.

It is not only visual contact with the mother that is important. Each twin also has eye contact with the other twin. The importance of the visual awareness of the other twin is touched on in an account of the treatment of a blind MZ twin by Omwake and Solnit (1961). They explore the difficulties faced by the blind twin, Ann, as they were exposed during her therapy from the ages of three to seven years. The mother was overwhelmed both by the birth of her twins, and by the fact that one became blind shortly after birth. The crucial mother-infant relationship was hampered by Ann's blindness and by mother's inability to help her infant deal with her handicap. As a result, Ann was neglected and consequently suffered in her development both physically and in her relationships. While the report is a fascinating study of the effects of blindness on the child's development (particularly her ego development), the twinship merely hovers in the background.

The authors believe Ann had little perception of being a twin both because of her blindness and the neglect she endured as an infant. The twins were cared for separately both in hospital and at home. The authors suggest that Ann only became aware of the concept of being a twin in her sixth year. She would, of course, have been affected by the fact of being a twin, as she had had to share the attention of the caregivers with her twin sister. Ann was reported to be confused about who took care of which twin.

It is difficult to ascertain without being involved in the therapeutic process whether or not Ann was aware of being a twin. However, there are indications in the case material presented that Ann *did* have an idea of her twinship. During her therapy, aged 3.5 years Ann used dolls as imaginary companions to express aspects of herself - a normal twinning process. At five years dolls represented the confusing concepts of both her blindness and of being a twin, as she saw herself as a baby in relation to her twin. It was her *secret* knowledge of being a twin that emerged when she was six. At age 6.5 years, Ann expressed her feeling that it was not fair that she had to share her mother and nurse with her twin sister, and she also expressed the 'dawning awareness of the difference between herself and her sister' (Omwake and Solnit, 1961: 354).

Commenting on the need for Ann to find sameness between her twin and herself (unusual in twins), G. Klein (1962) suggests that whereas twins normally seek to assert their differences in order to establish a sense of self, this child had to find in what ways she was similar to her twin sister in order to do so. She had to find the twinship that existed, and that she secretly knew about. Ann had to come to terms with her inequality with regard to her twin sister rather than any notion of sameness. I would add that Ann was blind, but not deaf or insensitive. It would be highly likely that she was aware of the presence of another infant even if the care of the infants was divided between mother and others. She would also have been aware of mother's unavailability to her and involvement with another baby.

Gains and losses in a twin relationship

While Leonard (1961) regards the twinship as a primary relationship, Arlow (1960) and Ablon et al. (1986) in contrast, regard the object tie to the twin as secondary to the tie with the parents. Arlow (1960) states that twins are individuals before they are aware of the twin relationship, and that their first experience of the other twin is as a rival in the relationship with mother, an intruder. Ablon et al. (1986) suggest that the tie between the twins facilitates the separation from mother as a primary object but delays the resolution of the oedipal conflict. The facilitation of the separation from mother is apparent rather than real because the difficulty is displaced onto the later separation from the twin. Ablon et al. observed similar developmental processes in MZ and DZ twins, unlike Leonard, who believes that twin inter-identification is not a problem for DZ twins.

Twins resolve difficulties in their relationship by complementarity, similarity and interchangeability, or externalization of the aggression between them by forming a gang of two against others (Ablon, 1986; Arlow, 1960; and Engel, 1975), like Castor and Polydeuces (see Chapter 2). Where the hostility in the twin relationship is directed inwards rather than outside the twinship, the effects on each twin may be profound and enduring, as for Jacob and Esau (see Chapter 2). Arlow (1960) describes a patient who so diminished his twin that he believed that he, as the firstborn twin, was the real child, the second-born being an afterthought which he identified with the afterbirth (a split described by Eric Rhode, 1994 – see Chapter 1). Both MZ and DZ, same or different sex, twins experience difficulties in establishing a sense of personal identity (Orr, 1941; Joseph, 1961 and 1975), indicating that it is the twinning processes that are the main factor interfering in usual developmental sequences, and not the genes or physical similarities between twins.

The use of a twin in a parental function is not a unique experience amongst children. Parens (1988) notes that even though the experience of siblings is usually less well defined than that of parental figures, and they are consequently less represented in the transference relationship in analysis, they do become meaningful from the middle of the first year. In a progressively more complex way, siblings become emotionally invested both libidinally and aggressively; both older and younger siblings can be used both jointly and alternately as parent-substitute and as peer, serving a bridging function; and siblings are used for development and adaptation. The attachment to siblings may be close in valuation to that of the parental relationship. While Parens notes that these processes operate between twins, he does not specifically address the nature of the relationship in twins.

Several authors suggest that the ego of one twin is incomplete without the other: based on the analysis of an MZ twin in an enmeshed twinship, Lacombe (1959) proposes that a twin's psychological unity and ego is split by the presence in the outside world of 'another self', an 'identical' twin who is persistently confused with him. He believes that the 'mutilating psychic damage' (Lacombe, 1959: 11) caused at birth by the twinship can only be repaired in analysis by manipulating the setting, to restore to the patient what was missing at birth, by concretely giving to the patient the remaining half share of attention that he was due. (This is discussed more fully in Chapter 6.) Thus, Lacombe suggests that the problem for a twin is that of a deficit in development, not a conflict.

The idea of a shared identity in twins is expressed by several authors: Jacobs and Mesnikoff (1962) report that psychosis in one twin precipitated it in the other because the twins were dependent on each other for their ego integrity. Ortmeyer (1970) also suggests that twins have a special unity – a 'we-self' (p. 125) of two personalities to some extent functioning as one. He focuses on a depleting complementarity in twins where traits are divided up between them in a way that is non-duplicative and non-identical. As a result, the twins function as one personality and the twins fill in the deficits for each other, rather than develop them within the self. The 'we-self' is intertwined with the developing individual identities of each twin:

> The author's thesis is that the psychological force forming the we-self is not a mirror image nor an identity. It is, rather, the complementary personality attributes that each offers the other, and the expectation of each that the other's personality traits are at his command. Without the personality of his counterpart, a twin faces the loss of traits necessary for his expected personality functioning (Ortmeyer, 1970: 129).

This will be discussed further in Chapter 6.

In contrast, Engel (1975) emphasizes the positive aspects of twinship while noting that the diffuseness of ego boundaries may lead to retardation in various aspects of development. He suggests that the twin relationship is intensified by attachment needs and behaviour towards the twin. The narcissistic advantages of twinship are a constant pull against the development of separateness. For twins the sense of a necessity to separate does not have the added impetus of the Oedipus conflict, as does the parent–child relationship. Instead the narcissistic advantages of the twinship may be used to evade the oedipal conflict. Engel notes the persistence of the twinship throughout life.

If the twins were to rely solely on each other as developmental objects, their mutual immaturity would ensure that there would be little emotional development. However, this is an extreme scenario, as if there were no parents to turn to and no parental intervention in the twin relationship. There are twins that remain interlocked in a rigid relationship with each other that seems to exclude all outsiders to the twinship. The twins described by Burlingham (1963) are an example of this (see Chapter 4). Even where there has been a greater degree of separation between twins and the development of a greater sense of personal identity separate from the twinship, the other twin remains a significant internal figure in the way the parental figures do. Because of the closeness of the twinship and the fact that the twins shared the womb, the importance of the twin in the psyche is likely to be greater than that of other siblings.

There are many factors that will affect each twin's development as a separate individual, and the extent to which the twin structure is favoured over individuality. Maenchen (1968) describes the need to develop two mother–infant couples to enable twins to develop as individuals. The degree of parental intervention in the twinship is of major importance in the creation of an adequate developmental space for each twin. The twinship may remain predominant either because the active intervention by the parents is lacking (through depression, being overwhelmed, neglect, etc.), or because there is a lack of willingness in the twins to allow this intervention. Some of these factors will be explored in the next chapter.

Chapter 4
Mothers and twins:
'a walking crowd'

Parental relationships with twin babies are complex and the parents' attitudes and experiences will shape their relationship with their twins and the development of each child in a number of ways. On the one hand, the parents may be reluctant to interfere in the closeness of their twins. Often the twins turn so automatically towards each other that the parents feel it is too intrusive to intervene. Sometimes twins resist any interference in their relationship and it may require quite some determination on the part of the parents to do so. Where parents do not intervene in the twin relationship, the twins may be encouraged to form a unit separate from parental interference. On the other hand, the parents may use splitting mechanisms to deal with the complexity of the relationships with and between the twins. This would encourage the attribution of different traits or aspects of the self to one or the other twin, creating a split between the twins that is based on an exaggerated division of qualities rather than true difference. The simultaneous presence of two same-age infants, and perhaps considerable similarity between the twins, involves the parents in a difficult balance: that of maintaining an individual and separate relationship with each twin that also takes account of the experience of the other twin at the same time. This requires the parents to manage not only the two infants, but also their own tendencies to cope by either amalgamating or splitting the twins.

This chapter is concerned mainly with the relationship between the mother and her twins. This is not to deny the importance of the father in his relationships both with his twins and with his wife. Clearly his relationship with his twin infants is vital to their healthy emotional development. Rather, the focus is on the primary caregiver, who is usually the mother, and hence for convenience sake is referred to as such.

Mothers of twins

I have used a number of sources of information other than psychoanalytic texts in this section, including newspaper articles and reports, and meetings with mothers of twins. I like the immediacy of the experience that these sources describe. They bring to life the concepts described in the sometimes ponderous professional literature.

I was invited to join a group of mothers of twins who meet regularly for support and help. They discussed a variety of experiences and I am grateful to the mothers for their enlightening comments, some of which I will draw upon. There is something special about twins, and many mothers have expressed satisfaction at the high status awarded them as the mother of twins. This is especially important as the task of mothering twins is so much more exhausting than dealing with one baby. The cuteness of their two babies is felt to be some compensation.

On discovering that she was pregnant with twins, Kellaway (1997) writes, 'I enjoyed being pregnant with twins. I forgot the first person singular. I was a walking crowd. I was always conscious of which baby was which. Their movements were quite distinct.' After birth, she felt as if she had to try to catch two balls at once, and that both she and her twins were panicking. She was thrilled at how unalike they were, but 'despaired of ever getting to know them as individuals, of looking into their faces, of playing with them'. She wondered whether it was going against the nature of twinship to separate the twins, particularly if the twins appeared not to want to be separated.

Elizabeth Bryan of the Multiple Birth Foundation has campaigned for the need to raise twins as individuals, to be given names that are properly distinct, to be dressed differently, and to be given 'the solitude and privacy that is the single child's birthright' (Kellaway, 1997), but parents face ambivalence about separating their twins. There is pressure to treat their twins individually, and yet they feel guilty about not treating them the same. Several mothers have expressed a wish that they had had only one baby, in the belief that they would have a harmonious fit with a single baby, without any of the dilemmas posed by twins. These days, it is unusual to see twins dressed alike and treated as if they were identical, though there are still situations where twins are regarded as a unit, even having the same name. The twin baby girls in the Internet adoption scandal (January 2001) were named Kiara and Keyara by the first adoptive couple – same name, two spellings.

It is a difficult task for mother to hold both babies in mind adequately, and the mother often feels guilty and neglectful towards each twin. Feeding situations are particularly problematic. Mothers with twin babies often feel frantic and guilty, as they are unable to give their full attention to either baby. If one baby sleeps while the other feeds, there is some peace. But this is not an ideal solution as it cannot be relied upon and it may be that the sleeping baby is avoiding overwhelming feelings by cutting off and sleeping. The babies will each have their own individual pattern of feeding and this might play on the mother's guilt about not treating both babies equally. One mother spoke of one twin who refused the breast, while the other twin breastfed satisfactorily. The mother then felt guilty that someone else had to feed one baby while she breastfed the other. Another mother described one baby breastfeeding well and feeling satisfied, but the other twin was too frantic while feeding to latch on to the nipple and was then subjected to a faceful of milk, leaving the mother feeling guilty. As a result, she stopped breastfeeding both twins at three months.

Mothers face a dilemma about whether to treat each child the same as the other or to allow individuality and therefore difference not only in them, but also in her attention to them. If the twins are fighting, should the blows be evened up? Should one or both be disciplined for fighting, even though one provoked it? Should mother talk to the twins individually about what they are doing, or as a pair? Mothers feel distressed at favouritism displayed by others towards one twin. So there is great pressure to create equality towards and between the twins, with an equal pressure to treat them as individuals. Burlingham (1952) describes the dilemmas mothers face in treating each twin, MZ or DZ, as an individual, but not wanting to be unfair to either.

Clearly there are differences between twins reared in a nursery like the Burlingham's (1952) study (see page 69), and those living at home with their mother. Demarest and Winestine (1955) suggest that the mother is bound to prefer one or the other twin at different times, a finding later confirmed by Piontelli (2002). Other members of the family (including the other twin) may be selected by the other twin as a substitute for mother, in an attempt to compensate for the loss of mother to the chosen twin. In an observation and therapy of twin girls, Demarest and Winestine (1955) note that the introduction of therapy upset the equilibrium between the twins, and that each twin needed to separate from the other twin as well as from mother for development to proceed adequately. In this study, the home life of the twins was such as to create a problematic twinship that was not resolved through the therapy.

There are, of course, all sorts of unconscious factors in the parents' relationships with their twins. Benjamin (1961) reports an observation of MZ twin boys and the differences in their development linked with differences in the mother's relationship with each twin. Mother identified with Charlie, the second-born twin, whom she saw as an intruder, unexpected and unwanted, as mother had herself felt as a child. Jimmy, the firstborn twin, was seen by mother as identified with father in particular, and men in general. Men were regarded as weak and hostile, while women were seen as strong. This view was echoed in the twin boys. Mother found Jimmy more difficult to understand and empathize with, and considered this to be his fault. The observers regarded Jimmy as more pathologically regressed than Charlie, who seemed to use his regressions more constructively. Charlie regarded father as an intruder in his symbiotic relationship with mother, and showed more evidence of overt fear of separation and loss of love. Jimmy seemed to share his father's fears of mother as a warm and loving but potentially castrating woman.

Parental attitudes may have a marked effect on the development of the twins. In a longitudinal study of eight families, Dibble and Cohen report a similar identification between a mother and her 'underdog' twin (Dibble and Cohen, 1981: 56) in one of the pairs observed. The twins each identified in a possessive way with one of the parents in order to avoid the intense rivalry of the twinship. Dibble and Cohen conclude that the attitudes of the parents in the study influenced the development of each set of twin infants, and that their view of the twins started before birth.

Some mothers of twins may face considerable difficulties in identifying with their babies (Burlingham, 1946). Mothers may experience a narcissistic injury as a result of having twins and also narcissistic pleasure in the attention the twins generate (Burlingham, 1952). Some feel that being the mother of twins is shameful, linked with animals having litters, while others believe it confers greater status on them, and take narcissistic pleasure and pride in the attention paid to their twins. This may lead the mother to stress the likeness between the twins. However, the mother also feels a need to differentiate between the twins. She experiences an inability to distinguish between them as a failure, as a lack of love. In order to express her feelings towards each baby and make close contact with them, she needs to be able to tell them apart, so she will know which baby she is directing her feelings towards. When they both look the same, she might feel confused about whether the right baby is receiving the right feelings. The twins need to have individual personalities for mother to identify with each one separately.

Burlingham (1946) also observes that mothers of both MZ and DZ twins try to treat the twins equally or alike as a matter of principle, so as to minimize jealousy. Concerns about jealousy make it difficult to give twins individual treatment, particularly where the twins want to be the same. Some mothers hate their twins to be separated, believing that they are a complete unit and could not do without each other. The twins express envy of each other and this leads to them being treated alike. Burlingham notes that in some twins there is a failure to develop different personalities. She concludes that the reason for this is unclear. It could be to do either with the twinship or with mother's attitude to them. If mother cannot tell them apart, and is driven by an inner urge to equality, she treats them as one, not two. As a result they feel there is nothing unique or personal about them, leaving them feeling misunderstood, angry and lonely. (Miss D, in Chapter 8, exemplifies this.) Where this occurs, the only person for whom the twin is unique is the other twin, and they may turn to each other for elements that are missing in their relationships with mother.

Twins and their mothers

Twins' own views of the benefits and difficulties of twinship vary, with some seeking sameness, others anxious for difference. William Wolff (1996) states that the fact of being a twin has been one of the most joyous and important facts in his life. Throughout his childhood and to the present day he is unable to speak of himself in the first person singular. However, his twin died, and since then he has been unable to celebrate his birthday. Michele Roberts

(1996) writes that at a profound level, she and her DZ twin are always there for each other. Their bond is unbreakable. As a child identifying with MZ twins at school, she sometimes puzzled about how their parents could know them apart, could know it was she and not her twin. 'Supposing we had been mixed up and given each other's names by mistake. Would I still be myself?' This is reminiscent of a story told to me by Peggy Jay of her daughters, the famous 'Jay twins', feted in the press in the 1960s. While she was in the kitchen, one of the twins was on the stairs out of sight. Peggy called to her, 'Is that you Catherine?' 'No,' replied Helen, 'It's not me'. The Surguladze twins (Stainer, 2002) believe they have complete understanding of each other, and are a perfect team. The Bradbury twins (Corner, 2001), in contrast, take pleasure in their difference and finding themselves as individuals. The ten-minute age gap in their births is seen as a welcome defining characteristic to them both.

Some twins are resistant to parental intervention in the twinship. It seems that the most potent factor in this eternal bonding is deprivation at an early stage. A failure of maternal containment, for whatever reason, leaves the twins to use each other developmentally. The failure of containment may be to do with the absence of availability in mother, or of mother's difficulty in holding both her babies in mind. It may be that she prefers one twin and focuses her attention on that infant. One twin may then be developmentally advantaged over the other and this may lead to the creation of a parasitic object relationship between the twins. Rosenfeld (1971b) suggests that in parasitic object relations in psychotic patients, massive projective identification takes place so that the patient believes he lives entirely inside an object, which is expected to function as his ego. 'Severe parasitism ... is not just a defensive state to deny envy or separation but is also an expression of aggression, particularly envy' (Rosenfeld, 1971b: 125). The combination of defence and aggression leads to an intractable state where not only envy and jealousy are avoided, but any painful emotion is defended against. The Gibbons twins (Wallace, 1996) would be an example of a parasitic relationship of this kind.

What factors lead to such parasitism in twins? As I will describe in greater detail in Chapter 5, Athanassiou (1986) suggests that parasitism between twins is based on the functional complementarity between them. She proposes that the interpenetrating projective identifications between twins leads to a state of fusion between them. The twin at the breast will have his experience with mother poisoned by his awareness of the excluded twin, who is presumed to be in a rage at this exclusion. Athanassiou believes that the twin at the breast is not sure whether it is him or his twin that is excluded, and that normal projective identification and introjection of mother's breast is then contaminated by this parasitic element. Thus it seems that the critical factors that lead to a parasitic twin relationship are considerable enmeshment between the twins and envy of such magnitude that it poisons the infant's relationship with its mother. As I describe below, a parasitic twin relationship may also be one in which one twin lives off the other because he has delegated some functioning to the other twin and then cannot manage life without him.

In a later paper (1991), Athanassiou describes her work with a child where the twinship had become a refuge from development through the mature medium of a maternal container (see Chapter 7). She explores the use of transitional phenomena in twins, particularly where they are used to avoid rather than to bear psychic pain, in the process of mourning, and in the development of a perception of separateness. Athanassiou describes twins who functioned as two parts of one self, splitting both functions and personality between them, with the result that each twin was regarded as part of the self and the split-off aspects were lost to the individual twin. She suggests that where an object of identification is too close to the subject in its qualities, separation becomes more difficult, as in the case of twins. The twinship is then used as a refuge from the pain of development.

Inter-twin complementarity is commonly described and may provide a useful solution in dealing with intense rivalry. Engel (1975) describes his relationship with his twin brother as 'close, intense, but extremely rivalrous' (p. 24). They were constant and exclusive companions until the age of twelve and thereafter shared friends rather than develop individual friend-ships with others. They attempted to deal with their aggression towards each other by developing equivalent aggression, and socially were highly complementary in their behaviour. They did lead separate existences in their early twenties, but remained competitive throughout their lives. The Engel twins used their complementarity constructively. However, where complementarity is based on massive projective identification between twins, there may be development in one twin at the expense of a retardation of development in the other. The projection of functioning parts of the self into the twin will create a narcissistic entanglement between the twins that will be detrimental to both, and it may encompass parasitic elements in which one twin lives off certain aspects of the other.

I am indebted to Estelle Roith who, arising out of her own work in progress, has drawn my attention to the fact that Engel's anniversary reaction to his twin's death after a heart attack is an expression of how powerful this unconscious narcissistic entanglement in twins can be, a persistent element at the core of a more healthy twin relationship. Although Engel seems to believe that he and his twin had dealt with their rivalry, had tamed it to manageable proportions by establishing an equivalent mutual aggression and developing a complementary relationship, it seems that unconscious elements prevailed. After his twin died, Engel waited with a sense of prescience for his own equivalent heart attack. This occurred one day short of 11 months after his twin had died. His immediate reaction was one of relief – he no longer had to anticipate the heart attack, 'the other shoe had fallen' (Engel, 1975: 25). He could now exonerate himself of the phantasied crime of killing his brother and the associated guilt (indicated in a phantasy that he experienced while in hospital). Engel had recognized his murderous wishes towards his twin brother, but he had not escaped the twinship. In the Judaic tradition, the period of mourning is exactly one day short of 11 months, and Engel's heart attack thus did indeed occur on the anniversary of his twin's death. In so doing, it phantastically united him with his twin again, recreating their narcissistic bond. The power of the unconscious phantasy of oneness with his twin showed itself with force and accuracy.

Constitutional factors in the twins may play the decisive role in the failure of maternal containment. Various factors may be at work. In a situation where the presence of two infants means that longer waits for attention are inevitable, the infants' innate difficulty in tolerating frustration may lead the twins to turn to each other for gratification, leading to a narcissistic entanglement. Envy of the other twin may be so powerful, whether innate or stimulated by the presence of the other twin, that it may engender an attack on the good link with mother, poisoning the relationship with her. In their immature state, a loving internal object may not have been securely established and would therefore not be available to ameliorate the jealousy of the relationship the other twin has with mother. Money-Kyrle (1971) suggests that when an infant has been kept waiting too long for gratification of its needs, 'spuriously satisfying' objects (p. 445) are substituted for the breast by the infant. For actual twins the wait is frequently too long and the creation of a phantasy twin or turning to the other twin as a spuriously satisfying object would not be uncommon. It is these 'spuriously satisfying substitutes' (Money-Kyrle, 1971: 445) that become an enduring destructive internal twinship that interferes with object relationships – as in Coen and Bradlow's (1982) 'persistent, stable transference paradigm of twinship' (p. 613).

The responses of others to twins also play a part in reinforcing the twinship. Burlingham (1946) suggests that the common phantasy of having a twin may lead an admiring onlooker to a spontaneous identification with twins. The fascination with twins would reinforce the twinship as the twins are made to feel special, attractive and interesting, and therefore superior. Twins face a conflict between the development of a narcissistic inter-twin relationship which may be seen and experienced as special but individuality-limiting, and the development of a personal sense of identity which allows greater autonomy but involves a limitation in the twinship. The infant twin faces two opposing maternal images: a mother who through her containment can aid development, and the same mother who in so doing, interferes in the twinship (Athanassiou, 1986).

Observational studies

The detailed observations of twins at Anna Freud's Hampstead Nursery (Burlingham, 1949) highlight some of the difficulties twins encounter in their development. Of course, it has to be borne in mind that these children were observed in a nursery, during the war, and separated from their parents. This would undoubtedly have affected them in their relationship with each other and with others in the nursery, staff and children, as well as with visiting parents. Burlingham notes that while the twins expressed their attachment to their mother at around five months, it was not until some months later that they seemed to notice each other. Current observations would place this inter-twin awareness at about three months (Gifford et al., 1966; Piontelli, 2002 – see Chapter 3).

The extraordinary study by Anna Freud and Sophie Dann (1951) of six children brought up as a group without parents in a German concentration camp until the age of three years, and consequently suffering catastrophic deprivation, provides insight into the developmental difficulties faced by children lacking reliable parental figures. The artificial twinning amongst these children was based on identification through common needs, anxieties and wishes, and on the similarity of age of children living in close proximity without adequate parental figures. They became insecure and anxious as soon as they were separated from each other. Without any parents, the horizontal relationships between these children were primary and all-important to them. The authors conclude with a note of warning about psychoanalytic assumptions regarding the importance of the maternal link for development. They note that while the children were not by any means problem-free, neither were they delinquent, deficient or psychotic. They had used their libidinal links to each other to master some of their anxieties and had developed social attitudes.

Sigmund Freud's (1900) acknowledgement of the importance of sibling relationships, and the above warning from Anna Freud and Dann in 1951 that horizontal relationships are extremely important in development, challenge psychoanalytic assumptions about the overriding importance of the maternal relationship. Freud and Dann's observations of these children and the use they made of each other to deal with their anxieties are of particular importance for twins and the way in which they may use each other as primary objects. However, the additional essential factor in twins is that not only might they use an immature twin as a primary object, but mother's attention is necessarily divided between the twins.

This chapter has focused on the relationships between twins and between each twin and its mother. Burlingham (1949) describes several aspects of the mother–twin relationships. As regards the twins' perception of mother and her relationship with each twin, Burlingham notes that in twin pairs the greatest emotional reaction towards each other is noticed in the feeding situation, and is different for each twin. It is common for one twin to wish to take the place of the other. In relation to mother, one twin tends to be active, the other passive, but this is reversible. It is dictated by whichever twin was in a stronger position at that time, forcing the other twin into a passive position rather than one twin choosing to be passive. Burlingham also notes that while children often imitate older siblings as an aid to development, the fact that twins are both at the same level creates an atmosphere of competition, forcing a less active child to achieve at an earlier age than usual.

This is especially so in trying to gain parental approval and noticing mother's pleasure at the other twin's achievements.

Burlingham also comments on the relationship of each twin with the other. She observed that they entertained each other through copying games in a way that excluded other children. Of particular note were the different developmental patterns shown by two twin pairs: Jessie and Bessie, and Bill and Bert. Jessie and Bessie imitated each other and this created a closer relationship between them, but their behaviour followed different patterns and their individualities became more marked. They were dependent on each other, but also independent and individually creative. It was noted that Bessie imitated Jessie more than the other way around, and in so doing, tried to take over Jessie's personality for fear of being left out. The twins acted as a team in relation to their mother, cooperating with each other to get the desired effect.

In contrast, Bill and Bert not only copied each other, but they also showed postural and movement similarities to a great degree. It is not clear whether this was the result of copying or constitutional identity, but they proved to be backward in development. Unlike Bessie and Jessie, they were unable to make normal contacts either with each other or with others outside the twin pair. They represented an enmeshed twinship in which the relationship did not further develop, and actually hindered contact with others. Under the influence of the dominant Bill, it was impossible for Bert's ego development to proceed normally.

The observations of two sets of twins described below illustrate very different attitudes both in the mother–twin relationship and in the relationship between the twins. These studies also differ in the outcome for the twins and highlight some of the major developmental factors discussed in this and the preceding chapter.

Bill and Bert

Burlingham (1963) follows the development of Bill and Bert from their arrival at the Hampstead Nursery, through their schooling, adolescence and post-adolescence. The detail of this observation offers a great deal of information about development in twins and the possible causes of an enmeshed twinship, for which I am indebted to the author.

Bill and Bert spent the first four months of their life with their mother in an evacuated baby hostel. They were admitted to Hampstead Nursery when their mother went back to work. They were never very welcome in their mother's home, partly because she found them so unmanageable, but also because they were the product of an affair with a married man, and mother later married someone else and had another child. Stepfather did not get on with the twins. After they left the nursery, they stayed with mother briefly, but were then placed in various institutional homes, and finally in a home for maladjusted children at the age of 12 years. In that home they were offered psychotherapy.

I will follow some of the elements that emerged that are particularly relevant to my thesis. Bert and Bill were so alike that both mother and the staff who dealt with them had difficulty telling them apart. They were frequently mistaken for each other and often called Billybert or Bertbilly. When separated as infants, each would mistake his image in a mirror for his twin. They were indeed mirror images of each other in posture and in movement, and were intensely competitive throughout their lives. The jealousy and rivalry between them was quite murderous, especially in their teens, and in therapy at the point when they were beginning to establish some sense of separateness.

In early observations a lack of superego formation was noted in the twins – any hopeful signs that it might be developing were quickly destroyed by the twins' greater involvement with each other than with an object external to the twinship. They constantly sought excitement and felt no guilt at hurting others. At school they showed some complementarity in their abilities as a means of coping with their rivalry. They felt murderous towards each other, but also totally absorbed with each other. They had no object relationships outside the twinship, but they attacked each other repeatedly. At other times they would act together as a gang of two, attacking the group of children at the school. They operated as a narcissistic system with a thin skin between the twins so that there was insufficient sense of personal boundary, and a thick skin around the pair, insulating them from all external objects. They were happiest when being totally destructive, reducing all around them to chaos. It was almost impossible to make emotional contact with them and they clung to being indistinguishable.

In Chapter 6, I will look at the enactment that took place with the twins' therapist in his attempt to get in touch with each of them as individuals. It was only by becoming sucked into the twinship that the therapist could get closer to the twins. This enabled a degree of differentiation so that they could each have psychotherapy with him. When he was able to establish separate relationships with them, various factors emerged in the therapy:

1. Both twins were afraid of formulating or verbalizing thoughts and feelings to their therapist because it felt to them like revealing themselves to their twin. It was as if the lack of proper boundary between the twins also existed between each twin and his therapist, i.e. the therapist became a transference twin to whom the boys clung. Thus the thin-skinned narcissism between the twins was enacted in the consulting room, with the psychic skin again enveloping the pair – the therapist and the twin.

2. Each twin feared that the other twin would murder him. Their murderous wishes were not contained and modified within the twinship. Their own

murderous projections were enhanced by those of the twin and were returned intensified instead of mitigated by containment. In this paranoid system the twins lived by the law of talion.

3. The twins identified with each other and assumed that the other twin had identical thoughts, as if the two twins were one person. Bert feared that he was a half-boy, defective, and he felt that he had lost his birthright to the twin born 20 minutes later. Bill felt he had no right to be born as mother already had a baby. He too felt incomplete.

4. Their main motivator was the competitiveness between them rather than any wish for self-advancement. Their aggressive enmeshment was expressed in homosexual sadistic love-play in which they engaged from early childhood.

5. While both twins were in psychotherapy, as they began to separate, each twin 'became a twin to himself' (Burlingham, 1963: 390). Both boys were placed at the same school and Bert tried to deal with the feelings of ambivalence towards Bill that this aroused in him. He felt both gratified and angry at being at school with Bill. He longed to be able to manage without Bill and was disappointed in not being able to do so. He was lonely and believed that this was because he was a twin. Thus, by creating a phantasy twin, 'being a twin to himself', he could replace his actual twin lost through separation and not have to suffer this loss. He wished to take back into himself those projected aspects of himself that he had lodged in Bill and were consequently lost to him.

Likewise, Bill became very anxious and felt that he was losing his identity when he could not be distinguished from Bert, and he too created a phantasy twin to try to resolve this dilemma. He phantasized that he was two people, a good right half where the left side was always left out, and a bad left side which was always angry at being left out. Thus in both twins we see an internalization of the twinning that had previously existed between them, a splitting of the self with aspects of the self projected into internal objects rather than into the external twin.

6. The damaging rivalry between Bert and Bill was such that neither could allow himself to succeed at anything for fear that he would be attacked by his twin. He would thus damage himself in anticipation. When one twin was damaged in some manner, the other felt responsible and would damage himself to prevent his twin's revenge. This uncontained aggression between the twins is in stark contrast to that described by Engel (1975) in which MZ twin brothers managed their aggression by adopting complementary roles. Bill depended on his twin for dissipating his aggression and he felt helpless without him. The sight of his twin was a reassurance that he had not killed him, and their horseplay was a safety valve for their aggression.

7. Bill felt unable to work when he was alone because he so longed for his twin, but when he was working with someone else he became ruthlessly competitive. This competition was necessary to both twins for their functioning, and they experienced a three-cornered situation as unmanageable. So they maintained a persistent twinship with no internal parental structure that would have allowed separateness and containment.

8. As is so common in twins, Bill and Bert had a mutual understanding without words. Emotionally, their strongest bond was to each other and this was of overriding importance in preventing other contacts. Their attachment was close and exclusive and their adaptation to group life nonexistent. The draw of the twinship caused their withdrawal from other objects.

Two factors were considered to be particularly important in the development of such an enmeshed twin relationship: the fact that the twins were a mirror image of each other, and that they were so similar in appearance that they caused confusion and consternation in both mother and their carers. Mother's attachment to the twins was weak, uncertain and changeable, and lacked regularity or warmth. As discussed above, the mother's relationship with her twins is a very important factor in their development of a sense of identity.

Burlingham notes the narcissistic unity and identification between the twins. The confusion for each boy between his own mirror image and his twin suggests 'that living in the presence of the twin was for them synonymous with living in the presence of their own reflection' (Burlingham, 1963: 403). Thus the loss of a twin through separation would represent a loss of a part of the self, a lost narcissistic element. She suggests that this narcissistic identification was resolved gradually when each twin realized that the other twin 'was not merely a duplication of the self, whose identical reactions heightened the wishes, needs, impulses of their own person, but also a rival to the self, capable of monopolizing wanted objects and means of satisfaction' (Burlingham, 1963: 404). Their rivalry and narcissistic investment in the twinship was such that they believed that a pleasurable gain for one twin automatically implied that the other twin had failed in their wish to possess a desirable object.

However, Burlingham notes that object cathexes in their early childhood other than the twin–twin attachment became evident in adolescence, as the twins each tried to avoid drawing the other twin into regressive incestuous phantasies, while the narcissism continued unabated. Thus, as noted with the Engel twins above, even when steps towards separation are achieved, a narcissistic core remains in the twin relationship.

As a result of their abortive relationships with adults and their defective superego development, Bill and Bert's struggle for personal identity, for each to be a person in his own right, meant for these twins having to be without a twin. (In Chapter 7, I discuss the murderous elimination of the psychic twin in a bid to find freedom from an imprisoning twinship.) For Bill and Bert, their extreme closeness and possessive intimacy in infancy, their copying games, understanding without words, constant companionship and the increase in power and efficiency in the twinship as opposed to being alone, all contributed to their difficulty in finding a separate identity. The absence of loneliness is another factor, and as seen in Chapter 1, an integral element in the establishment of separateness and symbolic thinking. Both the internal image of the twin and the external presence of the twin had to be got rid of and their loneliness faced, but there was a constant regressive pull back to the twinship, and a persistent preoccupation with the other twin. As I will discuss in Chapter 7, I think that the 'retardation' in their development is actually a regression to earlier levels of functioning rather than an arrest or deficit.

Burlingham suggests that various factors led to the antisocial development of the twins. A symbiotic relationship between the twins developed as a result of both the inherent twinship and the absence of a symbiotic relationship with mother or a mother substitute that could lead to the establishment of a good internal object. This twin–twin symbiosis intensified existing behavioural patterns by reciprocal infection and cross-stimulation. The narcissistic tie between the twins led to the overdevelopment of a narcissistic system between them. There was imperfect differentiation between self and twin as a result of which each twin lost his individual identity and instead his identification with his twin was exaggerated. The pleasurable interaction between the twins became a perversely exciting one that blotted out the need for an adult container. In this narcissistic system, the twins related to each other at an infantile level. With imperfectly developed object relationships, they used undue autoerotic behaviour and the narcissistic twinship in place of a good internal object.

It was only by intervention in the twinship and the analysis of their unconscious hostility towards each other that Bill and Bert could grow apart and form new relationships. Presumably the analysis of their hostility lessened its malignant power and enabled the establishment of a good internal object that allowed an adequate degree of separation from the twin. This made possible for each a withdrawal into the self and the enjoyment in solitude of a more mature personality.

Many factors operated to create a situation for Bert and Bill that was so deprived emotionally, socially and developmentally. They were illegitimate, born during the war and evacuated with their mother. They grew up in a nursery which, however caring, could not provide for them what a loving family home might. As they became more difficult behaviourally, the twins were rejected by their mother and stepfather. The fact that they were eventually able to emerge from the twinship and form loving relationships with others is testament to the quality of care offered them by the various professionals who worked with them and enabled them to forge better links with their family. In contrast, the Gibbons twins (Wallace, 1996) remained trapped in a defensive narcissistic twin system from which it seems impossible to escape even after the death of one of them.

In reviewing Burlingham's book, *Twins: A Study of Three Pairs of Identical Twins* (1952), Leonard (1953) suggests that in reality twins are more different than they are generally expected to be. The ubiquitous phantasy of having a twin colours our attitudes towards twins. Leonard suggests that the phantasy of having a twin idealizes the twin relationship and pictures it as devoid of feelings of rivalry and jealousy, providing instead a relationship of continued understanding and sympathy. However, anyone who has observed twins together will be quickly disabused of this idea, as was shown in Burlingham's study of Bill and Bert. Leonard suggests that rivalry starts earlier in twins than in other siblings. She questions Burlingham's view that the crippling and limiting twinship seen in Bert and Bill is the result of identification. She suggests instead that it is the continuation of a narcissistic state extended to include a second 'self'. She also wonders whether there is a possible retardation of ego differentiation in enmeshed twins, and whether the twin relationship as a rule has a tendency to delay the development of object relationships. Perhaps what is most relevant to development is the nature of the twin relationship, rather than its existence *per se*.

In an enmeshed twinship the loss of mother is less keenly felt because she has been replaced by the actual twin. Twins often feel like two halves of one, and develop complementary traits. But most important is the narcissistic basis of the twinship, as described in Chapter 1. The intensity of the love-hate relationship between twins is an aspect of the narcissistic nature of an enmeshed twinship. Each twin is treated as a part of the other, containing either desirable or hated aspects of the self, projected with great violence into the other. Each twin represents aspects of both the self and the other twin; twins occupy a narcissistic state not only as the individual members of the twin pair, but also the twinship itself is a narcissistic system. Where the longing for a twin finds its object in the reality of the other twin, the twins may remain in an intensely projectively identified state with each other, as if they were internal objects of a unitary system (like Britton's 'twin internal souls'; Britton, 2000: 3). Twins within such a twinship remain basically hostile to external object relations.

Mark and Luke

The report by Davison (1992) of an observation of infant twins, Mark and Luke, lies in stark contrast to the observations of Bert and Bill. As Davison notes, the environmental conditions for Mark and Luke were optimal, and the development of each baby in relation to its mother could proceed along normal lines. Within this situation, it was possible for each infant to develop a good relationship with the breast/mother as a primary object. Davison believes that for twins, as for singletons, the primary object can be the breast/mother, but the presence of the other twin impinges on this relationship.

Davison pays particular attention to the state of mind of the mother of the twins and she suggests that this is pivotal in promoting the individual development of each infant. In this observation, the mother's capacity to tolerate her own feelings of being left out was an essential element in helping her infants deal with the feelings evoked in an inherently triangular situation. Shortly after the birth of the twins, the mother expressed her difficulty in holding both babies in mind. Mother felt it was unnatural to have two infants at the same time. She was constantly concerned that her love and wonder for one infant at the breast also meant the exclusion of the other, and that they could not have exactly the same. In the early days the feeding of two babies felt particularly onerous and mother felt as if she had one enormously demanding infant that was too much to feed, and thus was unable to have a positive feeling towards either baby.

Mother identified with the excluded infant, especially at feeding times. At five weeks, she 'inhibited her first impulse to hold Luke's gaze, lovingly, for fear of leaving out Mark and provoking unbearable feelings in him towards herself and Luke' (Davison, 1992: 372). These feelings, which she recognized in both herself and her excluded infant, marred her pleasure with her infant at the breast. Although at that particular time Mark was asleep, this seemed to be a common feature of the observations. It is interesting that Davison attributes the left-out feelings to mother, i.e. that the 'left out' experience in the early stages is simply, or perhaps mainly, mother's projection. She does not seem to take account of the extent to which mother's recognition of her infant's experience was based on the infants' projecting unbearable feelings into her. However, Davison notes that all three participants resolved this difficult and painful situation by mother's feeding one twin while the other slept. It thus seems to me that each infant and the mother encountered the left-out experience. Mother tried to deal with it as best she could to minimize the pain for the infants, and they responded by creating the alternating pattern of sleeping and feeding.

At nine weeks, mother had firmly separated each infant in her mind. At ten weeks, each twin had established a relationship with a good mother, such that a good feed at a good breast led to a sense of being good inside and having a good mother who could be loved unreservedly. Davison notes that this development then led to competition between the twin babies for the same good mother, especially when one observed the other feeding. This stimulated possessiveness, as a result of which mother's breast temporarily lost its goodness. Davison suggests that it was only when each infant had established this good relationship with mother that competition between them for mother developed, and that it was based on possessiveness rather than hunger. However, she also notes that over the first two months, she had the illusion of observing only one infant, as the other was usually asleep. It seems that this is the way in which the rivalry between the twins was avoided in the minds of all concerned.

At three months, each twin was acutely aware of being himself, not the other twin, and it was mother who was central to each rather than the other twin. Thus, the development of a sense of separateness in each twin is intimately involved with mother's sense of the individuality of each of her infants. After three months and the establishment of a good breast relationship with mother, the rivalry between the twins was more obvious than an attachment to each other. Once mother's centrality to the twins had been clearly established, they would not make do with each other if she or another adult was present. The twins had to share mother's love and affection and the fact of not being the only one was painful for each of them.

With great sensitivity, Davison notes that it was a deprivation for mother always to have to be mindful of the pain experienced by the left-out twin and his limited capacity to deal with it. I think it is also clear that it was a deprivation for each of the twins as well, not having mother to themselves. Davison notes how the twin at the breast was disturbed, not by the presence of an excluded twin, but by mother's attention to the excluded twin, thus depriving him of her full attention and the social encounter that should have been more a part of the feed.

In supporting her view of the centrality of the breast/mother to each twin, Davison stresses that the most avidly searched for and depended upon object for each twin was the breast/mother rather than the other twin. At nine months, mother expressed a wish that the twins would bond to each other instead of primarily with her, as the mothers of other twins told her their infants did. This would at least give her some time to herself. It was observed that these twins did develop a bond to each other at the end of their first year as they played together and discovered each other as allies, ganging up against mother.

The question about what conditions promote normal development in twins, and what, instead, leads to the development of a narcissistic twin–twin dependency, is raised. Davison notes the late appearance of competition for the caregivers in Burlingham's studies of twins (at 10–12 months) as compared with the twins she observed (three months), and the enhanced inter-twin dependency in the Burlingham study. She suggests that the development of a narcissistic twin-system is due to the emotional deprivation suffered by the children in the Burlingham study rather than the existence of a twin *per se*.

Thus, Davison takes issue with the idea that it is inevitable that twins will use each other as primary objects and presents an infant observation where the optimal conditions allowed each twin to form a primary object relationship with the breast/mother. She believes that this is the norm and that it is only later that the other twin impinges on this primary relationship with the mother. Clearly the twins she observed found a way of dealing with their rivalry in a way that did not lead to an imprisoning twinship, and were greatly helped in this by a mother who was aware of their difficulty and had a considerable capacity to deal with it. She was able to tolerate her infants' projection into her of the experience of exclusion as well as her own feelings about it. A containing mother enabled her twin infants to resolve their rivalry and escape the trap of an enmeshed twinship.

Davison poses the question of whether

twins develop a bond with one another some time towards the end of the first year of life, a bond which deepens as they discover one another as playmates and allies, or whether they start life in a symbiotic state or syncytium which is only painfully and partially given up. In Stern's model of infant development each twin would be for the other an aspect of their environment which would gradually acquire, during the first six months, the characteristics of a 'core other' in mental representation and this core other would only become available for intersubjective experience at 7 months onward (Davison, 1992: 369).

As noted in Chapter 3, Stern (1985) does not believe there is an undifferentiated state between mother and infant or twin and twin.

From Stern's observations it would be expected that the twins' awareness of each other as a 'core other' would have internal representation and therefore form an object relationship at least from the age of seven months. As noted in Chapter 3, Gifford et al. (1966) and Piontelli (2002) both observed twin infants interacting from three months of age. What is troubling about Davison's account of her observation is that it appears that except for rivalry for mother from the age of three months, the twins appear to have no relationship with each other until they learn to play together at the end of their first year. Obviously in material from an observation, much must be omitted. But there is little sense of the twin boys relating to each other at all during their first year. Davison gives more information on the reactions of the older brother than any exchanges between the twins. It is as if in trying to establish that it is possible for twins to develop normally in their relationship with their mother, the fact of the twinship has been sidelined – treated as irrelevant.

The difficulty with infant observations is that they provide a subjective evaluation of observed behaviour, giving meaning when it is not really verifiable. Davison recognizes this and is tentative in the use she makes of what she observes. In the analytic situation, confirmation can be made via the transference situation, in all its complexity. It provides an opportunity to evaluate interpretations by noting the patient's responses and developments within the analytic situation.

In summary: The recognition of the breast/mother as the primary object of psychic life, rather than the twin, is essential to the development of each twin. However, the twinship is also a fundamentally important relationship to all parties. The twin will not only impinge on the other twin's relationship with mother and father. Even with the development of a good relationship with mother, there are aspects of the twin relationship that are unique and enduring. The internal twinship is a fundamental and powerful factor in twins. It will be an active force in the transference relationship with an analyst and is ignored at our peril, as I hope to illustrate in Chapters 7 and 8.

SECTION 2
THE TWIN AND THE
TRANSFERENCE

In this section, I will explore accounts of psychoanalytic work with a twin using material from both published papers and from my own work with twins. All the cases described are from work with individual patients who have an actual twin. The nature of the transference twin, and of the counter-transference sequelae, including enactments that occur within psycho-analytic work with these patients, will form the central theme of this section.

Each twin patient has a unique experience of him- or herself in relation to the analyst, not only with regard to the parental relationships, but – as importantly – with the transference twin. The nature of the twin in the transference varies both between different patients (each with their own experience of their unique twinship), and in the same patient at different times in the analysis. As the twin transference relationship between patient and analyst develops and changes, it would reflect all aspects of the internal twinship. This would include the major issues in the establishment of, and any difficulties with, individual difference and separateness in twins. The experience of the twinship, with both the regressive and the progressive moves, would be played out in the transference relationship with the analyst and would reflect the multiple dimensions and complexity of the twin relationship, including the relationship of the twin pair to the parents.

Chapter 5
The twin in the transference: a developing understanding

In this chapter, I will follow the development of the twin transference from three angles. I present case studies that demonstrate not only the presence of the transference twin, but also the ways in which the twin transference is expressed in and affects the analysis. My understanding of the development of the twin transference is grounded in my own work with patients who are twins, illustrated by case material from my own work. I also hope to elucidate the move through analytic work from the more regressive manifestations of the twin transference to the more progressive ones that serve the development of the individual.

The analysis of the transference relationship between patient and analyst that is central to understanding the patient's formative experiences, has focused almost exclusively on the internal parental objects, in both dyadic and triadic mode (see Chapter 3). Given that the parental relationships with the infant form the framework for development, a detailed analysis of the child–parent relationship is essential to understanding the core of the patient's psychic identity. However, with a patient who is a twin, the omission of an analysis of the twin relationship leaves important areas of the psyche unexplored, and aspects of the transference relationship with the analyst will remain fixed or unresolved. As a result, the analytic twin pair will remain entangled.

My work with patients who are twins has enabled me to understand better the nature of the twin transference and its specific and unique qualities. At first, I was aware that while some twin patients had left prematurely, for others, the planned ending had had an unfinished feel. This dissatisfaction is not in itself uncommon in that there is always more work to do, but I realized that with a patient who is a twin the lack of completion was strongly linked with a sense that aspects of the central core of relating had remained elusive and impenetrable. The experience of a lack of proper ending was mutual - such ex-patients might, for example, keep in contact with me for years with detailed letters about themselves and their lives. The tone of these letters was always intimate and confiding, as if there had been no parting. My own concerns were confirmed by several reports from twins who had been in analysis elsewhere who felt that something was missing, incomplete and that the twinship had not been adequately addressed in the transference relationship with their analyst. This had led to difficulties in separating at the end of the analysis.

The twin transference is a persistent dynamic in psychoanalytic work. All the aspects of the twin relationship will be revealed in the transference twin. The difficulties with ego boundaries may lead the patient to pursue a sense of merging into oneness with the analyst-twin, prompting the use of either reciprocal roles to share the twin identity, or rivalrous roles to lay claim to the more desirable aspects. The ambivalence about the twinship and consequent struggles to differentiate self from twin, both wanting to be twinned yet resenting it, are powerful forces in the analysis. The wish to use the analyst-twin to gratify narcissistic needs is an area that requires particular attention if it is not to lead to an enmeshed and acted-out analytic twinship.

While a twin relationship has much in common with twinning in any patient, and employs the same unconscious and conscious mechanisms, the experience of being an actual twin has unique consequences. This was recognized and indeed written about by analysts between the 1950s and the 1980s, mostly in the USA,[1] but also notably by Dorothy Burlingham (1945, 1946, 1949, 1952, and 1963) and others at the Hampstead Clinic. However, an understanding of the effect on the transference of working with a twin, and an awareness of its importance, seems to have all but disappeared from the analytic literature, and, perhaps, from the work of some analysts.

The evolution of the twin transference

The profound importance of the twinship to the patient, and its centrality in early development, becomes apparent through the evolution of different aspects of the twin transference. The transference relationship between patient and analyst develops and changes, sometimes rapidly, at other times more gradually. Different transference objects emerge into the analytic experience at different times in relation not only to the maternal and paternal relationships, but also to the twin relationship. Each transferential relationship is multi-faceted and multi-phasic, and its characteristics change with the state of mind and the predominant anxieties of the patient, and with the understanding gained through the analysis. The specific qualities of the patient's internal objects as experienced at the time will shape the nature of the transference relationship. Joseph (1983) notes that the transference is a living, changing set of relationships and that the 'whole complex system of object relationships, phantasy, anxiety and defences against anxiety is brought into the transference and countertransference' (p. 294).

The emergence of the twin transference and its development through analysis will be the focus of this section, using both published clinical

---

[1] Abraham, 1953; Ablon et al., 1986; Arlow, 1960; Coen and Bradlow, 1982; Dibble and Cohen, 1981; Engel, 1975; Glenn, 1966; Joseph and Tabor, 1961; Joseph, 1959, 1961; Lacombe, 1959; Leonard, 1961; Maenchen, 1968; Ortmeyer, 1970; Petö, 1946.

material and accounts of my own work with twin patients. I have found that in the early stages, the more narcissistic elements of the twinship (see Chapter 1) are likely to predominate. It is not uncommon for the analyst to feel imprisoned in an extremely controlling twinship transference with an adherent patient blocking any sign of separateness or independence. Where analytic intervention in this narcissistic mode of relating can be tolerated by the patient, other modes of relating emerge. The twinship is never absent from the analysis, though in later stages it may not be in the forefront of the transferential relationship.

The dynamics of the twinship that are predominant in the early stages of the treatment include not only the relationship between the twins, but also the twin patient's perception of the other twin's relationship with the parental figures. While maternal and paternal transference are not absent at this stage, it is frequently only when the twin transference has been analysed over a period of time that the parental figures gain an equally powerful position in the transference. (The analysis and interpretation of the twin transference is, of course, a containing, parental function.) Bion's work in the area of twinning (see page 88) clarifies the need for development from an 'identical' twinning transference to one where difference can be tolerated, before the oedipal conflict can be successfully addressed. The early twinning between patient and analyst may be hidden, and it may be denied by the patient, but it exerts a powerful hold on the analytic work.

The patient creates the analyst as a transference twin in the many facets of the twin relationship. Meltzer (1967) suggests that patients come into analysis with a pre-formed transference. With twins there is an unspoken expectation at the start of the analysis that the analyst is a transference twin. One aspect of this is that the patient may have difficulty tolerating difference (and hence analytic activity), whether this relates to peer or to generational difference. The patient may try to control the analyst either by insisting on sameness, or by denying the analyst's separate existence. Where an unwanted twin is projected into the analyst, the patient may treat the analyst with hatred, and as of no consequence other than as a bin for discarded projections. The analyst-twin is thus regarded as a narcissistic object (see page 86), which evolves through the complex pattern of transference/counter-transference experiences and a more detailed understanding of the transference twin in the analysis, towards a greater recognition of an external object relationship.

Initially, each patient brings into the consulting room experiences with a range of people who embody relevant relationships at that time. The patient's realization that these relationships represent his internal world emerges gradually and these figures do not immediately become alive in the transference. They take on their full potency and meaning as the analysis progresses. The twin emerges gradually as a transference figure that is both alive and available for analysis. Meltzer (1967) notes the importance of the setting – the analytic 'rules' and boundaries – in the creation of a relationship where the evolution of the patient's transference takes place. The constancy of the analyst in modulating the patient's psychic pain by the analyst's receptivity to the patient's projective identification, and the modification of this pain by interpretation, holds the patient in the setting. For a twin, an analyst functioning in this way may be felt to pose a threat to the twinship and to the patient's identification as a twin, as the narcissistic elements binding the twins in the twin relationship are gradually dismantled.

The earliest object relationships emerge into the transference with particular force, frequently via the patient's intense projective identifications into the analyst. At these times the analyst has a dual task: on the one hand it is necessary to remain receptive to the nature and effects of the transference (hopefully without enacting it). On the other hand is the need for openness to understanding both the patient's history and the analyst's own concept of mind. The analyst's counter-transference feelings become a particularly important source of understanding the patient's central formative relationship with the twin as the early preverbal experiences of the patient become active in the analysis. Difficulties in maintaining this balance are discussed in Chapters 7 and 8.

The narcissistic twin transference

The twin relationship is to a greater or lesser degree a narcissistic one and this will be reflected in the transference twin. The analyst is treated as a part of the patient – as a twin part who knows all about the patient, and who is controlled by the patient. As with other narcissistic patients, there is a lack of a sense of an external object. Britton (2000) notes of narcissistic patients, 'they cannot, at least initially, function in an ordinary way because they cannot form an ordinary transference relationship. Some remain aloof and detached, others are adherent, clamorous and concrete in their transference attachment but in neither situation is the analyst experienced *as both significant and separate*' (p. 2, author emphasis). This may lead in the early stages to an analytic encounter characterized by a sense of being excluded by, and irrelevant to, the twin patient.

The narcissistic nature of the twin relationship may lead to what Kohut calls 'pathological twinning' in the transference. Kohut (1971) regards the twin transference as a variant of the narcissistic mirror transference. He distinguishes (1984) between normal and pathological twinning in the transference. He maintains that normal twinning is a need based on the experience of the presence of essential likeness, the self-affirming and self-maintaining experiences of early childhood that are important in enabling us to feel human amongst humans, to have a sense of belonging and of participating. This type of twinning corresponds with Klein's (1963) concept of creating the breast as an imaginary twin in order to feel known, to belong, to mitigate essential loneliness.

Kohut maintains that pathological twinning in the transference is an attempt to repair structures that were damaged early in life. Thus a twin may seek analysis to enable the emergence from a limiting twinship by seeking to repair damaged or inadequate internal parental developmental objects by finding helpful parental objects in the transference. This reparative relationship means turning from the 'identical' twin to a different, external object. However, the patient may have come into analysis to repair the twinship, to reinstate the twin relationship in order to avoid rupturing a narcissistic twin system by turning towards external object relationships. This is pathological in that the twinship becomes a 'psychic retreat' (Steiner, 1993). The processes of both normal and pathological twinning operate simultaneously in the transference.

Not surprisingly, there is a tendency in twin patients to resist any change to the system that defines so much of whom they feel themselves to be – a twin identified within a twinship. The powerful narcissistic dynamics reinforcing the twinship are in conflict with the patient's desire to be separate from the twin. The resistance to interference or change in the twinship may take the form of excluding the analyst from the twinship, as the mother may have been excluded. The narcissistic twin patient in the consulting room seems to embody both twins and their interactions, and the analyst's interference in this enmeshed state is unwelcome and may indeed lead to a termination of the treatment (see Chapter 9). Even after the death of one twin, the internal twinship persists and the surviving twin patient may try to prevent the analyst-twin from coming to life by attempting to maintain a deadly control of the analyst, echoing the now-total control the patient has over the dead twin (see Chapter 12).

It is important to note that the creation of the twin transference is not, *per se*, a pathological state of mind. It is primarily a living out in the transference of one of the patient's most important internal object relationships and as such it is highly informative within the analysis (see Chapter 8 on the factors leading to enactment). It becomes pathological if the intention is to shore up the narcissistic elements of the twinship in order to avoid development that involves painful insights about the importance of the parental figures. This may lead to a situation in which the transference twin is not, or for whatever reason cannot be, recognized and adequately analysed. In this situation, the analytic twinning persists, to the detriment of analytic development, and it will be enacted to a greater or lesser extent by both analyst and patient (see Chapters 7 and 8). The transference twin persists in the analysis. It develops and changes from being the primary focus in the analysis to a less predominant transference relationship. This persistent presence and the sometimes intractable nature of the twinning are evidence of the very early origins of the twin relationship. Like the actual twinship, the transference twin never completely disappears, even when the analysis has ended.

As the analysis of the twin transference progresses, the patient becomes better able to tolerate the existence of difference and separateness. For a twin this means emerging from a perhaps imprisoning twinship into a state where a sense of personal and separate identity from the twin does not negate the twinship. *A move from an 'identical-twin' transference based on*

sameness, to a 'non-identical-twin' transference, tolerant of difference,
creates a milieu where the twin relationship is valued in addition to the
individual twin having a sense of personal, not shared, identity. This
development heralds the arrival of recognition not only of peer difference,
but also of generational difference, and the patient can make greater use of
developmental figures outside the twinship, the parental figures found in the
transference (Money-Kyrle, 1971). Bion's (1967) account of his work in 'The
imaginary twin' elucidates this.

Bion's imaginary twin

Bion (1967) describes the emergence of an imaginary twin in three patients,
only one of whom is an actual twin. As discussed in Chapter 1, 'twinning', or
seeking sameness in an external object, is ubiquitous and may serve several
purposes. It may be used to block an awareness of the other as a separate
person, to rid the self of unwanted aspects, or to gain more understanding of
the self. It occurs in both singletons and twins, and Bion did not differentiate
between a singleton and a twin using this mechanism.

Initially, the imaginary twin has a defensive function, in creating and
maintaining a distance from the analyst. It is important that the analyst
recognizes and interprets the twinning, as this may enable the patient to
separate himself from the deadness of an 'identical twin' from whom there is
no difference. Where this is accomplished, the twin transference may be
used to explore the otherness of the analyst as a 'non-identical twin'. Thus
where there is progress in the analysis, an 'identical twin' in the transference
that blocks any awareness of difference, gives way to a 'non-identical twin'
interested in both separateness and relatedness. At a later stage there may be
a shift from a 'non-identical twin' transference to a maternal transference that
allows freedom of thought and the possibility of further analysis.

I will briefly describe Bion's work with two of his patients:

Patient A was not a twin. Bion's account of this analysis contains the most
detail and it is this patient who was also most able to use his analysis to
further his development. He had a very disrupted and damaging early life,
punctuated by significant losses, parental separation, and illness. For the first
two years of his analysis, he spoke in a dreary monotone, drained of emotion
and filled with ambiguous statements that could not be clarified. The patient
used various methods of relating to his analyst in order to exclude any
meaningful intervention by his analyst. Then a twinning rhythm emerged in
the analysis: the patient's associations changed, alternating between boredom and depression, or regularly spaced phrases and pauses that suggested
to his analyst, 'your turn now'.

The patient's associations were stale and invited stale responses from his
analyst. Bion recognized that the use of stale associations to set up a twinning
rhythm of association–interpretation–association had induced the analyst to
become a twin of the patient. The twinning was aimed at the evasion of
analysis. This situation presented a dilemma for the analyst. He found that if

the twinning rhythm was broken the patient became anxious and/or irritable, but continuing with stale interpretations led to a dead end. This was a turning point in the analysis. The analyst's understanding of the function of the twinning brought the analysis to life. Peripheral associations that the patient had earlier brought to the analysis and that had not seemed significant at the time, now became meaningful. External relationships, about which the patient had previously spoken, came to life as these split-off parts of the patient were personified.

As Bion notes, the 'personification of the split-off portions of his personality' (Bion, 1967: 9), for example the patient 'using [Bion] as a personification of the bad part of himself from whom he wished to be dissociated' (p. 9), is an important factor in the emerging transference relationship and addresses the way in which transference objects come to life in the analysis. In a very defended state, the patient splits off aspects of himself in a way in which he loses immediate contact with them. Thus initially when patient A spoke of the people in his life, instead of them being felt to represent important object relationships, they seemed distant and unavailable. In fact, Bion also realized that conversations the patient had previously reported were frequently imagined conversations and that the patient had not distinguished between real and imagined events. When some understanding about the patient's splitting and projective processes developed through the analysis, the split-off parts of the patient could be owned and integrated into his personality. As a result, these object relationships were then available for projection into the analyst as a live transference relationship that could be felt, recognized and understood. The emerging imaginary twin was a personification of an internal object relationship that became alive in the transference when the split-off parts of the patient were reintegrated.

Bion questions whether the capacity to personify split-off parts of the personality is analogous to a capacity for symbol formation, particularly as observed in his work with patient A. Hinshelwood (1989: 377) writes:

> Klein showed that in their play, children turned their toys into persons, imaginary or real, who were of importance in their actual life, and they worried about the relations between those personified objects ... [and] that all mental activity is conceived with relationships between personified objects. She was impressed with the fluidity with which relations, affects and conflicts could be transferred to new objects.

Thus we are dealing with the capacity to represent important object relationships, to use symbolization, and to develop a transference relationship.

The initial twinning in Patient A was unconsciously designed to exclude the analyst from interfering in the projected twinship. The twin that was at first active in the transference blocked real contact with the analyst, and the patient confirmed this in a dream that he brought to the analysis. Bion's interpretation of the twinning led the patient to experience feelings of intense aggression and anxiety. However, he now seemed more able to tolerate these feelings. As a result, it became possible to draw attention, to recognize and analyse the patient's intra-psychic activity and the mechanisms he was using in the analysis. Because the patient was less fearful of his psychic mechanisms, he was able to tolerate working with the processes of projection, introjection, splitting and personification of the split-off parts of himself. This facilitated a move towards greater integration. The patient could now notice and tolerate difference so that the transference twin changed from an 'identical twin' fashioned into the shape desired by the patient, into a 'non-identical twin' who was allowed to be himself. However, at this stage the patient did not want his analyst to interfere in what he was thinking about. Bion notes that it was an important factor that patient A wished to bridge the gulf to reality, contributing to the hopefulness about the outcome of this analysis.

Bion contrasts the above patient with patient B who was an actual twin, and whom he describes as a more disturbed personality. Patient B also had phantasies of an imaginary twin, apparently serving the same function. But Bion notes that this patient's material seemed intractable, introjections were concrete and painful, and associations 'tenuous and fitful' (Bion, 1967: 16).

When patient B met another patient in the waiting room, this stirred up associations connected with his real twin, and the imaginary twin emerged in the transference. However, patient B seems not to have had the emotional equipment needed to phantasize about his real twin, to explore his intra-psychic tensions, or for contact with reality. Instead he twinned himself with his analyst magically, claiming that thanks to his analysis, he had the ability to see right into the minds of others. He complained that real analysis, in contrast, made him feel ill, as if he had been poisoned by his awareness of another patient/twin. At this point, interpretation of the transference, of the analyst as the imaginary twin, had become possible. However, while patient B indicated his interest in a greater capacity for exploration of intra-psychic conflicts and reality, he remained unable to see his analyst as anything other than an 'identical twin'. The patient seems to have had a more limited capacity for phantasy than patient A, and he took little sustenance from the analysis. It is as if he remained trapped in his internal twinship, with a consequent lack of capacity for development towards a tolerance of difference and symbolic thinking.

Prior to the emergence of the imaginary twin in the transference, work relating to the oedipal conflict remained superficial in both these patients. The development towards awareness of difference leads to recognition of the 'facts of life' (Money-Kyrle, 1971), the good breast and the creative parental couple. In a patient where the 'identical twin' transference remains intractable, development is hampered. For each of Bion's patients, the emergence of the transference twin was crucial in providing an opportunity for understanding and hence for development. The use each patient made of this depended upon their own capacities and personality structure.

Splitting and projective identification may serve several functions. Projective identification may be used for the purpose of communication, in which case the transference relationship will feel alive and active. However, it may also serve as a means of ridding the self of unwanted aspects of the self in a concrete manner. In this situation, the split-off parts of the self lack personification. (In Chapter 8, I explore the role of the analyst in relation to the powerful processes of projective identification linked with the patient's earliest experiences.) The twin emerges in the transference as the split-off aspects of the self become personified and gain vitality in the transference relationship. Prior to this, the twinning with the analyst remains hidden and deadening. The internal twinship is personified in the imaginary twin. Bion asks why the emergence of the imaginary twin in patient A was so important, and given its importance, why it remained peripheral for so long, rather than central to the work. He suggests 'that the imaginary twin goes back to his very earliest relationship and is an expression of his inability to tolerate an object that was not entirely under his control. The function of the imaginary twin was thus to deny a reality different from himself' (Bion, 1967: 19).

Bion does not explain why he thought patient B was unable to develop these capacities, despite the possibility that emerged for the patient to use his psychic apparatus to enable him to explore further. He regards patient B as 'a more disturbed personality' (Bion, 1967: 16) but does not amplify this comment. I think it is notable, however, that this patient is an actual twin and this will have had important consequences for his intra-psychic development. Bion's allusive comments invite questions and speculation. Perhaps patient B remained so bound up in the internal twinning with an actual twin that he felt unable to turn to his analyst as a mature developmental object. Perhaps his analyst did not take sufficient notice in the analysis of the importance of the fact that patient B was a twin. No doubt many factors will have contributed to patient B's developmental difficulties. However, the lack of reference to the effect of the actual twinship either on patient B's development or on the nature of the transference relationship and particularly the transference twin, raises these questions.

The initial defensive stage of twinning may remain impenetrable to analysis. The analyst is regarded as an intruder into this enclosed twin world and the patient may well leave the analysis if the analyst is successful in penetrating the twinship (see Chapter 9). As described above and in the clinical work following, there is a feeling of dullness in the work, of being excluded, and even rather patronized.

The patient creates an imaginary twin, a secret blocking twin to try to alleviate anxiety about an encounter with an analyst who is different from himself and not under his control. The imaginary twin is created out of a very early experience of terror of fragmentation, a fear of nameless dread engendered in the process of separation from both the twin-breast and the actual twin (see Chapter 8). As the imaginary twin becomes alive in the transference the patient develops more confidence in his capacity to use his psychic apparatus to explore his internal state as it is experienced in the consulting room. The capacity for observation of self and others develops within the framework of the triangular relationship with the parental couple (Britton, 1989). In the absence of such a capacity, the patient will be faced with the experience of loss of meaning, chaos, and nameless dread.

The simultaneous analyses of twins

The accounts of the simultaneous analyses of MZ male twins (Joseph, 1959; Joseph and Tabor, 1961) illustrate the differing nature of the twin transference in 'identical' twin patients. For each twin, the transference to the analyst reflected the essential nature of the patient's experience of the twinship. Although the transference twin varied and developed within each of these analyses, the central mode of relating remained very different for each twin. It is a particularly interesting case study not only because the simultaneous analyses of both twins by two analysts is rare, but also because it demonstrates the fallacy of an idea of MZ twins being 'identical'. Each of these twins has had an individual experience of the shared family and of the twinship in a way that has been formative for their personality development and relationship with the world.

Patient B sought analysis with Tabor as a result of acute anxiety. Patient A thought that if his twin was in analysis, he must need it too. Joseph (1959) notes that throughout their lives the twins had been inseparable, sharing college, army, women and travel. Patient A regarded mother as dominant and father as weak and submissive. There was a confusion of ego boundaries between the twins and they divided up different personality attributes between them. Patient A was identified as more 'feminine' than B. His femininity was an important way of distinguishing himself from his twin brother, as evidenced in a hallucinatory experience: on seeing his reflection in a shop window, he was not sure whether it represented him or his twin. 'Suddenly the image that he saw was perceived as that of a beautiful woman with a glamorous figure. He then knew that the reflection was himself' (Joseph, 1959: 192-3).

Patient A used his body to express his thoughts in the analysis and this became an important source of information (see below). He referred to himself as 'we' rather than 'I', but within this twin unity he felt intense rage towards B. However, he denied his feelings of rage because he also felt genuine love for B, and he felt guilty about his murderous wishes towards him. He gained narcissistic gratification from B and was thus terrified of being separated or different from his twin.

At the beginning of the analysis the twins lived together. Towards the end of the first year of analysis patient A impulsively moved out of the shared flat to live on his own. (He had become anxious about emerging homosexual phantasies about his twin.) Patient A became lonely and tried to assuage this by lying on his bed in front of a mirror, telling himself that the reflection he saw was his twin. He began to eat a lot and gained a great deal of weight.

There were three phantasies associated with this. He identified with his older brother who was 3.5 years older and considerably larger, and the phantasy was that the older brother was bigger than the twins because his own twin was inside him. Thus patient A believed he had incorporated his twin by becoming larger. There was also a protective element to this phantasy, as A believed that either twin alone would perish.

Joseph notes that the mirror gazing and overeating occurred at the end of a year of analysis, when the patient moved out of his flat/analysis, and was alone, separated from his twin and his analyst. Although Joseph does not directly link this eating and mirror gazing activity with the patient's wish to incorporate his analyst-twin in his absence between sessions or in a break, it must surely reflect his wish to do so. Joseph does go on to describe how the patient used the same visual introjective mechanisms with his analyst. The patient believed himself to be like the analyst because they read the same magazines. Patient A would stare fixedly at his analyst for a moment before leaving sessions, representing a visual taking-in of the analyst (like gazing at his twin-image in the mirror), as if to gain the strength to last until the next session.

Joseph links the patient's incorporative wishes with his earliest experiences of wanting the breast completely to himself, and not to have to share it with his twin. He feared that there was not enough milk to feed them both. By incorporating his twin, the patient believed he could make his twin disappear and thus deal with his insatiable greed, at the same time protecting both himself and his twin from starvation. The wish to incorporate his twin was also the basis of his phantasy that was enacted in his homosexual relationship with his twin (see Chapter 11). In addition, he projected out the unwanted aspects of himself (his homosexual tendencies), denying that they were his.

As with Bion's patients, we again see the 'identical' twin transference in which patient A creates his analyst in his own image. This is reflected in the visual introjection of his analyst, the oral incorporation making the two into one, and in the homosexual phantasies. Joseph and Tabor (1961) note the passive compliance of patient A, which masked the twinning in the transference. Thus the patient often accepted interpretations 'only if he repeated them himself with the phantasy that hearing them in his own voice meant they came from his twin who knew what he was thinking' (Joseph and Tabor, 1961: 283). However, as the analysis progressed, the patient felt he no longer needed to take over his analyst's interpretations as the analyst had now become his twin. The patient felt it was unnecessary to state many things because he assumed that his 'twin-analyst' already knew them. The twin had emerged as a live presence in the transference.

Patient B, in contrast, remained identified with an 'identical twin-analyst'. B was the second-born twin. He regarded father as depressed, and having a deep-seated love of knowledge. In his view, father treated mother as a precious, fragile thing whom he adored. It seems that the parents delegated personality attributes to each other, as did the twins. He too saw mother as dominant and driving. Identifications with mother and father were different for patients A and B, and influence the homosexual enactment linked with this. This theme is explored in Chapter 11. Patient B's view of the family differed from A's, concordant with his pathology. Patient A had divided the family into two groups, one containing mother and older brother (the stronger group), with father and the twins in the other (the weaker group). Patient B, in contrast, isolated his twin and himself into one group, separated from mother, father and older brother. This indicates his investment in the twin relationship rather than a relationship with a parental couple. However, he also saw the twins as devalued and degraded, as 'wormy runts' (Joseph and Tabor, 1961: 286). For him the twins were a self-sufficient unit and he had no friends.

Patient A was more open to other relationships, despite an initial tendency to twinning with the other person. He initially viewed his wife as a twin, before discovering her difference from him. Patient B remained more isolated and bound in the twinship. He used his secretary to take his twin's place. 'He used her as his guide into the world of people' (Joseph and Tabor, 1961: 289). As with Bion's patient A before the emergence of the personified twin in the transference, Tabor's patient B also produced vague, unclear accounts of his life. However, unlike his twin brother and Bion's patient A, he was not able to develop much further in his relationships. He wanted to use his analyst as he did his secretary-twin – for guidance and counselling. There was a lack of linking and connectedness in his material and where he did recall anything of value from his analyst he attributed it to himself or to someone outside.

Later in the analysis patient B competed with his analyst-twin for interpretations but he nevertheless kept fragmented the information he had gained. He denied his deep need for his twin or his analyst-twin. He did develop sufficiently to recognize, 'I'm not him, but who am I?' (Joseph and Tabor, 1961: 290) but seemed to remain stuck there. It was as if he had lost one identity and not found another. For patient B there was little twin-transference understanding and the twin did not emerge into the transference in a way that could be analysed. His development and his use of the analysis were much more limited than that of his twin brother, patient A.

Joseph and Tabor note the striking differences between these twins and this is clearly reflected in the transference relationships with their analysts. Patient A is less narcissistic and develops a loving, tender relationship with his wife. Patient B can only establish relationships based on either mother–child or twin–twin identification. Patient A had a greater sense of identity, while patient B remained more lost between a 'we' and an 'I'. Patient A was more mature, had a stronger sense of reality and a more helpful superego and was therefore better able to deal with his feelings of guilt. Patient B remained governed by primitive defences, using denial, isolation and projective identification more extremely. As a result of these differences, patient A was able to use his analyst in a developmental capacity while patient B remained locked in a narcissistic twin rivalry with his analyst.

As the authors note, the 'twinning reaction' leads to a loss of ego boundary between the two individuals and a loss of identity. This will apply not only within the twinship, but also in the analysis. Joseph (1961) regards the analytic relationship as a situation *par excellence* for creating a twin relationship, with the resultant difficulties that arise in relation to the transference while analysing a twin:

> There are two people who share a common purpose, develop a secret language in a common room, etc. Inevitably, therefore, the patient's need to re-create the twin situation is fostered by analysis. This results in a 'sticky' type of transference. Problems of terminating the analysis are increased because the twin fantasies a perpetual analysis with his 'twin-analyst' (Joseph, 1961: 162).

As noted above, these two twin patients differed in their analyses. Patient A could allow the analytic twin to emerge and exist in the transference, though this was felt to lead to 'certain technical difficulties' (Joseph and Tabor, 1961: 295). Patient B resisted the emergence of a twin in the transference. The authors explain this in terms of B's rebelliousness versus A's compliance in the analysis. But compliance is a hidden rebelliousness, and I suspect it has more to do with A's greater ego strength, maturity, sense of identity and a greater ability for reality testing. This would create a situation where he felt more secure in allowing the split-off parts of his personality to become alive in the transference, to be explored and integrated, without feeling too threatened by it. Patient B, who, like Bion's patient B, sounds like a much more disturbed personality, was unable to allow the emergence and personification of the splits in the transference.

Joseph and Tabor (1961: 297) conclude:

> The transference reactions of each of these individuals have been strikingly different. We have considered the possible role of difference in the personalities of the analysts as playing a part in the different transference reactions, but it is evident from the material that these reactions seen in the transference are repetitions of attitudes that were present in all of their relationships outside the analysis. Therefore, it has been felt that the personalities of the analysts have not materially influenced the nature of the particular reactions, so that these are in reality valid findings of the analytic situation.

The effect that the particularities of any analyst might have on the analytic process has come into much closer focus with the recognition of the importance of the counter-transference in understanding the patient's communications. Sandler (1993), in his summing up of papers at an international psychoanalytic conference, comments on the very personal internal psychoanalytic map each analyst uses, even when there are points of overlap with others in theory or technique. Not only does the analyst follow his own internal map, but what is awakened in it is the result of a complex dialogue between analyst and analysand at that particular moment, within the context of the analysis at that time. While this does not invalidate Joseph and Tabor's findings about the differences between the twins they analysed, it does grey the area somewhat. Each of the analysts involved in this study would have had an active personal internal world into which the patients' projections were received. Their counter-transference feelings would have shaped their understanding of the patient's material. Each analyst also has a personal conceptualization about the functioning of the mind. Both these important factors would have influenced their reactions to and understanding of each of the patients in analysis.

Adhesive twin transference and the fear of separation

Where the twin relationship involves an extensive sharing of ego boundaries and a consequent lack of sense of an individual self, separation from the twin (and from any twin transferential objects) poses a serious threat to the identity of each twin. The twin transference relationship will have an adhesive quality (Meltzer, 1975) based on a fear of disintegration or death as a result of separation.

Opposite-sex twins may engage in extensive twinning and Glenn (1966) notes the marked effects on the transference in his work with a DZo twin. A man with a twin sister sought analysis because amongst his other anxieties, he feared he would die of a heart attack and the associated chest pains. The patient's enmeshment in a narcissistic twin relationship was evident in his phantasy that he and his sister were two halves of one person derived from the splitting of one fertilized egg. He believed they had embraced in the womb with no membrane between them. The patient also phantasized that his sister had stolen half of his penis. He felt like an incomplete person and 'longed for contact with his other half' (Glenn, 1966: 739), like the Platonic beings described in Chapter 2.

The patient and his twin sister were brought up very close to each other and shared a room until they were 19 years old. While the parents were out at work, the twins were responsible for cleaning the house and they mimicked the parents in their frequent fights, the twin couple identifying with the parental couple. The closeness of the twins and the lack of a sense of generational difference from the parents probably contributed to the creation of an enmeshed twinship. The twins formed a narcissistic unit and the patient also twinned with others in his life including his wife and his business partner. He believed that he was cheated by his partner, as he had been by his twin sister.

The transference twin was a prominent figure in the analysis:

Mr. C. had a strong desire to picture the analyst as a twin. This ... had both a gratifying and defensive aspect. He could thus experience hate and love for a twin not actually his sister. He offered me his old clothes – not only to deprecate me as a poor relative but also to get me to dress like him. He was constantly disappointed that I did not dress to his taste. In the process of picturing me as his twin, he

imagined that we were the same age, had a similar family and similar income. At
the same time he felt that I robbed him and he wished in turn to steal from me.
Finally, he feared I would hurt him in reprisal. Much of this type of interchange
revolved around the fee, which he tried to keep as low as possible, lying about his
income. He would often confuse what he thought with what he believed the
analyst thought (Glenn, 1966: 730).

The twin transference had an adhesive quality and the patient believed that
separation from his analyst-twin would result in the death of the analyst.
This fear was based on the patient's fear of separation from both his twin
sister and his mother, representing a loss of his twin self and of the
imaginary twin-breast. It was apparent that this fear was linked with the
symptoms that brought him to analysis – the chest pain. The patient, in his
desire to be one with his sister, phantasized that he and his sister were
joined at the breasts. Thus the pains in his chest 'were associated with the
imagined severing of the twins at the point of attachment' (Glenn, 1966:
742), the breasts. A later association also linked these symptoms with the
patient's desire for his mother to place healing hot cups on his chest as she
did on her return from work when he was ill. Glenn suggests that this
phantasy is based on a wish to be united with a protective mother. I would
add that it also represents the patient's wish to reunite and identify with
mother's breast – his imaginary twin. The anxiety experienced about
separation would also have been heightened by the phantasy that the twins
had been joined at the penis.

This is an interesting study in that it elucidates the links between the
imaginary twin/breast and the narcissistic twin–twin identification. It is as if
one conceptualization is shaped in the image of the other and they become
fused.

Enmeshed-twin projections

The adhesive quality of the relationship with the twin and the transference
twin is more prominent when there has been less development towards an
individual identity. The internal twin and the self remain insufficiently
distinguished, resulting in an enmeshed internal twinship. Where there has
been massive mutual projective identification that has resulted in impaired
development in the twins, the transference twin becomes more complicated.
Perhaps one of the most difficult tasks in analysing the twin transference is
that of separating what belongs to which internal twin.

Maenchen (1968) describes therapy with a seven-year-old boy who is an
MZ twin, and whose twin was in therapy with someone else. The parents had
not expected twins, and mother was depressed for the first year after their
birth, later describing that year as a nightmare. The twins were left alone
together for long periods and clearly used each other to alleviate anxiety in
mother's absence and unavailability. They developed a private language with
which they excited each other, becoming so absorbed in it that they retreat-
ed into their own world, excluding all around them. The highly libidinized

sounds filled the gap left by an unavailable mother and kept primitive anxieties at bay by creating excitement (as observed in Bill and Bert, Chapter 4).

Although Maenchen states that the twins were psychologically identical, it is apparent from the case material that they adopted complementary roles. Despite the fact that one therapist was an older woman, the other a younger man, each twin treated their therapist as if they were identical, that is, as a twin – the 'identical twin' in the transference. Maenchen's patient attached himself to her as he did to his twin and was determined to find similarities between them in order to allay his terrible anxiety. When he did find similarity, he no longer felt alone and he merged with his therapist. He felt a great need to have close bodily contact with her, the adhesive identification being bodily as well as emotional. He repeated her interpretations endlessly as if he had taken them in and stored them without any process of digestion. His thought processes were disturbed and his thinking concrete, thoughts becoming acts. With his lack of ability to symbolize, he had difficulty tolerating any delay and used compulsive talk and rituals to alleviate his anxiety. He was possessive of every minute of his time with his analyst. He feared bodily disintegration and resorted to grandiose ideas about himself to protect himself from intense anxieties.

The patient had a severe disturbance in his sense of self. He felt himself to be 'only a half' (Maenchen, 1968: 444). He wished never to be separated from his twin and his real identification was with his twin, not his parents. Like Tabor's patient above, he viewed his family as divided into parents and other children on one side, and the twins on the other, and he was caught up in an enmeshed twin relationship that was represented in his adhesive clinging to his analyst. The aggression in the twin relationship was expressed towards his analyst in the transference, as he mocked and ridiculed her, and wanted to take possession of her and all her things. The patient attempted to impose on his analyst the *folie à deux* that had developed between him and his twin.

Maenchen notes that this patient suffered from confusion between himself and his mirror image, his twin – 'the twinning which confuses the distinction between self and object' (Maenchen, 1968: 453) – and that this was reflected in the transference. 'The core tie was to his twin, and the representation of other objects contained that of the twin. All later ties were pseudo ties.' (p. 448). The patient complained that 'the wires in his brain were crossed' (p. 453) and he had difficulty differentiating between internal and external reality, a difficulty that was exacerbated by the presence of a 'mirror image' twin. As a result, what were originally thought to be straightforward projections in his therapy, turned out to be much more confused – a combination of the patient and his twin.

When twins are very alike, the confusion about who is who will be not only between the twins themselves. The mother (and father) is also likely to experience confusion in relation to each of her twins. The twins' confusion will thus be compounded by mother's, and by introjections from mother that may at times 'belong' to the other twin. This will further undermine any clear sense of personal identity. This cumulative trauma will be a factor in the fear of separation. The twin encountered in the transference will at times reflect these confusions, containing elements of 'self-twin' and 'other-twin', and both the self- and other-twin in relation to mother.

A parasitic twin transference

In the triangular set-up that exists between a mother and her twins, various different pairings arise based on both constitutional and environmental factors. The ideal situation is one in which mother can relate to each twin individually, creating the optimum situation for growth and for allowing the twin relationship to develop without the twin pairing becoming too dominant. Each twin will make what he/she can of the given situation. As Athanassiou (1986) notes, 'A human being in fact truly reveals himself in what he makes of both his neonatal impedimenta and of what his environment does or does not offer him' (p. 329). This allows for individual development in both MZ and DZ twins, as well as for the possibility of change within the psychoanalytic situation, according to the use the patient makes of the objects found in the transference, which is the theme of this chapter.

Athanassiou distinguishes between two of the variants of pairing in the mother–twin–twin triad. She believes that a symbiotic relationship between the twins precedes the symbiotic relationship of each twin with the mother, but that inter-twin rivalry may lead to an 'anti-symbiotic trend' and to the 'parasitisation' of the relationship with the maternal object. In the symbiotic type of twin relationship each infant develops a mutually projective relationship with its twin – essentially a dyadic relationship leading to a confusion of identity between self and object. The movement to a symbiotic relationship with mother ameliorates the confusion and allows for individual development. However, a parasitic twin relationship may develop in which confusion of identity between the twins is not paramount. Instead the three-person relationship between mother and the twins creates a situation where one baby is always excluded, and therefore enraged. The baby at the breast identifies with the rage of the excluded baby, so poisoning its own experience of the breast, creating what Athanassiou terms a parasitic relationship between the twins. While the symbiotic relationship can evolve and eventually be put to the service of understanding, the nature of the parasitic relationship in twins blocks the development of a relationship with mother.

Athanassiou describes a patient who was a DZ twin and who came to analysis when her twin sister had just married. The separation from her twin had awakened paranoid phantasies of her birth in which she believed that she had been catastrophically deprived of the presence of her sister. Her own relationships were fleeting and insubstantial. She had experienced the marriage of her twin sister as catastrophic as it brought about the break-up of the parasitic relationship with her twin.

The patient tried to plug the gap created by the marriage of her twin sister. She projected the parasitic twin into passive men with whom she associated, and for whom she played the part of an 'ideal twin'. At the start of the treatment, the patient fought to remain in a twinship external to the analysis, from which the analyst was excluded – the rival mother being spurned for the preferred independence of the twinship. She went to her sessions for her regular feed, but failed to benefit from analysis. Her analyst felt paralysed by the split-off parasitic twin who controlled the analysis.

The patient experienced the analyst's unwanted interpretations as an external twin who was no longer under her control, a twin who made nothing but a parasitic noise, i.e. an intrusive parasite that invaded her while she was being fed by mother. An interpretation was also the voice of a mother intruding in the twinship, a mother that could only be experienced through the twinship, but not directly. The parasitic twin prevented any direct contact with mother. It was only when the patient's material could be used creatively to separate her from the parasitic twin that she was able to contemplate the move from the parasitic twinship into a real-life analysis, forming a direct relationship with a maternal object for the first time.

I think that what Athanassiou is addressing is in essence an envy of one twin by the other that so poisons its own relationship with the mother, that the infant is unable to take emotional sustenance from her and turns instead to the twin. In poisoning the relationship with mother, her intervention in the twinship is prevented because she too is considered poisonous. A parasitic twin relationship is a particular kind of enmeshed twinship – it is a twinship that is dominated by the envy of the other twin in a relationship with mother, so binding the twins together. In an enmeshed twinship of another kind, an overvaluation of the twinship may arise when the twins turn to each other as a result of neglect or other factors connected with mother's unavailability.

Unresolved residues of the twin transference

As with the maternal and paternal transference relationships in analysis, the twin transference is never completely resolved, whether it is a narcissistic enmeshed relationship or one more tolerant of separateness. The powerful hold of these transference residues from the earliest relationships can be seen clearly in the ending of an analysis, as the issues of separation come to the fore. While the separation through adolescence from the early parental relationships has a developmental dynamic based on the movement into adulthood, separation from a twin is of a different order. It has more to do with finding a personal identity through separateness and difference than the 'growing up' of the adolescent. Because of the narcissistic and therefore adhesive aspects of the twinship, separateness and separation may feel life-threatening in a way similar to the infant–mother relationship.

Ablon et al. (1986) describe the conflicts experienced by a patient as the ending of analysis and the resolution of the maternal and twin transference approached. The patient was an MZ twin who had started analysis because he experienced panic attacks. The authors note the prominence of the twin in both dream material and the transference, both as a sibling and as a substitute for parental transference figures. In the analysis the patient created a tie with his analyst as a securing figure, an analyst-twin, to replace his 'identical twin'. This ameliorated his anxieties but it also trapped him in a twinship with the analyst in which he felt he had either to merge with the analyst-twin or to escape from him, as if there were no possibility of finding a developmental object. He saw the analyst-twin as either an omnipotent mother-twin who was deeply involved with him, tending to his most intimate needs, or as a 'phallic' twin who wished to be separate.

The authors interestingly refer to a combined mother–twin–analyst transference tie that had to be worked through in ending the analysis. They suggest that the patient's mother was a nurturing mother and that this fact made it more difficult for the patient to relinquish his tie with his twin. The patient's relationship with his twin mitigated the separation from his mother and may have delayed the separation-individuation experience from the mother, 'which further potentiated the pull to union with the twin' (Ablon et al., 1986: 255-6) – using the twinship as a more permanent refuge, regressing to the dyadic mother–child/twin–twin level.

The conflicts involved in separating from his analyst-twin were graphically illustrated in three episodes in the final phase of this patient's analysis. I will take the liberty of expanding on the authors' understanding of these events because I believe they contain fascinating insights into the nature of the transference relationships. I am, of course, aware that this is speculative, as my interpretations cannot be confirmed in the consulting room. However, I think there is an indication in the authors' discussion that this may be what was understood.

In the first event, the patient had a phantasy of being in a lake and his analyst pushing him away from the side into deep water saying, 'You can swim' (Ablon et al., 1986: 247). This was linked with the patient's recognition that the analyst would never be his lover, and his concern about whether he could ever become a man without leaving her. The oedipal theme is clear here, but the analyst's active pushing him away in the phantasy indicates the difficulty in severing a powerful tie linked with pre-oedipal mother–infant/twin–twin relationships – the phantasy twin of both breast- and actual-twin origin.

The second event occurred while the patient was on holiday. He was swimming in the sea and had drifted out of his depth. He called to a woman on the shore for help but she could not hear him above the sound of the waves. He managed to use his own resources to get back to shore. The patient told his analyst that he had to prepare to leave the analysis even though he had not achieved all he hoped for. He was afraid 'not of drowning but of collapsing' (Ablon et al., 1986: 248) in what seemed like a never-ending struggle. He had to 'break free of the strength of the undertow' (p. 248). I think this material indicates that the patient felt that the analyst-mother was unable to hear him calling for help because of the interference of the twinship – the noisy waves and the undertow (the compelling pull of the twinship). He needed the mother-analyst to help him free himself from an inhibiting twin relationship, but found he had to do this on his own. Perhaps the complex inter-twining of breast-phantasy-twin and internal-actual-twin in the transference made turning to the mother-analyst for help problematic.

The resolution of this difficulty seemed to come in the final week of his analysis. The patient reported that he had been swimming in a lake, and he stepped off the shallow end and swam into the deep water on his own – in the lake there was no undertow so this was more manageable. He linked the third event with 'growing up' (Ablon et al., 1986: 248) and leaving his mother to live his own life. It is significant that he had chosen a safer place to swim, where there was no chance of being drawn back in by an undercurrent that could not be ignored. I suggest that he realized that there were aspects of the twinship that could not be severed, reflected in the transference, and that would have to be put aside in recognition of the fact that the twinship continues to exist in a powerful way throughout life.

The patient longed for the dyadic relationship of the twinship and this was linked with a powerful pre-oedipal maternal transference. As the authors note, oedipal conflicts were underscored by the conflict created within the twinship between the need to merge and the need for separateness. This, I think, is at the heart of the fierce 'undertow' that the patient felt he had to escape, and could never adequately resolve. He could not just grow up and leave his analyst-mother. He also had to break away from his analyst-twin by force, the 'phallic twin' exerting his power.

This material illustrates beautifully the concept of 'buoyancy' as described by Quinodoz (1993). 'With the progress of the analysis ... the manifestations of separation anxiety are reduced in intensity and frequency because the quality of the transference relationship evolves and changes' (p. 172). Both the analyst and the patient perceive a sensation of buoyancy of the internalized object as the patient gains greater autonomy relative to dependency, 'and as an affirmation of the identity of the analysand, who feels himself to be becoming truly himself, thus auguring well for termination of the analysis' (Quinodoz, 1993: 172). The material in the above case also clearly shows the enduring power of the twinship, both in external life and in the transference. I will trace the nature of the transference twin, in material from my own work with a patient, in the next chapter.

Chapter 6
From narcissistic twin bond to an individual sense of self

I will discuss some aspects of my work with Mr P to demonstrate the changing nature of the transference twin, and the insight this offers into the effects that being a twin had on Mr P's development. There are many aspects of this work that I will not address in this account, but will focus instead on what is relevant to this particular subject.

Mr P, an MZ twin, was in his fifties when he was referred to me. Following the ending of a romantic relationship, he had suffered what appeared to be a psychotic episode during which he had become anxious and disorientated, and was in a rather grandiose and hallucinatory state of mind. At the start of treatment, his acute state had passed and he recognized that he needed psychotherapeutic help.

Although he had been married for many years, Mr P's relationship with his wife was problematic. Throughout the marriage Mr P had had a series of affairs. His wife was aware of these extra-marital relationships and although she was greatly distressed about them, Mr P and his wife nevertheless remained inseparable. For both partners, the marriage was like a troubled twinship where neither could enjoy being either alone or together, and from which neither could escape. Mr P had ended his latest affair because he felt he could no longer tolerate being torn between his mistress and his family. Later, his mistress had become involved with another man whom she subsequently married. In losing her, Mr P felt he had lost a vital part of himself and he feared he would disintegrate. It seemed that he had formed an eroticized twin relationship with his mistress. He thus had a cold, unrewarding twinship with his wife and an eroticized twinship with his mistress. Losing the latter felt like a devastating loss of self – a taster of transference issues to come.

Mr P told me his 'birth story': he and his twin were born interlocked. Mother was only told when she went into labour that she was giving birth to twins. They were delivered by Caesarean section, so neither was older. However, inequality showed itself in other ways. Mr P was the weaker twin and had had to be resuscitated. He believed that his twin brother had strangled him in utero, and that after birth he had been neglected, 'left for dead', while all the attention went to his twin. Mr P thought that mother had always favoured his twin and he felt greatly aggrieved about this. He felt he had been cheated of his birthright as his twin was the bigger, stronger, and more dominant of the pair. Like Jacob and Esau, this twinship was constructed around murderous rivalry. The birthright that was stolen from Mr P was the primary place in his mother's attention.

The crushed-twin/tyrannical-twin transference

In the early period of the treatment, Mr P was in a fragile state, and at times he was involved in a rather delusional system, believing he was a secret descendant of royalty, or at another time, that he was a champion athlete. This sense of being special manifested itself in my consulting room. He not only filled up all the space with a dominating presence, but in various ways he managed to get my consulting room organized to his liking. He persuaded me to reduce the lighting in the room (a counter-transference enactment as I colluded with his belief that he needed special treatment because he was so fragile[1]). At the beginning of each session he created a seductive atmosphere, taking off his jacket, tie and watch, letting go of any formal accoutrements, as if he were visiting a lover. He noted and commented on what I wore, to try and get me to wear what he liked (as he explained at a later time). He would then begin a hard-edged, flat recital of his activities or ideas, getting more and more worked up about his grievances, until he was shouting in an angry and dominating way for most of the session.

At this time, Mr P rarely mentioned his twin. However, he used projective identification to keep me informed about his current experience of being a twin. He talked and shouted at me relentlessly to push me into a corner like a crushed twin-baby, a twin not noticed, a twin 'left for dead'. Meanwhile, he identified with his beefy twin brother and occupied all the space, giving him pride of place. His clinging, abrasive, intrusive voice came at me from all sides, emasculating and controlling me. He stripped my interpretations of meaning by quickly taking them up and intellectualizing about them, and by rating my interpretations ('thank you, that's a good interpretation'), followed by a sterile examination of them. He started each session with his own analysis of the previous session. Throughout this period he found it intolerable not to understand something before I did, as he fiercely competed with me.

Mr P seemed to have no sense of my actual presence in the consulting room other than as his creation. As a transference object, I was to be a cold, un-giving, unsupportive, hate-filled twin who wanted to push away the beefy bullying twin to gain some space for myself. He would go through the motions of analytic work with me, bringing lots of material, including dreams, but it seemed that the only way to make contact with him or to enter into his private tormented world was as a transference twin. He experienced my interpretations as intrusive and threatening and as an indication not only of my separateness from him, but also of my wish to dominate him.

---

[1] The role of the analyst in colluding with the patient in an attempt to avoid an experience of terror, a fear of annihilation, or anxieties of a psychotic nature is discussed in Chapter 8.

Mr P reported a dream that illustrated this frame of mind:

He and his twin sat in the public gallery at the House of Commons. His twin was shouting at the members, interrupting the procedures, and getting involved in the debates. His twin was eventually arrested by the police. As they were taking him away, Mr P pleaded with them to release his twin brother.

Mr P felt disappointed that he could not immediately interpret his dream himself. I suggested that the shouting and debating twin was Mr P, here, observing my analytic thinking (the productive parents/MPs at work) and trying to prevent any activity. He experienced my interpretations as the police trying to stop him being so disruptive. He was afraid of exposing a smaller vulnerable twin-self. Instead, an angry, shouting, bullying twin got in the way so that the other needy twin couldn't tell me what he had come to say.

While I think this interpretation was correct, and Mr P agreed with it, it seemed to carry no meaning for my patient. He had no idea of me being able to offer him anything other than restrictions to his freedom and a depriving twin relationship. We seemed to be trapped in a limiting and unrewarding twinship in the transference relationship, as Mr P continued with his angry complaints and his self-analysis.

The angry tyrannical-twin was counterbalanced by the crushed-twin, and both were active in the twin transference relationship with me. The confusion of ego boundaries between the twins exists not only between the actual twins, but it is also represented in the internal twinship. A situation is then created where the transference twin might represent any of a number of aspects of either twin. It was clear that Mr P identified with both sides of the above twin balance. Thus, shortly before a break, Mr P demanded to be seen at a weekend, like an infant who could not tolerate any separation, the weak twin who was supposedly about to be 'left for dead'. He was incensed at my refusal to see him, and demanded that I explain to him why I would not accede to his wishes. He found it intolerable that I did not answer his questions in the way he expected me to, and became more and more insistent, creating a tyranny in his relationship with me. While he believed he was a weak, needy twin who could not endure without additional sustenance, he enacted a tyrannical twin, hiding his neediness and blocking out the help that the needy twin cried for.

However, around this time another transference object came to the fore.

The eroticized mistress-twin transference

Mr P began to behave in a manic, excited way. He engaged in athletics, which involved him in a considerable amount of training and physical activity. He became more aware of his physical appearance and he dieted and bought new clothes, all accomplished with a great deal of preening. He felt he could not successfully compete with a twin-me, so instead he became seductive. His relationship with me became increasingly eroticized, and although it was apparent from the start of the work that he regarded me as his new mistress, this now became a florid preoccupation for him. He brought me flowers and gifts, sent me apparently appreciative cards, agreed with my interpretations of his eroticization of me, and remained untouched by them.

I had become the eroticized mistress-twin in the transference. As became evident later, the eroticized mistress-twin was based on the eroticization of the maternal relationship (discussed below). Likewise, the cold wife-twin transference was linked with a mother who was not sufficiently available for Mr P. The twin-breast and the actual twin relationship became fused in this multiple transference representation.

Mr P reported seeing a picture of a woman with big breasts alongside armoured tanks displaying big erectile guns. He imagined himself inside one of these tanks, echoing his engagement with macho sports, exhibiting his newly slim body to me, but remaining armoured and impenetrable. He thought I looked sexy, and that I found him sexually attractive, and that the only reason I did not admit my feelings was because I was 'obeying the rules'.

It was evident that Mr P was using a pre-symbolic mode of thinking, using his body as a 'phallus' (Birksted-Breen, 1996), creating an illusory state that gave him a sense of potency, completeness and omnipotence. In this frame of mind, he split his objects – I was now seen as a warm, caring, sexy mistress-twin, while his wife-twin was felt to be cold, negative and persecuting. It was apparent that he believed he could use his eroticized phantasies to possess his mother-analyst. He had grandiose thoughts of being a prince. Later, I came to understand that as the tyrannical twin, he hoped to possess the sexy mother. The alternative was that he felt he was nothing – a weak and dying twin who got the cold, uncaring mother.

In this omnipotent state of mind, Mr P bound himself to me as an idealized love-object. This protected him from painful and difficult feelings, like the terror he had experienced before coming to see me, a fear of falling apart, of disintegrating. As with the tyrannical twin, he used this eroticization to prevent the needy twin from emerging. He did not want a needy twin to be born here, and he hoped for a magical Caesarean birth from me without having to endure the struggle of a real separation. He alternated between the two modes of relating to me: when his erotic phantasies were punctured, he became again the tyrannical-twin.

The duality of the split object was again evident in the transference. Although Mr P harboured romantic phantasies about me, he simultaneously felt me to be withholding, inscrutable, and wilfully denying him what he so desperately wanted, like a split-off cold mother. He used his romantic phantasies to protect himself from feeling bleak and alone. He felt that I was the depriving mother who was too preoccupied with herself and his twin to have time for him. So he created a phantasy of a romantically attached mother who would be solely his. In fact it later transpired that mother had named him after a romantic novelist whom she had much admired. This seemed to confirm that his confusion was also stimulated by her unconscious phantasies.

Meltzer (1974) refers to the development of a particularly 'sticky' erotic transference that is based on narcissism. He suggests that the eroticization fastens itself onto individual qualities of the analyst, arousing counter-transference interference in the analyst's capacity to investigate. Only insistence on the analytic method, exploring the infantile nature of the desires and feelings and the masturbatory nature of the excitement felt in the consulting room, will eventually reveal the narcissistic organization, and 'the violence of the Oedipal jealousy and the cruelty of wounded vanity' (Meltzer, 1974: 316).

I think that what had become apparent was that Mr P's functioning at this time was based on a narcissistic internal organization of the twinship. Both his experiences of being a twin and of having a mother who was not adequately available to him as an infant left him having to turn to the twinship for gratification and help. As a result of the immaturity of the infant twins, this led to a narcissistic twin relationship. The narcissistic twinning transferred to all his relationships - with his wife, his lover, his son, and his analyst. The eroticization protected him from a fear of experiencing his smallness and neediness in what he believed was a hopeless situation. He was filled with a masturbatory sexual excitement about being in my consulting room and being on the couch. Unconsciously, he phantasized that by being there he had penetrated and possessed me. On a conscious level he acted out this phantasy in his excitedly sexual manner and his wish to give me gifts. Every indication that he had not possessed me sexually stimulated his outrage and hurt.

It is now possible to understand that in this excited, omnipotent delusional state of mind, Mr P used a more borderline position to avoid a state of fragmentation. His eroticized narcissistic twinning with me gave him a sense of togetherness that protected him from intense anxiety. He espoused coherence on the basis of delusion, a state of mind that Britton (1998) refers to as a pathological depressive position. Rather than face the incoherence and uncertainty of a more paranoid-schizoid state of mind that might have helped him in his development, he instead entered into a manic and omnipotent state to provide a false coherence as a defence against his terror of the unknown. He used his dieting and athletics to give him a sense of invulnerability. His persistent delusion that he and I were secretly having an affair protected him from any awareness of loneliness, of exclusion and of difference. It acted as a psychic organizer holding his thoughts together.

However, as Steiner (1993) and Birksted-Breen (1996) note, the use of this sort of omnipotent state in the search for a reliable structure leads to a rigid and restricted internal world. In such an omnipotent state of mind, the patient feels he has no need for a real mother and father. The oedipal constellation consisting of mother, father and infant, within which the capacity for thinking develops, is avoided. Instead a manic and concrete solution is used to replace what is felt to be a lack of internal parental structuring function. The aim of the omnipotent state of mind is to protect the individual against fragmentation and chaos. It is a solution resorted to only too often in a situation where an infant turns to its twin as a primary object rather than finding a maternal object who can prime the infant to engage with the oedipal couple.

Gradually Mr P began to relinquish his idealized, eroticized object. In an important developmental move indicating the recovery of his epistemophilic instincts, he discovered more historical information by researching his background. It emerged that mother had been depressed and ill after the birth of her twins and was not much available to them, as a result of which they were left to each other a great deal. As he found a containing mother rather than an eroticized object in the transference, Mr P became increasingly jealous of my other patients, whom he saw as the preferred twin. He began to fear that I would take his twin into treatment, instead of him.

The parasitic-twin and the poisoned mother

Mr P's twin had become a palpable presence in Mr P's mind in his sessions, and he spoke about his twin brother. Whereas formerly he had been a silent but active twin, he now became an alive and personified twin. Mr P perceived all my other patients as the twin, filling me up and taking all my time. His anger and jealousy of his twin now poisoned his relationship with me, in a similar vein to the parasitic twin relationship described by Athanassiou (1986) (see pp. 99-100). He believed his twin was in the favoured position vis-à- vis mother. Mr P described a dream:

> He was in a cafeteria. While he was still eating the first course, another person was
> eating a huge parfait. Mr P felt unable to continue eating, as if his food had become
> poisoned.

In his associations the cafeteria represented his sessions and the person being treated to the huge parfait was his twin. It was clear that he felt that his analytic food had been poisoned not only by the transference presence of his twin, but by the jealousy this stirred in Mr P. In the next session Mr P spoke about his warm, loving aunt whom his mother had tried to poison him against. So mother was now split and while his twin got the loving mother, Mr P got a poisonous cold mother.

Mr P arrived for his next session brandishing a bunch of flowers for me. I did not accept the flowers and in consequence he saw me as the poisoned mind of mother, as a clever, cruel vicious woman stripping him of his defences, a rejecting mother preoccupied with his twin brother. I was a transference mother who gave special food to his twin and not to him. Although he hated me as this unrewarding object, he chose to cling to this view because he was afraid I would change into someone less familiar.

The narcissistic-twinship transference

To protect himself from such poisonous feelings I now became an 'identical' transference twin that Mr P recognized. He copied my words and phrases and analysed himself, as if trying to be me. Whereas he had previously tried to crush me out of existence, he now created sameness. He was afraid of separateness and difference, and felt he could not disagree with me, that he had to be one with me in order to be safe. He twinned with me as a defence against a narcissistic injury occasioned by the dissolution of the binding twinship and therefore a fracturing of his identity. He believed that disentanglement would lead to his annihilation.

Mr P described how his twin had always demanded attention from mother while he had put himself second, getting attention instead by adapting to mother's needs, becoming mother's confidant, her mini-husband and his twin's mini-father. He felt this had been damaging to him both in his relationship with his father and to his sense of identity as a man. This mother–son relationship was played out in the consulting room at this stage of the work. I was a mother–twin and he remained compliant as a defence against my separateness and maternal function. It was as if we were glued together.

Further work led to the recognition of this twinning and the personification of the transference twin. Mr P then became able to explore the nature of his relationship with his twin. He measured himself against his twin, and also felt admired by him. However, he became violently angry with me because he felt that I had intervened in the twinship. He expressed his anger in his tone of voice and machine-gun delivery. He spoke with relish about killing wasps and flies with poisonous spray. He felt I had exposed him to an unbearable reality in the presence of the twin for whom he felt such intense jealousy. He concealed his jealousy in his pseudo-concern for other patients, as he described brushing the leaves off my doorstep to stop them from slipping.

The violence of his feelings was illuminated in a dream:

> Mr P was lying on a couch and his ex-lover was lying next to him. She told him that she had been let down by her husband, but she had someone else lined up to marry. She was going away with him, and she had to repeat three times where she was going, as he could not quite hear it. It sounded like the 'County of Isis'. He thought she meant Leicester, near Stafford. He felt sad that she was going and had not chosen him.

He associated to his dream: the County of Isis was Essex, the family home where his parents had previously lived. They had then moved, and mother 'took father to the country', where Mr P felt there was no longer a home for him. Leicester was where his twin brother went to university. Mr P felt mother had two men she preferred to him: his father and his twin. Mr P was furious that he did not possess mother. He linked this with his sexual relationships with women. He believed that in stealing his lover from her older boyfriend, he had stolen mother from father. As a result, he felt guilty and afraid, and he therefore preferred that father should have mother while he had a phantasized clandestine relationship with her, as he did with his lover and his analyst. He saw himself as emasculated in relation to mother as he listened to her incessant complaints about father and his twin. Mr P then spoke of the iron bar he had noticed in the street after he had left his last session (his sadistic, murderous phallus).

It was some years later that I understood the complexity of this dream and its links with the myth of Isis and her elder brother Osiris. As described in Chapter 2, Osiris chose Isis as his consort and they ruled happily and successfully together in what could be regarded as a narcissistic twinship. Osiris was assassinated and dismembered by Set, their jealous younger brother. The distraught Isis secretly regained Osiris' dismembered body and magically rejoined the parts, but without the phallus, which had been eaten by a Nile crab. She embalmed Osiris' body so as to restore her murdered God-brother-husband to eternal life.

I think the dream represents the various splits and dynamic experiences that Mr P was undergoing in relinquishing his eroticized mother-twin-analyst, a developmental move that led to the recognition of different aspects of his internal twin relationship.

Mr P, the twin in a murderously jealous /Set frame of mind believed that his twin-lover-on-the-couch/Isis (the omnipotently created clandestine lover-analyst) had chosen his Leicester-twin/Osiris rather than himself. He had to be told three times where the couple had gone, representing the three sessions per week in which Mr P kept an eye on the mother-lover-analyst who was unfaithful to him in choosing his twin rather than him. The telling three times would also represent the three corners of the oedipal triangle that he resisted recognizing as well as the three-cornered twin–twin–mother relationship. He was furious with the analyst-mother for dislodging him from his delusional phantasies of possessing the eroticized mother, and with the mother-lover-analyst who chose Osiris-father rather than him. He felt displaced and homeless as the parental couple moved to the country (the parental bedroom) where there was no place for him. Mr P wished to restore magically the eroticized Isis–Osiris twinship with me. This magical reparation would enable him to avoid the pain of his loss of the eroticized mother and the emergence of jealousy in the twinship. But he realized that the omnipotently restored Osiris-him was impotent (the missing phallus), and that the magical twinship was not a generative relationship, as was the parental one.

As proof that I was the unfaithful mistress-Isis-twin, in his next session Mr P commented on the footprints he had noticed on the doorstep. In a further defensive move, he became fiercely competitive with me.

The birth story

Mr P made the discovery in discussion with his father that the 'birth story' that he was 'left for dead' was not quite as it had been portrayed in the account often retold by his mother. He had, in fact, had some difficulties at birth, but he had received special attention from a nurse who had resuscitated him. His phantasy of being 'left for dead' was thus based in part on his murderous rivalry (the Set-twin) with his twin brother (the Osiris-twin), which had become a potent force in the transference. He had established a twinship with me that was a totalitarian state, allowing of no dissent, as indicated in the following material.

As the Christmas break approached, he described a poster that he had seen, featuring a child with its hand over one eye, with a caption, 'he won't enjoy Christmas this year. How can you?' - a message clearly intended for me. The one-eyed child was his twin-self with one eye for mother and one for his twin. He kept himself in a state of deprivation by neglecting himself and his health, martyring himself for me. He felt that I was a deaf, insensitive mother. He tried to terrorize me into giving him care by shouting at me. He used his anger to deal with his paranoid suspicions that I would only be nice to him under duress, if he shouted at me. His sexualized relationship with me was a screen against contact with an infant-him whose mother was preoccupied with his twin. I was again the cold depriving mother who became a hard person who abandoned him at Christmas.

Mr P reported that in a conversation with his mother she had said that both twins were her favourites. He could not understand this and clung to a phantasy of an aggressive sexual mother who split her twins, rather than a nurturing one who could hold both in mind. Again, this linked with his birth story - he felt alive only when he created sexual excitement, like the baby 'left for dead' who conjures up a sexual mother. He identified with this sexualized mother and this had implications for his sexual identity (see next section). He denigrated women and was contemptuous of women who 'prattle on', are predatory and 'might as well be men', while at the same time he preferred sexually dominant women.

Now that Mr P was confronted with an alive transference twin, he resorted to splitting. He regarded twins as two halves of one person, split so that one was good and the other bad. He resisted integrating these split aspects of himself with omnipotent phantasies of tall, bizarre buildings that he referred to as 'erect follies', in recognition of his self-mocking pseudo-phallic versions of potency. He split his mind and body as he regarded his mind as a parasite on his body, i.e. he hated his ability to think and to develop insight. He did not wish to recognize the way in which his own jealousy poisoned his relationships or that his twin was a separate person, not just a carrier of Mr P's cast-off feelings.

The feminine-twin and sado-masochistic rivalry

The sado-masochistic rivalry with me that ensued was in part an attempt by Mr P to identify himself and establish his own boundaries. He had started a process of distinguishing himself from his twinned objects.

In recognizing the existence of his psychic twin, Mr P also recognized that he had boundary problems with his actual twin whom he saw as a mirror-twin. He recognized that his ex-mistress was a mirror of himself who had represented an idealized twin. However, she had been toppled from her idealized perch and he now saw in her what he disliked in himself - he felt he was greedy, avaricious, self-centred, a misogynist, a 'rapist'. She was now a denigrated twin with whom he identified. Mr P expressed his fear of collapsing with the alteration of the twin boundaries. He resorted to violent, sadistic sexual phantasies to try to deal with his boundary confusions. On reading a newspaper report of a horrific gang rape of a woman over a period of five hours, he identified in phantasy with the gang of men.

This led to the emergence of Mr P's identification with a feminine role in the twinship and his gender confusion. He reported a dream:

> He was preparing to go out. He went up to the bathroom and found that the cabinet he had put on the wall had been knocked off, and was lying in the basin. He went to the kitchen. Both the kitchen and bathroom were like his mother's. His son was messing about with a friend. When his son admitted to knocking the cabinet down, Mr P pushed him around. He put his son outside the back door although he was dressed only in his pyjama pants. Mr P then went upstairs. He cut his hair so as to accommodate a wig. He put on a wig with an overhanging bit covering his forehead and nose, like a big cockscomb. He went to a restaurant where other men were dressed as women.

Associating to his dream, Mr P said he thought he played the feminine role in the twinship. His twin-son-analyst had damaged his sadistic masculine image of himself (the cabinet/phallus knocked into the basin), so he knocked his son (his young vulnerable twin-self) about and excluded him (split him off). He then inflated himself with a big 'cockscomb' – a phallus – while identifying himself with other men dressed as women. He had thus resorted to using an omnipotent solution to a narcissistic injury, inflating himself in identification with an aggressive masculine woman.

This inflation was evident in a second dream:

> He was in a tall building with a tower. The lift shaft had a ladder thing on top, fitting into the tower for support.

Mr P thought the tall building and tower were phallic and he said his dream book indicated it had to do with disguising his masculinity. Thus, he was confused and felt insecure in his masculinity. He felt that he was feminine, but that mother and his analyst were not feminine. Instead they were like men. In his gender confusion, he took his mother's-analyst's femininity for himself. It is apparent that he saw my interpretations as a father-me stripping him of his masculinity, barring him from, and interfering in, his twinship with a phantasied mistress-mother.

Clarifying boundaries: the separateness of twins

As the boundaries were slowly clarified, Mr P tried to blur them by wanting to get right inside me. I had not given him a birthday card and he was furious with me. He complained that he never got the attention he wanted and that I just took him apart. This linked with his belief he had been 'left for dead'. He said he wanted to leave his shoes in my room to make the space his, to leave a part of himself, to have a 'foot in the door', and his 'shoes under the bed'. He explained that this was to do with his concern for maintaining a safe place for himself, and he believed that my refusal meant his shoes were in danger (the split-off vulnerable, needy infant). Unconsciously, he wanted to secure the womb for himself, not to allow any others (twins) in.

The idea of leaving one's shoes under the bed also, of course, has sexual connotations, and Mr P phantasized that he had a sexual relationship with me. His wish to leave his shoes under the bed represented the semen that he would leave behind, inside me. He tried to shout me into a corner. He expressed his intense jealousy of his twin and my other patients and he started prying, wanting to know who and what existed in my life. He felt I had been profoundly unfaithful to him and he believed that he came to his sessions three times a week primarily to check up on me.

Whose shoes was he now in? He wanted to step into my shoes as he had stepped into father's shoes as a boy (mother's mini-husband). He felt his personal boundaries were unclear. He looked in the mirror and saw a mask, not recognizing himself. He felt his real self was not abutting on anyone else – that he was alone. He felt bereft and his jealousy of his now separate twin was vast and consuming. It was at this time that he learned from his parents that his twin had been extremely ill as a child and had been in danger of dying. Mr P recalled that he had felt furious with mother for both separating him from his twin and totally ignoring him, giving all the attention to his twin as he felt I did at weekends, 'leaving him for dead'. He was beginning to recognize the narcissistic side of himself.

Mr P's anger at being abandoned by his twin as he found the separateness between them was illustrated in the following session. On arrival, he saw something on the couch that I had not noticed (actually a chestnut placed there by my dog). Mr P quickly picked it up and handed it to me before I could get to it, saying that my last patient had left some 'nuts'. He then associated to a dream:

> He was coming here, but he was late. His twin was with him. He ran from the tube station, and his twin kept shouting after him as the distance between them increased. His pants kept falling down, so it was hard for him to run. He got here but the building was different. It was big and square. He came inside. In my room there were a lot of people, all my patients. He was surprised at how many there were. The meeting had been called because someone had threatened to buy the building, to take it over. Then it would all be different. Everyone was offering money to save the building. Mr P had less money than the others did. He also didn't know what was going on, and it was as though the others had been to meetings before but he hadn't. He handed two of the women an address card each, but he didn't have any more to give to the others.

Mr P said he felt embarrassed at the idea of his pants falling down and someone noticing. He felt I had deliberately put something on the couch to put him down, to swat him like a fly. I interpreted his feeling exposed (caught with his pants down) in the previous day's session when he expressed his intense jealousy of his twin. As a result, he felt angry with me that I had seen how vulnerable he felt. When his parents had given a lot of attention to his twin when he was so ill, Mr P felt that he was left with nothing. He felt that here too, the other patients/twins got all my attention and love. He believed other people's 'nuts' were taking his place. (Later, I came to see this as his 'ballsy' twin or aggressive masculine women.) He feared that because of the anger he expressed here the day before, openly as his twin would do, his hidden twin was actually here with him. He had brought his twin with him. He believed I would not tolerate his anger with me and that I had left the 'nuts' on the couch to put him down, to 'swat him like a fly'. So now he wanted to buy me out, to take over and have me all to himself. But he recognized that he did not have that power; that he had to share me.

Mr P confirmed this interpretation, saying he realized how angry he was yesterday after he left – his head was spinning on the train. He had arrived here this morning feeling angry again, and he then felt totally squashed by the 'nuts' on the couch. It was evident that he felt displaced by an aggressive masculine twin-rival.

The competition with the 'non-identical' transference twin

The awareness of separateness ushered in a period of exploring difference. Mr P saw me as a bullying, depriving, omnipotent twin who was cleverer than he was and knew things before he did – like his twin brother did. He recalled his competitiveness with his twin, and that his twin got into the best grammar school while he barely scraped through his 11-plus exam. He then had to go for an interview for a place at an inferior school. He could not understand what had happened, because he had learned to read before his twin. He thought the head teacher at his school took an interest in him only because he was a twin, and the fact that the other twin was at the best school. So he believed that the head was trying to prove something and was not interested in him for himself. He was never good enough. He was never valued like his twin. He was compliant with me, which led me to think that he was hiding his murderous anger.

However, it transpired that the schooldays were not quite as he had recalled. Mr P met his twin and they talked about their teenage years. He learned 'secrets' from his twin: that Mr P had originally been allocated to a technical school miles away and father had had to intervene and fight for him to go to a grammar school. He also learned that his twin had got into a lot of trouble at school, with truanting and detentions, and that he was nearly expelled. Thus, Mr P began to discover further facts of his life – a father who took care of him, and a twin brother with problems.

Mr P went to see the Tom Stoppard play *The Real Thing*, a work that explores what love really does mean in relationships. Mr P was angry with me because I had exposed him to the existence of other patients/a twin. He felt that I had for the past two years withheld from him the reality of his intense competition with his twin. He was enraged at discovering in me the 'competitive twin', the 'real thing'. He now believed that his phantasy of me as a seductive mother-mistress was a red herring, a defence against the 'real thing' of a competitive twin. In the ensuing period, Mr P tried to deal with his feelings of emptiness at the loss of this eroticized phantasy mother-twin, and the deadness and sham in his life. He oscillated between regression to the narcissistic defences of twinship and involving himself in further discoveries of the facts of his life.

Thus the twin transference has both regressive and progressive elements. As Mr P's capacities to tolerate his separateness developed in the move from a narcissistic twinship to a twinship of difference and competition, he became more able to recognize the different movements and to observe his state of mind.

The loss of the enmeshed twinship and the discovery of a companion

Mr P then experienced an inner bleakness, despair, isolation and intense pain. He felt hurt and aggrieved, 'no good, invisible, sick, devalued'. He looked into the mirror (analysis) for his reflection (twin-self), but he could not find it. He felt he had no echo with me and believed he had lost me, and indeed, I did at times feel disconnected from him. He telephoned me at weekends for company. He complained in his sessions in the hope of gaining my attention. He felt I had separated him from his twin and would now give my attention to his twin instead of to him. He missed the companionship of his enmeshed twinship. He wanted to contact my other patients to fill the void of the missing twin. I would now add that I had become the hated father who had separated him from both his twin and his eroticized breast-mother.

As Mr P spoke of the void created by the absence of his twin and the loss of his phantasy breast-twin, he found it difficult to believe he could survive alone. Life was empty without his twin. He relived his birth legend by identifying with a news story about a toddler who had been locked up and left to die. He was angry that I had pushed him into the void and he saw me as an uncaring insensitive mother who did not know how bad it felt for him; a mother unable to contain his fears about his survival.

Mr P alternated between, on the one hand, desperately trying to find a twin to fill the void by making two people into one-and-a-half (as he saw his wife and himself), i.e. wanting to merge with a twin-analyst; and on the other hand, communicating with a separate analyst-mother. Sometimes he would suddenly find himself feeling comfortable in the silence with me, listening to the birds. In an important progressive move, he recognized how he had used a re-enactment of his past, his relentless and aggressive twinning, to push people into getting what he wanted. I realized that I was no longer experienced as persecuting and uncaring in relation to him.

Mr P recalled that mother had said that she had not been expecting twins and that it seemed she had not been well prepared for the birth of even one baby. He had believed there was no place for him, as he had been given the box room while his twin got the bigger bedroom. However, he also recalled feelings of closeness with his twin, as they gossiped together about their parents. He remembered their being strapped together in their pram and leaning on each other. So Mr P had now found memories of an internal representation of a twin with whom he had satisfying and shared mutual support, during times when things must have been difficult for his mother and father. A companionable twin thus enabled him to tolerate the deprivation he suffered in the company of a depressed, inadequately available mother – and a separate analyst.

Mr P began to take pleasure in the competitiveness of the twinship. He also began to realize that progress in the work was leading towards an ending, and he had dreams of me pushing him out too fast. He wanted to remain at the breast constantly to prevent access to the other twin – the enduring rivalry of the twinship. Mr P also tried to preserve his permanent place at the breast through the twinship, with a dream about moving on and making way for other patients with whom he had twinned himself, so as not to lose me or his place with me.

Separation felt dangerous to Mr P as it exposed him to the oedipal father, as evidenced in the following dream:

> Mr P was scrambling backwards into an aeroplane. However, it took off before he had got inside and his legs were hanging outside. The plane banked and he was in danger of falling out. He called to his twin who grabbed him under the arms and pulled him into the plane, saving his life. He then discovered that his father was the pilot.

The reckless, dangerous pilot was the hated father that would intervene between Mr P and the breast-twin, as he approached separation from his analyst. In this dream Mr P turned to the twinship to save him from this threatening, primitive oedipal father, a further indication that the twinship had provided a refuge from conflictual oedipal issues at a time when Mr P felt he had not had a sufficiently containing experience with mother.

Containing the conflicts of ending

In a discussion with his parents, Mr P learned that they had been concerned about the welfare of their twin babies and had taken them to a psychologist who had found nothing wrong with them. Mr P had sought and found caring, concerned parents. He now became more aware of his parents' difficulties and inadequacies in a way he felt he could tolerate. He could recognize that they had done their best in difficult circumstances. His developing sense of guilt and his concern about his objects, particularly about my 'stickability' and capacity to survive his attacks, led to his wish to make reparation. Now he could begin the process of mourning.

Fearing that he would lose me through the success of the analysis, Mr P again relived the now-discredited birth legend by neglecting himself, martyring himself, until he reached a state of near-paralysis. On recognizing this, he discovered in himself an overwhelming sadness at missing out on the affection he had craved as a little boy, something that was brought into sharp contrast by his relationship with his own children. He felt he gained loving attention vicariously through his children's relationship with him.

As the issue of ending became more prominent, Mr P reported a dream:

He was in a room with his twin and others. There was a window that opened upwards. He and his twin argued about opening it. The twin opened the window and dived out headfirst. Mr P was horrified. He rushed to the window and looked out. He saw that his twin had dived into an open manhole full of water. He felt relieved but noticed that he had damaged his hand.

Mr P associated to a room on the 19th floor where he had lived for five years. (I lived in the postcode N19!) He knew that the previous occupant had jumped to his death from the window in that room. It was also the same room in which he had broken up with his lover, prior to coming to see me. After the ending of his relationship with her, Mr P had locked the door and sobbed for a long time. He added that his twin brother was celebrating a wedding anniversary, but Mr P had intervened between his twin and his wife about arrangements for the party.

Mr P was reluctant to allow me to analyse the dream, to open the window (arguing with his twin about the window). He felt that to do so was an interference in our long 'marriage', as he had intervened between his twin and his twin's wife. Mr P wanted to avoid knowing about his separation from me, fearing that the separation would cause his death (jumping out of the window of N19). However, he recognized that life goes on (his twin survived the jump), and that he had buoyancy (Quinodoz, 1993) – the water in the manhole enabled him to swim, to be a man.

In his anger with me about the ending, Mr P felt I was like a parasitic twin, like an 'Alien', who put my thoughts/ideas into him so they could hatch and destroy him. He was afraid that he could not survive parting from me, my separateness from him, and an ending of the analytic work. Oedipal issues now predominated. He thought I looked tearful and he assumed I had suffered a bereavement of a parent, i.e. he was killing off a parent so that he could take the parent's place.

Mr P was angry at my not treating him as 'normal' instead of as a patient, and he contrasted a woman therapist he had met who had spoken to him as a colleague. This had excited him. In contrast he felt I was like a rich father who deprived him of what he wanted, so condemning him to poverty and misery. He felt he exhausted himself trying to make me into a friend, to deny the ending of a relationship that embodied a generational difference. Mr P envied me my knowledge. He decided he would train as a psychotherapist and spent weeks talking about his wish to train, poring over the prospectus, wondering whether to apply. Eventually he was able to relinquish this wish to be so identified with me, to be the same as me, to be my twin. He found a compromise solution in a related profession, which offered him similarity, but not sameness.

Mr P now saw his twin-analyst as an insensitive bully and he wanted to separate himself from his bully-analyst. He found it difficult to believe that someone would replace him here, and complained about my 'battery farming' – a mother who produces twins! In his rage he made me into a 'dead but beautiful mummy figure', both to express and to cover his painful feelings of loss. Difference became an important issue for him, both from his twin and a generational difference from an analyst-mother.

Mr P was put out to see me wearing glasses. He thought that I had been weeping, as he believed that I shared his grief. He thought that I might have an eye infection. He recognized that he had gradually become able to see himself through less infected eyes, as someone who had changed and developed internally. He felt better about himself, but realized that he was not the beautiful swan he had wanted to be. However, he could accept his limitations without grievance and get on with his life. Like his twin in the dream, Mr P now had buoyancy (Quinodoz, 1993). He was becoming himself, and he felt he could carry himself rather than having to depend on a narcissistic twin object for his survival. As Quinodoz notes, this sensation leads to a feeling of jubilation, flying out of the window, floating in the water – of buoyancy. Mr P was also aware of his sadness at losing his object, linked with his recognition of the inevitability of death.

Chapter 7
Enactment of the transference twin: individual development and regression

In researching the literature on the psychoanalytic treatment of twins, I have been struck by the number of published cases in which the analyst has enacted a twin transference relationship with a patient, rather than deal with it through interpretation. In addition, some analysts have justified the enactment, claiming that it is the transformational factor in the analysis.

Ordinarily, a patient phantasizes about projecting an experience or object relationship into the analyst. The analyst is nudged into living this experience in the transference relationship with the patient and is then able to recognize and interpret it. The patient has brought alive the transference relationship in the analyst's mind by pushing the analyst intra-psychically to 'actualise' (Sandler, 1976: 45) the transference relationship. Sandler (1993) defines 'actualisation' as 'a process in which the object is pushed, by a variety of subtle unconscious manoeuvres, both verbal and non-verbal, into playing a particular role for the patient' (p. 1105). However, in an enactment, the analyst *becomes* the transference object and enacts the assigned role instead of analysing and interpreting. As I will discuss in the next chapter, enactment is a product of both the patient's projective identification and the analyst's own counter-transference reaction.

A great deal has been written about projective identification and the counter-transference reactions of the analyst (see Hinshelwood, 1989). I will briefly outline some of the processes that lead to enactment. In unconscious phantasy, the patient splits off aspects of his own experience and projects them into the analyst (Klein, 1946). The patient then believes that these aspects of the self are located in the analyst, as a result of which the patient's perception of the analyst is changed (Spillius, 1983). Thus the patient would in phantasy project an object relationship into the analyst and then believe that he/she is in that particular object relationship with the analyst. The analyst's response to the projected phantasy would depend on many factors, including the motive for the patient's projective identification.

In this respect, Bion (1959) notes that projective identification is the link between the infant and the breast, and between the patient and the analyst. He distinguishes between normal and pathological projective identification, depending on the degree of violence and omnipotence in the phantasied projection. In normal projective identification, the patient communicates an experience of an object relationship for the purposes of understanding. It is intended 'to introduce into the object a state of mind, as a means of communicating with it about this mental state' (Hinshelwood, 1989: 184). In pathological projective identification, the motive is to rid the self of an unwanted experience or relationship. The intention is 'to evacuate violently a painful state of mind leading to forcibly entering an object, in phantasy, for immediate relief, and often with the aim of intimidating control of the object' (Hinshelwood, 1989: 184).

Rosenfeld (1983) further distinguished between defensive, communicative and empathic projective identification. Analytic empathy would be a benign form of projective identification in which there is no loss of a sense of reality or confusion of boundaries. However, in pathological identification, the boundaries between the self and the object would be destroyed. The early object relationships, notably those with mother, father, twin and other siblings, especially preverbal relationships that are more difficult to express in verbal terms, may be communicated in this way and may exert considerable pressure on the analyst to enact rather than analyse the transference relationship (Joseph, 1978).

Some degree of enactment is inevitable in the analytic crucible as a function of the nature of the analytic relationship. The process of actualization offers an opportunity for the patient's phantasy to become 'known' to the analyst. Patients seek in the analyst a resonance that corresponds in some degree to their own experience, and in this way the analyst is pushed or nudged (Joseph, 1987) by the patient into living out the experience of the projected transference relationship. The patient's projected phantasies impinge on the analyst's feelings, thinking and actions in a necessary step beyond projective identification and before interpretation becomes possible.

However, where an actual enactment occurs, the analytic stance is, at least momentarily, lost. The enactment is a transference/counter-transference experience since it involves unconscious processes of both the patient and the analyst. It is likely that the enactment will be based at least partly on the analyst's own unanalysed conflict, which has been awakened by the patient's projective identification. As a result, both the patient's projection and the analyst's own unresolved conflicts may lead to considerable pressure to discharge the unbearable tension through enactment of the transference relationship. If this tension is not recognized and thought about, the analyst may consequently be prompted to act in a manner that would ordinarily be considered to be outside the analytic repertoire. Such enactment precludes the use of the projected material for the purposes of understanding and interpretation unless it is subsequently acknowledged and analysed with the patient. Enactment damages the analytic setting that is vital to the analysis. Repair to the setting can only occur where the lapse has been properly addressed psychoanalytically.

Twins tend to seek twinships in many of their external relationships, and the analytic setup provides fertile ground for the twin relationship to emerge. The pressure on the analyst to become a psychic twin may, at different times and with different patients, vary in intensity and it may be expressed in different ways. There may be a number of reasons for the readiness of the analyst to respond to the pressure from the patient to enact the twin relationship, and these may be both emotional and theoretical. (I will explore some of these through the case material in this chapter.) The intimacy of the analytic relationship activates unconscious experiences in the analyst as well as in the patient. Amongst these experiences is the fundamental ubiquitous longing for a twin (Klein, 1963), stemming from the sense of loneliness inherent in being separate. Some of the 'special' pairings that occur in analyses, the feelings that a particular patient is 'special', will fall into this dimension of experience.

Of the examples I describe below, some are from analyses a long time ago, and our understanding and technique have developed a great deal since then. Nevertheless, it seems to me that these enactments in the analyses of twins warrant some attention. The case studies also raise important questions about the causes of the difficulties that twins may encounter in analysis. Is the analytic twinning encountered in working with twin patients the result of the dynamic nature of their inter- and intra-personal object relationships, of regression to a more protected position in the face of unmanageable anxiety, or is it due to an arrest or a deficit in emotional development? I will explore these issues in discussing the cases. The links between possible differential brain development in twins within the context of the early affectional bond with the mother, and its effects on object relationships (explored in Chapter 10), might have some bearing on this issue.

In the following reports of transference/counter-transference enactments taken from a number of published papers, I will pay particular attention to the context in the analysis within which the enactment occurred. I believe the material that follows supports a number of proposals:

1. enactment does have a particular significance in psychoanalytic work with a twin.
2. enactment may occur more frequently in twins than other patients because of the particular psychodynamics of the twinship.
3. enactments occurring in the analysis of twins frequently occur at a point of transition in the analysis, when the patient is engaged in a process of psychic separation from the other twin, and as a consequence is facing what are felt to be unbearable anxieties. This will have a powerful effect on the transference relationship between patient and analyst, where the twin relationship is not only reflected, but is played out to its fullest extent.

The use of analysis to avoid the terror of psychic separation

An account of the analyses of both twins by the same analyst graphically indicates the way each twin used the analyst as a transference twin at a time when he was faced with both actual and psychic separation from the other twin.

Petö (1946) reports that when Peter had been in analysis with him for nearly three years, his twin, Paul, also entered an analysis with him that lasted for three months. The two analyses overlapped in time. Petö does not question either the ethical or psychoanalytic advisability of taking both twins into treatment simultaneously with the same analyst. These days, with our current understanding of object and transference relationships, an analyst would be most unlikely to take both twins of a pair into treatment. But perhaps the fact that Petö did so was influenced as much by the dynamics of the twinship, as by differences in analytic approach. It is significant in this regard that each of Petö's twin patients took 'refuge in analysis' (Petö, 1946: 126) at the point of separation from the other twin, when they might have committed themselves to a heterosexual relationship. Petö notes that both the analyses began with a strong homosexual transference to the analyst but he does not report on his analysis of the homosexual transference. He analyses only the parental transference figures, where there may of course be an important homosexual element. However, it is as if the transference twin, in this situation the obvious homosexual twin, was of no relevance to the analysis.

I suggest that at the point of separation from his twin, each of Petö's patients was seeking an 'identical' (homosexual) twin in the analyst to try to maintain the twinship. In seeing both twins for analysis, Petö was drawn into an enactment of the twin transference in each case and became the 'identical' (homosexual) twin to each patient, enabling the twin patients to remain bound in the twinship. He acted as a go-between for the homosexual aspects of the twins. It is significant to this case that the twins suffered the very early loss of their mother, and were brought up by a cold, severe aunt/stepmother whom father later married. Father was largely absent, but when present he was experienced as brutal and unloving, traumatizing his vulnerable twin sons still further. As Petö notes, the twins 'knew no mother's breast' (Petö, 1946: 128), and would have relied on each other heavily in these adverse circumstances, as a consequence creating an enmeshed twinship.

(The difficulties created for the twin relationship when either one or both twins are in psychoanalytic treatment are discussed in Chapter 9.)

Enactment to restore a 'mutilated identity' or personality deficit

Some analysts regard twins as individually incomplete, and believe that the twin pair forms a psychological unit. They suggest that twins suffer a personality deficit as a result of the experience of being a twin. The personalities of the twins are composed of mutually shared aspects that are complementary, not duplicated. Thus neither twin has a complete identity, but shares it with the other twin. Together the twins form one whole personality. As a result, there is an inadequate distinction between the personalities of each twin, affecting both cognitive and functional aspects of the personality.

A theory of deficit regarding the structure of the personalities of twins has implications for the treatment of twin patients, and I believe that it encourages the enactment rather than the analysis of the transference twin. I will explore the cases of two analysts who espouse a theory of deficit. Both the analysts regard their enactment as *the* transformational factor in the analysis, and they believe that such enactment restores to the patients that which they supposedly lack. Contrary to their views, I believe that their material indicates that the analysts have played into the patient's delusional system by engaging in a transference enactment that is then justified in relation to the theory of personality deficit.

Lacombe (1959) describes the analysis of an 'identical' twin with a severe obsessional neurosis and a masochistic compulsion to cheat. In Lacombe's view, this twin patient suffered from a mutilated identity as a result of being a twin. He explains that the 'identical' twin is faced with a double of himself in reality, not just in phantasy, as a result of which his psychological unity is damaged. In the analysis, the patient was obsessive in his pursuit of his wish for the reconstitution of his mutilated identity (a factor that must have added to the pressure on the analyst to enact the transference twin). The analyst was finally nudged into compensating for the patient's supposed psychological damage by filling the gap vacated by the twin. I will give a brief summary of the main features of this reported analysis, and will then explore the way in which Lacombe's theory influenced the analytic encounter.

The patient was the firstborn twin and the twin boys did everything together. The patient regarded his twin as 'the other leg of the same body' (Lacombe, 1959: 7) and it seems that the twins were enmeshed within their relationship. In support of his theory of a personality deficit or mutilated identity in twins, Lacombe notes that at the start of the analysis, the patient said nothing about his parents, and also maintained a 'dead silence' about his twin: when the analyst addressed this, the patient explained, 'They [twins] don't count', and 'We are only halves of the same being' (Lacombe, 1959: 7). As children, the twins fought violently with each other, despite, or perhaps because of, their closeness. As also becomes apparent from the material, the patient wished to annihilate his twin brother rather than separate from him, a wish that I think was achieved psychically through the analytic enactment.

The pivotal point in the analysis arose when the patient stopped talking in his sessions, supposedly as a result of his strong feelings of guilt about his attitude to life, his manipulation of events so that he had everything and his twin had nothing. He reproduced this cheating in the analysis as he used his silence to deprive the analyst-twin of his free associations, so that the analyst also had nothing and the patient had everything. Analysing this silent resistance in its many aspects over a long period of time apparently did not resolve the block. Instead, Lacombe dealt with this impasse by removing it. He offered the patient double sessions, with the justification that 'the double session will symbolically mean to Jack the permission and opportunity to realize his unity in this new atmosphere of analytic affective experience. In fact the double session would mean a double share to Jack, who at birth had received only half of his share' (Lacombe, 1959: 9). Thus the analyst was manipulated into creating a concretely corrective emotional experience.

The patient responded positively to the doubling of his session time. He felt that the two hours were really just one (a denial of reality), and that he was now getting his full share of attention. Consequently, he gave his full share of material, dreams and associations to his analyst. Lacombe states, 'The double sessions, by *symbolically* returning to Jack his full share, allow him a full identity and virility no longer reduced by half' (p.10, my emphasis). In a further confusion of theory, Lacombe refers to the introduction of the double sessions as a 'symbolic realisation technique', quoting Sechehaye (1951): 'The symbols were reality to the patient, in fact, the only reality; they were symbols merely for the analyst' (Lacombe, 1959: 10). In current terms, I think we would regard this concretization, the doubling of sessions to compensate for loss of 'the other half' (p. 8), as a 'symbolic equation' (Segal, 1957: 41) and lacking the representational value of a true symbol. This confusion is central to the delusional system that was enacted in the analysis.

The analyst reports that the focus of the patient's conflict then moved on to oedipal issues and he regards this shift as evidence of the success of the enactment in enabling the patient to develop. The patient's sessions were later reduced to single ones. During the ensuing work, the patient believed he had changed from being an 'identical' to a 'non-identical' twin, while his actual twin had remained the same. In 'his final emotional dissociation from his twin', the patient relegated his twin to being 'simply ... another brother' (Lacombe. 1959: 10). So Lacombe and his patient believe that he is no longer a twin. Thus, Lacombe believes he has achieved his aim to liberate the patient from a 'mutilating union' (p. 10) with his twin, via the analysis and by the doubling of sessions.

Lacombe regards the doubling of sessions in order to compensate for the supposed deficit in the patient as *the* crucial step in transforming the patient from an 'identical' to a 'non-identical' twin, and in the dissolution of the twinship. As Lacombe notes, the richness and detail of the analysis is lacking in the report, so it is not possible to understand the precise dynamics that were operating. However, the dramatic shift from the twin-transference to oedipal material suggests that instead of a gradual process of recognition of difference and separation, the enactment repressed or bypassed something that was felt to be too difficult to bear. This created immediate relief for both patient and analyst, but the enactment was not a resolution of the transference/counter-transference difficulty. In fact, I think the material the patient then produced confirms that this was a bypass rather than a resolution of the impasse: the patient reported a dream that led to an understanding that the patient had cheated by taking his twin's share and that he felt guilty about so doing – I think he had succeeded in cheating his analyst.

Lacombe describes the complex transference relationships that he regards as the patient's attempt to reconstitute his mutilated identity. His understanding of these relationships is based on his theory of a mutilated identity in twins. I will outline these transference relationships and comment on the consequent psychoanalytic difficulties engendered by this theory:

The fused-twin-transference: Lacombe proposes that the patient fused transferentially with the analyst (and others), thus creating an 'identical twin' to whom he clung. Lacombe stresses that this is *fusion*, not *confusion*, with the analyst, as the two halves become one whole. Thus the analyst filled the gap left by the other twin, without whom the patient was considered to be incomplete. In other words, the analyst had to *be* the transference twin for the patient to be able to function, rather than analyse the twin transference in a true maternal function that would have painfully distinguished each twin. In enacting the twin transference, I think that the analyst has entered the patient's delusional belief that a twin is half a person, and that by restoring the other twin to him in the form of a substitute, the patient would become whole. The reality of there being two people in a twinship and two analytic hours in a double session is subverted in the name of a theory of mutilated identity, including a hope that there could be reparation by compensatory emotional provision.

The split-twin-transference: The patient believed that he and his twin brother were a two-faced unity and that therefore all other people must be too. In a kind of echoing double vision, the patient thought that likewise he had two mothers and two fathers, and two analysts. I think that in adhering to a view of fusion rather than confusion both between the twins and with the transference twin, the separateness of the two can only exist through splitting. The doubling must be based on splitting processes in relation to ego functions that would indeed leave the patient feeling depleted.

The double-mother-transference: The patient wished not only to get 'his full share' (Lacombe, 1959: 10) back from his twin by withholding his free associations. He also demanded an extra share from the mother-analyst. He cheated all the people in his life, echoing the way in which he believed he had had to steal his mother's love, since he only got half of it. The analyst enacted the patient's doubling phantasy, becoming a double-mother by offering double sessions, as if this would make good his patient's loss.

The cheated-twin-transference: It is inevitable that with such splitting, the twins would believe that they had suffered the loss of aspects of the self to the other twin. Thus, Lacombe notes that the patient wished to take away from his twin the half share that he believed that his twin had taken from mother. In this vein, he married his twin's girlfriend and cheated him in various other ways. I believe that this was the crucial transference encounter that was enacted by the analyst. The analyst-twin was not only cheated out of the patient's associations, but also of his own analytic capacities.

I suggest that in doubling the sessions, Lacombe did not function as a true maternal container. Instead, the analyst enacted a transference twin in the guise of a double-mother who gave to the twin-patient that which was his own (the analyst's). In the enactment, Lacombe became a twin-analyst who gave up his birthright of analysis, instead being a mother-analyst who could contain his patient's anxieties and feelings of loss at not having mother to himself. He compensated the patient for not having a solely possessed mother, and for having to share mother with his twin. In so doing, Lacombe succumbed to the idea that something with symbolic significance in the patient's internal world could be converted into a concrete reality. The analytic setting was manipulated to restore the supposed 'mutilating psychic damage' (Lacombe, 1959: 11) of being a twin.

The analyst played into his patient's delusion that as a twin substitute, he could replace the half that was supposedly missing from his patient's personality. He became the delusional double-mother-twin that was created by the patient in his own (split-twin) image. The enactment allowed the avoidance of an encounter with an analyst who was not an 'identical' twin and whom the patient could not cheat. Lacombe claims that this enactment and analysis brought about a successful resolution of the twinship and the development of a separate identity by the patient who was no longer a twin. He refers to the patient's 'dissociation' (Lacombe, 1959: 10) from his twin, suggesting again that the mechanism used was splitting, rather than differentiation. This confirms my view that in the enactment of the phantasy, both patient and analyst colluded in the belief that the other twin had been psychically eliminated. In psychic reality a twin is always a twin, and always will be, even in the event of the death of one twin (see Engel, 1975), but that does not mean he is 'identical' or shares a personality with his twin.

Intertwined twinship and the complementarity of the twin pair

Like Lacombe, Ortmeyer (1970 and 1975) postulates that twins suffer a deficit as a result of the experience of being a twin. The disadvantaged twins develop a psychological unity, a 'we-self' system (Ortmeyer, 1970: 125) instead of an individual identity. There is insufficient distinction between one twin's personality and the other's. The two personalities blend in such a way that some traits are complementary, i.e. non-duplicative and non-identical. These traits endure and each twin will have particular traits more fully developed and structured than the other twin. The twins do not distinguish between their own and their twin's personality but instead use each other's personality as an adjunct to their own. Each twin will therefore experience difficulties at an individual level.

The twins interact with each other and the external world as a 'we-self' unit. The absence of the other twin creates anxiety that may become acute, because of the loss of certain personality traits that are needed for the individual twin to function. Rather than develop his/her own capacities to compensate for the supposed deficit, the twin expects the other twin or a twin-substitute to fill the gap. The analysis will then focus on the necessity of resolving the identity fusion (not confusion) of the twin patient.

Ortmeyer (1970) describes psychoanalytic work by a therapist with a twin patient, paying particular attention to the intertwined nature of the twinship and the complementarity of the twin pair. He notes that the parents of the twins had apparently encouraged the development of an enmeshed twinship. I will describe some of the material that led up to the enactment of the transference twin by the therapist.

The 'identical twin' patient seemed to have no sense of herself as separate from her twin, and she used the pronouns 'she' and 'I' (for her twin and herself) interchangeably. The therapist commented on the confusion between the patient and her twin. After this, the patient lapsed into a prolonged silence. When asked by her therapist what was happening in the silence, the patient insisted that the therapist knew (as she presumed her twin would). The therapist then interpreted the patient's silence as resistance. He interpreted that in the transference he represented the patient's repressed ambivalent feelings for her twin. Getting no response to this interpretation, he then variously interpreted her denial of her competitiveness with her twin, her need for constant affection from her twin, and her frustration at having to share with her twin. All this led to further silence. It seems, however, that he did not interpret his patient's wish for him to be her twin, to fill the gap left by the absent twin, that is, her nudging her therapist to enact the transference twin.

The therapist considered his counter-transference and realized he had become annoyed and anxious about the patient's silences. It then transpired that the therapist was himself a 'fraternal' twin who, like his patient, had assumed that his twin knew whatever was on his mind without him having to say it. He recalled feeling annoyed and rejected when his twin did not understand him. He had been convinced his twin knew everything and remembered his pleasure in this. So, the therapist recognized the transference twin, but it linked too closely with his own unresolved experiences for him to have the necessary distance to analyse it.

Instead, the therapist then enacted this transference/counter-transference relationship with his patient. He became the thought-reading twin, speaking his own thoughts about his patient and some aspects of his own life to his patient. He enacted the twin transference instead of interpreting that he was experienced as the patient's twin – he became the twin substitute. The patient relaxed and said, 'she felt whole again when the therapist talked' (Ortmeyer, 1970: 132). She felt he had spoken her thoughts for her (although not always accurately), as her twin would have done.

As the treatment progressed, the patient occasionally became mute and rigid, and the therapist's silence led to an increase in her rigidity and a fear 'that she might begin to act uncontrollably' (Ortmeyer, 1970: 132). The therapist recalled that as a child, his own upset was relieved when his twin verbalized his feelings for him. Using this counter-transference information, the therapist then talked actively and assertively about what he thought was bothering the patient and again the patient relaxed. The therapist hypothesized that when the patient became rigid, images of love and hate for her twin, and transferentially for her therapist, were emerging into awareness. Thus he again recognized the twin in the transference, but he continued to enact this role rather than interpret the patient's wish to get him to take over aspects of her own functioning. The therapist believed that the patient had neither the security nor the skill to verbalize her own feelings and that her twin had relieved the patient of this personality function, as he was now doing. The patient confirmed that she did tend to act out her images rather than express them verbally.

In Ortmeyer's view, the therapist had entered into the 'we-self' by enacting the transference relationship. He notes,

> The author did not find that these attributes [an ability to express her feelings and memories] were simply repressed in her and that lifting the repression revealed the fully developed trait. It was not sufficient to interpret the resistance and transference to her. The therapist supplied the personality functions that the other had. He at least partially gratified the patient's needs by playing the role of the other twin. By entering in the we-self, he made the patient aware of her deficit, and helped her via identification and discussion to overcome it (Ortmeyer, 1970: 133).

Ortmeyer maintains that the enactment was necessary for there to be any progress with this patient, as the intertwined twinship had created a deficit in each twin that could not be remedied through interpretation.

In analysing transference material, we hope to develop and transform our own and the patient's understanding of the transference object, so that what is internalized by the patient is not just the same object relationship that has been lived out again in the consulting room. Given that the therapist above enacted rather than analysed the transference twin, this raises the question of what the patient might have identified with that would have enabled her to make progress. In enacting the transference twin, the therapist enacted both the enmeshed relationship between the patient and her twin sister, and his own unresolved conflicts in relation to his twin. The patient would, as a result, have introjected a compound twin relationship. Filling the gap, as described, would support and reinforce the complementary-twin structure rather than elucidate the anxiety-provoking internal relationship the patient was struggling with. She might have been enabled, through a containing relationship, to develop her own capacities to articulate her feelings. Her relaxation after the enactment may thus have been relief at the reinstatement of the twinship, Ortmeyer's 'we-self', rather than an indication of any real progress in understanding the nature of her transference objects.

The question arises as to whether we are really dealing with a personality deficit in twins, a developmental arrest, as both Lacombe and Ortmeyer suggest, or a confusion of identities between the twins as a result of porous ego boundaries, with some areas of complementarity between the twins. Lacombe and Ortmeyer stress that the complementarity between twins is based on deficit and that personality traits are allocated to one twin or the other, but are not duplicated in them both, as if one personality is shared out between the twins. However, it is apparent from other work (notably Engel, 1975, and Joseph, 1961) that complementary traits are more likely to be based on the emphasis of one trait or another in each twin in an attempt to deal with rivalry between them, rather than absence of that trait in either.

Regression to earlier modes of functioning

What are the elements of the twin relationship that stir such enactments in analysis? The level of mental functioning may certainly be one factor. Twins are likely to suffer a greater level of frustration than a single infant does, as they have to wait longer for attention and feeding. Unless there is more than one carer (with whatever problems that itself might bring; see Chapter 4), one infant is always waiting while the other is fed. Thus the existence of a twin creates a situation where optimal amounts of both gratification and frustration are interfered with. Excessive frustration inhibits the development of a capacity for thinking (Bion, 1962a). As a result, twins may experience difficulty in moving from primary process thinking to secondary process thinking. The excessive frustration is a source of the rage that the infant experiences in relation to both mother and twin. The rage will be a destructive element in the development of symbolic thought (Glenn, 1966).

Twins in an enmeshed twinship occupy a borderline state of mind. The question arises as to whether this is as a result of deficit based on absence or of regression. Fonagy (1991) suggests that the impairment of object relations in borderline patients leads to a fragmentation of their sense of identity that is crucial in developing the ability to take account of one's own and other's mental states (a 'theory of mind', p. 620). He suggests that the deficit in borderline patients is self-imposed and partial, brought on by the disavowal of the mental existence of the object as unbearable psychic pain is anticipated. Fonagy is quite clear that regression to a state where there is confusion of boundaries should be understood not as a developmental arrest, or as changes in the ego, but as a re-employment of structures that were used earlier in development. The capacity for differentiation of self and other is impaired in borderline patients as a result of regression to earlier and obsolete structures, and is not due to a developmental arrest.

Britton (1998) also regards regression as a retreat to a pathological organization that reiterates the past and evades the future. Normally we move from a position of greater psychic order to one of less cohesive functioning, and back again in a continuous, lifelong, cyclical development through both paranoid-schizoid and depressive positions. Either position may be used defensively in a wish to end uncertainty and the fears associated with fragmentation. Thus the patient may move from an emergent position of uncertainty and incoherence in a new paranoid-schizoid position, to a 'coherence on a basis of delusion' (Britton, 1998: 73) in a pathological depressive position. I believe that this was the case with Lacombe's patient.

Collusive complementarities

It is not only in long-ago analyses that enactments have occurred with twin patients. Wolf (1991) describes the analysis of a female twin whose closest relationship was with her twin brother. She had married an emotionally distant man and developed various symptoms that brought her to analysis. Her analyst 'listened with empathic interest' (Wolf, 1991: 130) and notes that her symptoms began to fade. I will quote Wolf, as the material speaks for itself:

> She began to trust and confide in the analyst as she had with her twin brother. At the same time her need for her husband diminished, as she could recognize her need for a more closely attuned mate. Using the analyst merely as a listening alter-ego selfobject, she discussed her choices and options without requiring any deep dynamic insight into the infantile roots of her needs and symptoms. The twinship transference was interpreted and accepted by the analysand without any experience of significant affect (Wolf, 1991: 130).

The patient left her husband and married someone who, it would seem, became a twin substitute, as her analyst had been.

Wolf suggests that the patient made sufficient gains from an undisturbed harmonious therapeutic ambience with her analyst to provide her with a 'strengthened self' (Wolf, 1991: 131). He does note that rivalry, eroticism, hostility, aggression, and oedipal transference were absent from the work, and that he is not sure whether more intensive treatment would have brought these themes into the analysis. He concludes, 'The therapeutic relationship was perceived by the analysand as a self-enhancing selfobject experience that resulted in renewed self-cohesion' (Wolf, 1991: 131). I would put it more simply: in enacting the twin transference, the analyst had reinforced the internal twinning of this patient so that she was no longer troubled by anxieties relating to separateness and difference. This allowed her to enter into a twinned relationship with her new husband.

Absence of the other twin and regression to earlier modes of functioning

In another contemporary account of counter-transference enactment by the analyst, Athanassiou (1991) describes her psychoanalytic work with Lucie from the age of 18 months. The analyst perceived Lucie's relationship with her twin brother in terms similar to those described above, as a unit consisting of two complementary twins. Lucie used the twinship to avoid external object relationships, which she found too arousing. She mediated her anxiety through the twinship, allowing for no transitional space and therefore no symbolic thought, creating what was essentially a borderline state.

Athanassiou describes the twins as a symbiotic twin couple in which mutual dependency was based on the delegation of functions between them, rather than the sort of dependency that could lead to autonomy as with a maternal container. The rigidity of this twin organization was used as a defence against any possibility of change, i.e. Lucie used the space as a refuge rather than as a possibility for growth.

Athanassiou suggests that the twin brother and sister shared a common part of their psychical organization and that mother saw the twins as a single person divided into two halves. Ego functions that are normally split within a personality were instead divided between the two, so that the internal working together of parts of the personality became instead an external cooperation between the twins. In this way the twin brother became the strong but less sensitive negotiator with the outside world, while Lucie was the over-sensitive inner self, with little direct contact with her objects. Her contact with external objects was mediated through her twin brother.

The twin system precluded any separation between the twins and therefore impeded the development of object relations. Athanassiou observes that in play, Lucie used a mirror as a mediator between herself and the observer, as she used her twin brother. Without the intermediary of mirror or twin, Lucie felt penetrated by the observer's look. However, this experience of mediation in relation to her objects was not one that could usefully be introjected and as a result she lacked a sense of internal security which would have allowed her to deal with change and development.

Lucie's difficulty in engaging with an external object created an impasse in the analysis. Athanassiou used an enactment of the twin transference as a solution to this impasse. The analysis was conducted within the context of a nursery that both twins attended. At the start of the analysis, Lucie could neither leave her twin brother in the group room to be with her analyst, nor could she stay with him while her analyst was in the other room. The analyst decided that the way of overcoming this impasse was to convey sameness between herself and the child (enacting the twinship). Thus when Lucie cried, the analyst also made crying noises, as if an 'echo in the night' (Athanassiou, 1991: 59). When Lucie screamed, the analyst screamed even louder, creating confusion about where the noise was coming from.

Having created 'sameness' in this way, Athanassiou claims she then created difference from Lucie by using a different tone of voice when she screamed. She postulates that in doing so, she conveyed an object that was separate from the child, and that separated the child from her twin, but that could be as close as her twin. She suggests that in this way the analyst introduced a transitional space into the sessions, and by echoing the child, the analyst demonstrated the close proximity between self and object, the merging of one with the other. The different tone she later used supposedly created a perception of separateness that caused enormous anxiety for the child. However, the difference also created a space for the possibility of an object that was capable of helping the child deal with her anxiety, rather than avoid it in the refuge of the twinship. Athanassiou believes that through her enactment, a good maternal object became available to Lucie.

Like the analysts reported above, Athanassiou also theorizes about a shared-personality system between twins, a two-acting-as-one personality, and believes that her enactment was necessary to fill the gap created by the absence of the other twin, in order to resolve an impasse in the analysis. Lucie's separation from her twin provoked unmanageable anxiety that the analyst dealt with by enacting the transference twin. While it does seem that Athanassiou helped Lucie overcome her difficulties, I suspect it was by some factor other than the enactment of the transference twin, which again cannot be considered as maternal containment.

A theory of absence (rather than regression) in relation to development in twins implies that there are inherent deficits in each twin. I believe that this theory increases the tendency to enactment in the analysis as a corrective measure. In an attempt to make good the assumed deficit, the particular nature of the transference at any moment and the object relationship it represents is enacted rather than interpreted. The analyst fills the gap of the missing twin, recreating the enmeshed twinship, and in so doing compromises his analytic capacities with regard to that patient.

Where the impasse is understood in terms of regression to a past defensive position in the face of unbearable anxiety, there is a possibility for analysis rather than enactment. The setting has not been breached and the analyst remains receptive to the patient's projections, recognizes the actualization of the twin in the transference, and considers his counter-transference. The interpretation based on all of these factors will allow the transference twin to be understood rather than enacted and so enable further development.

The impenetrable 'gang of two'

Finally, I want to go back to some material that I referred to earlier (Chapter 4). This case illustrates clearly the enormous difficulty that can be created in dealing with an enmeshed narcissistic twin relationship. Sometimes it seems that only enactment can address the intransigent nature of a rigid twinship. Unlike the other cases reported in this chapter, the following material is not based on a theory of personality deficit in twins, rather on the pathological nature of this particular twinship.

As described in Chapter 4, Burlingham (1963) wrote a detailed and moving account of the development of twins including material from observations, testing, and psychoanalytic treatments while they were in a home for maladjusted children. She describes the 'identical' twins, Bert and Bill. These enmeshed twins had a very difficult time in their early years in a way that seemed significantly to accentuate the twinship and hamper their individual development. At the age of 12 years the twins were placed in a home for maladjusted children where they received psychoanalytic treatment.

Barron, who ran the home, reports that the twins 'had no object relationships except in attacking each other, or together, as a gang, attacking the group' (Burlingham, 1963: 383). Barron tried repeatedly but unsuccessfully to establish contact with the twins in order to develop a relationship with them. For the first four months he could not even tell them apart and whenever one developed a distinguishing characteristic, such as a boil or a red nose, the other twin would quickly develop the same symptom. Throughout this period, the twins persisted in their disruptive behaviour.

Having failed to make individual contact with either of the twins, and feeling hopeless about doing so, Barron tried the ''Aichhorn technique'[1] (Burlingham, 1963: 384). This technique involved Barron in action 'to show myself to each boy the sort of person he showed by his behaviour that he admired' (Burlingham, 1963: 384). He shocked the twins into submission, as they did to others. As examples, Barron cites having swearing matches with them; and driving them in his car so fast and wildly that he frightened them.

'This worked like magic' reports Barron (Burlingham, 1963: 384) – the twins now developed a dependent relationship with him. (In fact, this 'dependent' relationship was more than that. It was clinging and adhesive – an enmeshed twin relationship.) The twins competed for Barron's attention and literally followed him wherever he went on public or private business. They interfered in his conversations, as if threatened by the presence of others. While they ignored even the most intense expressions of feeling or experience by anyone else, they took note of 'every nuance of feeling, every nuance of voice' (Burlingham, 1963: 385) of Barron's, and responded to each detail.

It then became possible to distinguish between the twin boys and to develop separate relationships with each. The twins also enabled this by allowing distinguishing signs to show. However, Barron adds a note of warning, that *it was only on the basis of including me into their gang* (Burlingham, 1963: 385 - my emphasis), that they could tolerate being involved in a relationship with him.

Again we see that a counter-transference enactment – the analyst joining the twin gang – created a shift. The new dependency that the twins developed in relation to Mr Barron was put to the service of analytic work that had

---

[1] It is interesting how an unorthodox technique is called into action again to provide a platform for an enactment, similar to that used by Lacombe, who employed the 'Sechehaye technique' – see earlier in this chapter.

not been possible before. Barron had in his enactment *become* a twin to Bert and Bill, apparently as the only way to get near them emotionally.

There is a further difficulty with this work, echoing the case reported by Petö, but in this case recognized by those concerned. Mr Barron was the only therapist available in the hostel. This resulted in him seeing both twins for psychoanalytic work, both starting on the same day. As a result of his enactment (joining their twin gang) and the situation as regards analysis, each of the twins immediately regarded Barron as a twin. Each was afraid to express their thoughts to Barron because it seemed equivalent to exposing himself to his murderously rivalrous twin. However, it seems that at this point, Barron had enabled each twin to begin a process of separation from the other twin.

Both twins accepted therapy in the hope of both getting rid of the internal twin, and finding some separation from the external one. Barron notes that their unconscious enmity became apparent in the treatment as they became aware of their murderous feelings towards each other. Their preoccupation with the other twin was persistent. However, one of the twins was more able than the other to use the therapy to lessen his narcissistic relationship with the analyst in favour of a more object-related one, and hence to separate from his twin.

The narcissistic aspects of the twin relationship may lead to a greater propensity in the twin patient towards splitting and projective identification. The relative neglect of all sibling relationships in analysis, and specifically the twin transference, will leave these unconscious forces as a powerful transference dynamic – a perfect recipe for enactment. Agger (1988) suggests that patients who are more prone to splitting and projective identification tend to use these mechanisms to induce sibling roles in others in order to satisfy their own narcissistic needs. Sibling transference relationships may act as a 'silent variable' in the analysis (Agger, 1988: 7). Likewise, the patient's intense wish to bind the analyst into an enduring twinship may lead to an enactment of the narcissistic twinning that damages the analytic setting. However, it appears to be a particularly difficult analytic impasse to address both prior to and during the enactment.

As was noted in Chapter 5, it is essential for the analysis that the analyst utilizes his consciousness for the purpose of verbal thought, and not for action (Meltzer, 1967). By containing the infantile aspects of the patient's mind and only communicating about them, the analyst contributes to the patient's capacity for insight. Within the analytic setting 'the transference processes of the patient's mind may discover expression' (Meltzer, 1967: xii) and can be interpreted. Interpretation modifies anxiety, while the maintenance of the setting by the analyst modulates it. As Meltzer states unequivocally, 'This modulation occurs through the patient's repeated experience in analysis that there is a place where the expression of his transference processes will not be met by *counter-transference activity* but only by *analytical activity*, namely a *search for the truth*' (Meltzer, 1967: xii).

A breach of the setting has consequences for the continuing analysis, and while the enactment may be worked with and used as an aid to further insight, it cannot be undone or eradicated. Interpretation of the transference relationship relieves anxiety at deeper levels, but enactment may enable the analyst and patient to gloss over the difficulty (as I believe occurred in the cases described above). Therefore, enactment must be followed by a re-establishment of the analytic setting to achieve an understanding of the processes that led to the enactment at that time in the treatment, and to enable further development in the analysis.

The enactment itself is not transformative although, as I hope to show in the next chapter, it may happen at a transformational time in the analysis. Where enactment bypasses the difficulty, the relief experienced after the enactment would be more likely to be the result of repression, not resolution, of the transference/counter-transference impasse. However, enactment may be useful in exposing hidden phantasies that have kept the analyst and patient bound in a twinship and this information can then be analysed.

Glenn (1966) provides a useful summary of some of the hidden phantasies and characteristics of twinning, several of which have been identified and enacted in the case material and transference relationships with the analyst, in this chapter:

(1)   the unconscious fantasy of being half a person and the associated belief that he was deprived of half his body in the womb or in infancy;
(2)   the desire for revenge toward his mother and sibling for imagined or real deprivations;
(3)   the wish to make things even;
(4)   intense rivalry intertwined with intense libidinal attachment;
(5)   lifelong identification with the other twin and the prominent use of identification as a defence;
(6)   uncertainty about separation of self-representation and object-representation;
(7)   through displacement and projection the world will appear to be populated by people who have these characteristics and who are pictured as twins;
(8)   the twins may complement each other, each one taking on traits opposite to his sibling

(Glenn, 1966: 380).

What is it about a twin that encourages enactment in analysis? Why did it seem necessary to the analytic work above that the analyst enacted the twin in the transference in order to deal with an impasse? What is the nature of the impasse and the pressure on the analyst to enact? In the next chapter, I will attempt to unpack the various elements that lead to enactment and use case material to illustrate my views.

Chapter 8
Enactment in transition and the fragmentation of the self

The pressures that precede a transference/counter-transference enactment are complex and may be experienced as compelling. I believe that particular aspects of the twin relationship that are reflected in the transference create an atmosphere that predisposes the analytic pair to enactment. I will begin this chapter with a theoretical discussion tracing these ideas. This discussion links the last chapter on enactment and my own clinical material that follows later in this chapter.

First, I offer my hypothesis, followed by an exploration of the underlying dynamics:

> In the analysis of a twin there is a central dynamic that pressurizes the analyst towards a breach of the analytic setting by an enactment. This dynamic is the fundamentally unbearable quality of the paranoid anxieties and the fear of fragmentation. These qualities arise as the patient emerges from a bound narcissistic state with the analyst-twin into a state of individual differentiation and a sense of being separate.

In outline, the process is as follows: the patient creates a transference twin that contains elements of the earliest experiences of the twin relationship, as well as the earliest twinning relationship with the breast. The transference twin is projected into the analyst, who then lives out the projected relationship transferentially. In this way a primitive inter-twin relationship is established between the patient and the analyst in the transference. The analytic twinning is based on extensive projective identification and the primitive nature of this communication puts considerable pressure on the analyst to do something other than analyse (Joseph, 1978). However, information provided by communication from sources other than verbal associations, dreams, etc., particularly the analyst's counter-transference reactions, provides invaluable information about very early experiences that would not otherwise be known (Joseph, 1985, 1987). The early, unresolved twin relationship with the breast and with the actual twin would be communicated in the analysis via nonverbal means, echoing both the understanding without words with the twin breast and much of the communication between the twins themselves.

The narcissistic twinning that has been created in the analysis is a refuge against psychic change in the way that an enmeshed actual twin relationship is. This rigid twin structure is maintained by schizoid mechanisms. Emerging from a state of mind governed by such mechanisms creates unbearable pain (Joseph, 1981) and a fear of fragmentation. The narcissistic twin refuge provides a false container offering a fixed sense of identity (Emanuel, 2001), with no possibility for psychic development. *Separation from the psychic twin is experienced as abandonment into the void and generates a terror of non-being* (as experienced by Miss D – see pp. 145–7). The refuge that the narcissistic twinship offers is precarious. On the one hand, it leaves the individual in a state of constant fear of breakdown (Rosenfeld, 1987) because of its rigidity and instability. On the other hand, it protects the analytic twins – the patient and the analyst as transference twin – from the terror of facing uncontained experiences of a psychotic intensity (Segal and Britton, 1981).

For twins bound in a narcissistic twinship, the functions of true containment have not been adequately internalized and are therefore not available for use in translating and dealing with new experiences. As noted in Chapter 3, the twin relationship lacks the quality of containment provided by a parental object. The narcissistic inter-twin projective identification does not offer understanding and insight. Instead each twin has an experience in which projections are stripped of meaning and 'nameless dread' is re-introjected, rather than an experience of fear made tolerable by containment (Bion, 1962b: 309). In contrast, the reparative capacity of the internal parents and their creative intercourse can transform nameless dread into an experience that is tolerable (Meltzer, 1968). The analyst fulfils this role by using his capacity for thinking. Where he instead enacts the twin transference, he does so at the primitive levels of the inter-twin relationship, and in so doing, sacrifices his capacity for containment at that time.

The primitive transference twin based on the early twinning with the breast and with the actual twin represents an archaic object relationship such as those described by Feldman (1997). The lack of fit between the projected archaic twin relationship and the actual relationship with the analyst-twin creates a disturbance for both the patient and the analyst. This leads to a pressure on the analyst to become an 'identical' twin as if the patient is unable to tolerate or make use of the discrepancy, i.e. the fact of difference. Feldman notes that the pressure towards identity

> goes beyond and seems to conflict with the need to feel understood, or reassured about the capacity of the object to take in and to 'contain' the projections. The lack of this identity between the internal and external reality may not only stir up envy, or doubts about the object's receptivity, but create an alarming space in which thought and new knowledge and understanding might take place, but which many patients find intolerable (Feldman, 1997: 232).

I have suggested in Chapter 3 that in an enmeshed narcissistic twinship, the twins occupy a single, thick psychic 'skin' that forms a common identity membrane around the pair. In contrast, the psychic membrane between the twins is especially thin, is highly permeable and allows extensive projective identification to take place between the twin pair. Psychic movement away from the other twin is experienced both as a loss of part of the self and as exposure to a void outside the common psychic membrane. Analysis threatens to rupture the narcissistic twin membrane and enables the twin patient to develop an identity separate from the enmeshed twin relationship. But the separation of the psychic twins also engenders terror and a fear of fragmentation.

Enactment is particularly prevalent in thick- and thin-skinned narcissistic patients[1] at the point of transition from one narcissistic state to another, just when interpretation becomes therapeutically effective (Bateman, 1998). At this time, both the patient and the analyst may experience unthinkable anxiety that has a quality of incomprehensibility to both patient and analyst (Joseph, 1981). This anxiety may lead the analyst to collude with the patient to cover up and avoid the analysis of the narcissistic twin transference relationship in the hope of avoiding separation and the terror of fragmentation.

This collusion is an enactment of the twin transference that may be brief or chronic and is aimed at preventing the unconscious highly destructive and archaic traumatic relationships from emerging and being known (Cassorla, 2001). Cassorla suggests that the collusion may be not only a resistance to uncovering traumatic experiences. From his case material, he suggests that a period of collusion may also be 'a stage of waiting, maturing, in fragile extremely sensitive patients' (Cassorla, 2001: 1167). The acute enactment that exposed the collusion occurred as Cassorla's patient shifted from a thick-skinned to thin-skinned narcissistic defence. Cassorla suggests that unconscious perceptions indicated when the time was right. The collusion could be exposed by an acute and intense enactment of the phantasy relationship because patient and analyst both felt able to face the mental anguish created by the recognition of the analyst as a separate person, 'no longer a narcissistic extension of the patient' (Cassorla, 2001: 1167).

It is not clear how a chronic collusion in the analysis would, as Cassorla suggests, prepare the patient for this difficult task. Perhaps the patient's anxiety has been reduced by the constancy of the setting (Meltzer, 1967), despite the analyst's failure to interpret the intense unconscious anxiety. This amelioration might then enable the patient to feel strong enough to face the terrifying unconscious phantasies that are hidden by the collusion. However, there is also another possibility that may have operated in some of the cases described in Chapter 7 (Lacombe, 1959; Ortmeyer, 1970; etc.). Perhaps an acute or active enactment following chronic collusion occurs in order to avoid insight, rather than because the patient is ready for the insight that might be gained. It may be that either the patient or the analyst does not have

---

[1] See Chapter 1 on twinning as a narcissistic state.

the capacity to face the hidden issues at that time. In this situation, the enactment takes the place of analysis rather than informing it.

The twinning rhythm that had been set up in Bion's (1967) analysis of patient A (described in Chapter 5), with the participation in it by both patient and analyst, might be seen as a period of collusion. I suggest that in offering stale interpretations in response to stale associations the analyst was unconsciously enacting the transference twin. However, the recognition and interpretation by the analyst of the twin transference provided information that led to insight. This understanding resulted in the emergence of the imaginary twin into the transference at a time when the patient could tolerate looking at his psychic apparatus and the split-off parts of his personality could be recognized and owned. But although patient A used twinning in the transference relationship with his analyst, he was not a twin. An actual twin (Patient B) did not respond so favourably to the analysis of the twin transference and it seems that it was not possible for Bion to extricate himself by analysis from the assigned role of transference twin with this patient.

Enactment to some degree is inevitable in analytic treatment (see Chapter 7) and is a function of both the nature of the projections into the analyst and the analyst's own state of mind. If the analyst's counter-transference reaction connects too strongly with his own unresolved experiences (as in the case described by Ortmeyer, 1970, see Chapter 7), he may be less able to distinguish what belongs to him and what to the patient in order to maintain his analytic functioning. As a result the pressure to enact the transference twin rather than analyse it will be even greater. The analyst's counter-transference reaction is a joint creation by the patient and the analyst. The projective identifications belong to the patient, but the counter-transference enactment contains subjective elements of the analyst's internal world. The analyst's own conflicts and internal object world will dictate the final shape of the enactment (Gabbard, 1995).

It seems, therefore, that the collusive twinning between analyst and patient that culminates in an acute enactment occurs in a situation where either the analyst, or the patient, or both, are hampered by their own limitations in tolerating the intensity of the anxiety generated by the prevailing unconscious phantasy at that time. This situation may be temporary and the analyst may regain the capacity for analytic functioning. However, where the patient has less capacity to tolerate mental pain in the process of development, the enactment will serve to reinforce the archaic regressive structures such as an enmeshed twin relationship.

The clinical material that follows illustrates the nature of the anxieties that confront the analytic pair as a twin patient is enabled to develop from an 'identical' twin into a person who has discrete individual boundaries. The pain of separating from a narcissistic entangled twinship led to an experience of fragmentation that was intense and, at the time, incomprehensible. The analytic setting was altered in two ways, one of which may have been an enactment prior to important psychic changes.

Clinical material

I will give a rather condensed description of my work with Miss D as a background to a more detailed account of particular aspects that illustrate the nature of the anxieties that were aroused in the transition from a narcissistic twin refuge to a sense of separate identity.[2]

Miss D, an MZ twin, was highly motivated to find an identity separate from her twin sister, despite her great anxiety and pain in doing so. She found herself trapped in a suffocating relationship with her 'identical' twin, Jane, a relationship made especially painful and frightening by the fact that Jane had been diagnosed as schizophrenic. Miss D had researched the statistical figures on the heritability of schizophrenia and was clearly afraid she might share Jane's madness.

Miss D was the second born and unexpected twin and she believed she was a 'total shock' to her parents rather than a lovely surprise. Her parents seem never to have recovered from this shock and Miss D felt unwanted and that she existed for her parents only as a problem. Unlike her twin, my patient was not named for some time after birth. She had suffered from projectile vomiting as an infant and her parents had worried that she might die. As emerged in the analysis, the violence of the projections between the twins echoed her infantile feeding difficulties and her life and death struggle to find an individual identity.

Miss D felt that her parents had denied the separate existence of their second-born twin. She believed that mother saw only one baby, especially as the twins were so alike. The parents dressed both girls exactly alike and insisted on absolute equality between the twins even when this meant depriving one of them of a hard-won scholarship. Miss D felt she had no identity separate from her twin. She was regarded as Jane's shadow or reflection and felt that her parents had 'erased her existence'. She saw herself as like a charcoal and chalk portrait that could be rubbed out. Even as adults, both twins were frequently referred to as 'Jane'. When they were children, a cousin had thought that there was only one twin, and had called both girls with a double name comprising each twin's name (like Bill and Bert, Chapter 4). It later emerged that it felt safer for Miss D to merge with her sister as a shadow than to be recognized in her own right – she was punished excessively as a child and 'invisibility' provided some protection for her.

As a result of both parental insistence on sameness and a lack of adequate maternal containment, a narcissistic twinship was established. It became apparent in the analysis as Miss D struggled to find an identity separate from her twin sister that the twins were deeply enmeshed with each other in a love-hate relationship. The intense feelings generated in relation to each other and violently projected into each other were unmodulated by either a maternal container or within the twinship. Consequently, the twins felt that they were engaged in a life and death struggle as if they could not exist satisfactorily within the twinship or independently outside it.

---

[2] Some other aspects of my work with this patient were described in Lewin, 1994 and 2002.

The narcissistic 'identical-twin' transference

In the initial stages of treatment, Miss D seemed to regard me as a necessary ear for her thoughts but an outsider to her musings and complaints about her relationship with her twin. It was as if I had no significance for her as a maternal container. This brought to mind Joseph's (1981) description of a patient who expected to be given 'understanding' (p. 91) while her analyst seemed barely to exist for her. Joseph linked this with the patient's fear of psychic change.

Alterations to the nature of the twin relationship necessitate considerable changes in the inter- and intra-psychic world of the twins. Miss D had created a twin-barrier against my intrusion into the narcissistic twinship that provided a refuge from change and development. She was protecting herself from the kind of contact with me that she both longed for and feared. She longed for the warmth and containment of a maternal breast-twin. However, she feared unleashing intolerable psychic pain by using the analysis to extricate herself from the enmeshed twinship. The intensity of the anticipated traumatic experience is the central feature of this account.

The sadistic-twin transference

In order to make any live contact with Miss D, I had to break into her communion between herself and her phantasied twin-listener. However, she experienced my intervention as cold and critical of her. It seemed that I had become a sadistic transference twin who punished her with my coldness and criticism. I believe that Miss D felt that my interpretations were a forceful and illegitimate intrusion into her private, controlled 'identical-twin' world. This experience reflected her internal world in which an absent mother did not see her and a forceful, punishing father did not provide protection for her vulnerable self or allow her to differentiate herself from a mad and frequently violent twin.

The psychically and physically violent narcissistic twinning was thus a potent force in the analysis as the psychic mechanisms of splitting and projection were echoed in the twin transference relationship. Miss D felt that my interpretations were a violent re-projection by me of the hated feelings she had projected into her twin. Interpreting these splits was complicated by the fact that Jane was not only very ill, but also deeply resentful of any separateness between them. I think Miss D experienced me as trapping her in the analytic twinship, either by trying to force a very ill twin back into her, or as a mad twin by forcing back into her projected feelings that had been distorted and stripped of meaning. Either way I was experienced as being cruel.

Miss D had difficulty in expressing her feelings of anger and she usually projected them into Jane and dissociated herself from them. She openly expressed her hatred of Jane and she wished to eliminate the look-alike that carried and expressed her anger. She told me that she had thought of bringing me a photograph of Jane and herself so I might see how alike, indeed how indistinguishable, they were. However, she had not brought the photograph. In her anger with both Jane (for representing a side of herself she did not want to own) and me (a potential 'non-identical' twin-analyst) she tore it up. In so doing, she hoped both to destroy the twinship in order to free herself from a crippling bond, and at the same time to destroy the possibility that I might see some difference between them, and so separate them. She hoped to eliminate the differentiating insight that would free her from the tyrannical trap of a narcissistic twinship.

I interpreted that Miss D split off and disowned the angry, sadistic side of herself and then felt she had to protect herself from a sadistic transference twin that represented both her twin's and her own sadism. A significant change then occurred in that Miss D became openly angry with me for the first time. She complained that my interpretations were 'too close to the bone'. Having been more directly angry with me, she then expected a punitive response to her complaint: retaliation from a sadistic transference twin. When I did not respond in this way, she felt relieved that I listened to and understood her feelings. Gradually, Miss D felt she had begun to free herself from Jane who was so ill, and who had frequently been violent to her. I felt that the silent and deadening effect of the projected sadistic twin had begun to lift.

Tasting a possibility of freedom from an imprisoning twinship, Miss D became more free in her thinking, and dared to acknowledge her secret thoughts. She expressed a wish, even an expectation, that her twin sister would die. It seemed that she believed death was the only way to be rid of the hateful intruder-twin. This magical solution increasingly became a focus of the analytic work. It was only when she had emerged from the terrifying experience of separation from her psychic twin that she could feel more compassionate and less duty-bound towards Jane. Given the nature of her anxieties about separation, the struggle was intense and dramatic.

The manic solution – a life and death see-saw

Miss D began to feel very anxious about acknowledging her wishes that Jane would die, especially as she discovered that at the very time she had spoken about this wish, Jane was being admitted to hospital with severe depression. Miss D now felt responsible for having caused her twin's deterioration. She believed that her omnipotent wish to kill Jane in order to separate from her had almost come true. She felt she had always been engaged in a lethal balancing act with Jane. She had always envied Jane, who had previously been more successful than she had, and who had been the firstborn baby, accepted and loved by mother. Now the tables were turned, and she was the one who was embracing life while Jane seemed to be not far from death.

There was a persistent malignant see-saw between the twins. As Jane recovered, Miss D felt that Jane was gaining what she was losing. Each time Miss D began to feel a little more separate from Jane, Jane became depressed, and several times she overdosed and was again admitted to hospital. It was not surprising that Miss D became panicky whenever she achieved any degree of separateness from Jane. Miss D felt extremely alarmed and guilty about her twin's deteriorating condition and she was afraid that she was responsible for it. Each time Jane recovered, Miss D began to wonder whether separation was possible without killing off her twin. Although she could see that she had not omnipotently killed Jane, she was aware that advances in her own development might be implicated in her twin's decline.

As we worked through these issues Miss D gradually became more reflective about herself and she said that people had noticed that she was different. This created a dilemma for her. Separation of the twins was repeatedly associated with the elimination of one or the other. Clearly, Miss D's attempts to establish a separate identity from Jane had a profound effect on a twin who was an extremely vulnerable woman. Miss D's omnipotent wishes for her twin's death merged with the real illness her twin suffered. As soon as Miss D appeared different in any way, Jane would copy her, trying to re-establish the twinship, the narcissistic sameness. If Miss D rejected this sameness, she felt responsible for Jane's decline. Yet to go along with it meant her own psychic suicide.

The struggle to separate from her actual twin reflected Miss D's difficulty in separating the psychic life- and death-twins of her internal world. In this omnipotent, narcissistic internal twinship, it seemed that one twin could live only if the other was dying, as if the life and death instincts had been divided up between the twins. As long as the twins remained fused in the narcissistic twinship, the deathliness could be moderated. Separation seemed to mean that unabated destruction would lead to the death of one or the other of the psychic twins. Rosenfeld (1987) suggests that the life instinct mitigates the power of the death instinct when they are partially fused or bound together. However, in states of mind governed by the primitive forces of a paranoid-schizoid kind, the life and death instincts become almost completely defused or unbound. This separation of instincts results in an increase in the intensity of the destructiveness of the death instinct – 'a pure culture of the death instinct' (Rosenfeld, 1987: 127).

From 'identical' to 'non-identical' twin

The see-sawing twinship was now played out in a milder form in the transference. On her return from a break during which she had felt more substantial in herself, Miss D said she was afraid that although she had begun to feel different, she felt that I would not see this. It was apparent that in her mind I had become the transference twin who could not allow her to change and be different, a clamorous transference twin-sister seeking sameness. This interpretation again allowed Miss D to feel a little more free of the imprisoning twinship and she felt immensely grateful to me for allowing her to be different, and to begin to find herself as a real person, not just to remain Jane's shadow.

Some months later, shortly before the summer break, Miss D was shocked to find that she was wearing a skirt that was similar to mine. She wondered whether we were 'identical' twins again. The atmosphere of the session was alive and grounded. Miss D associated with a dream:

> Miss D was looking for me in a house, but I had moved and she could not find me. She went up to the attic room. It was a public house called 'The Mermaid'. She felt confused.

I suggested that the dream linked with the pending summer break, and Miss D was wondering whether I would continue to be here for her. Who would I be on my return? Would I be like the mermaids that lure the sailors into the sea and then leave them to drown? It seemed that she had made a psychic move into a relationship with me as a 'non-identical' transference twin, and she now believed I had lured her into deep waters only to abandon her as I went on my summer break. (In retrospect, this dream had added significance – to be discussed below.) I was both the 'identical' twin from whom she was separating, exposing her to being alone in the world, and an absent mother who was not able to see and manage her infant's fears.

Miss D indicated that she enjoyed her feelings of closeness to me that did not depend on sameness. She told me that she and her twin sister had spoken a private and exclusive language that no one else understood. They still used this language in adulthood, including their special names for each other. Now that she was withdrawing from an enmeshed twinship, she spoke in less coded terms to her twin. This development was reflected in the analytic work as she began to speak more openly and directly with me.

In her ambivalence about separation from her twin, Miss D moved in and out of the refuge of the twinship. Whenever her anxieties about her separateness became too great, she returned to her twinship retreat until she was ready to risk venturing out again, or until the closeness to her transference twin became too unbearable – a claustro/agoraphobic dilemma. During this time, Miss D had begun to recognize my capacity for a containing function, a psychic move that was important in allowing her to emerge from the enmeshed narcissistic twinship.

Memories of a painful past

A month later, I informed Miss D that in about six weeks I would be moving to a different consulting room for six or more months. Miss D expressed some anxiety about this verbally, and gradually she began to tell me about painful experiences that she associated with this move. However, the full emotional reality that this move (both psychic and actual) held for her became apparent only after I had relocated my practice.

I will outline the various linked factors and phantasies that emerged prior to the move of rooms. Miss D spoke of her distress when, as a teenager, she had been expelled from a group of friends at the instigation of her twin sister because Miss D had established herself as different from her twin in some way. Miss D had felt devastated by this exclusion from both her twin and her friends, and she had led a very lonely life for some years as a result. Again (as in the mermaid dream), it seemed that in finding a 'non-identical' twin-analyst in the transference, Miss D was afraid that by moving from a familiar place I would expel her into an unknown and lonely state.

It was at this point that an alteration was made in the setting prior to my move. Was this an enactment? The timing and the changes it ushered in indicate that it may well have been. It had became evident over several sessions that Miss D was experiencing intense anxiety that did not seem manageable within a single session. I suggested to Miss D that we should extend the length of the sessions to one hour and twenty minutes.[3] This idea did not come out of the blue, as Miss D had asked for this extension for some time. However, the timing of this change was significant. Miss D had a very long journey to her sessions as a result of which she was unable to attend more than once weekly. The sessions never seemed long enough as she tended to be stiff and withholding at the beginning of the session, only gradually feeling able to be more forthcoming and less controlled and controlling. The session always seemed to end at a point where we had reached something important and could not pursue it. We had explored this many times, but the difficulty did not abate.

Miss D did not immediately accept my offer. She thought it over and in her next session she accepted the increase in time. Miss D then told me that she remembered her family moving home frequently when she was a child. On several of these occasions she was expected to travel by train from school to a new station. There was no one to meet her at the station and she had to find her way, alone, to the new family home. Each time this occurred she had felt as if she had been dropped into a void – a forewarning of what she came to feel with me. As I will describe, I was later able to understand how my increasing the session times at this particular time was linked with Miss D's terror at the loss of her psychic home.

In the last session before my move Miss D said that her twin sister had been admitted to hospital in a floridly psychotic state. Given her intense identification with her psychotic twin sister, Miss D was clearly referring to her fears about her own mental state and her concerns for her sanity. As I have described above, moving my consulting room had revived memories of several experiences that Miss D had faced as a child, and she was in touch with and able to verbalize this. But what ensued next was of a different order, and more closely linked with her psychotic twin.

Descent into the void of fragmentation

The next session took place in the new rooms. I had taken care to maintain as much continuity as I could, taking all my own consulting room furniture, plants, pictures and rugs to the new room, which was, however, in a different

---

[3] This increase in the session time is similar to that described by Lacombe (1959) in Chapter 7.

part of London. Another major difference was that my desk and computer were in a 'study-corner' of the room, whereas they had previously been located in a room private to me, not seen by my patients.

When I went to meet Miss D in the waiting room, I found her standing with her back glued to the wall, facing the window, staring at a picture on the wall next to the window. She looked terrified. As she walked into the consulting room, she became extremely disturbed by the presence of the computer. In an earlier session, Miss D had associated a TV monitor with her mirroring 'identical' twin.[4] In her current state of mind, it was as if her twin were actually present in the room. She said she felt compelled to sit at the desk in front of the computer, but she resisted doing so. Nevertheless, she remained staring at it for some time. She looked fearfully around the room and complained about the walls having ears. She said she could not sit with her back to the window (the position that the chair was in) because she felt she had to see who was there, and especially to keep the computer in view. She spent the session sitting on the floor, against the side of the couch, facing the window. She felt trapped as she had in a traumatic childhood incident. She recalled that as a child when her mother was absent over an extended period, she had hidden in rooms behind a chair (as she was doing now). At that time people had come in and out of the room, unaware of her presence while she was able to see them.

Over the next few sessions, Miss D relived the pain and confusion of what she had experienced as a rupture from her twin and abandonment by her mother. In both the transference relationships and in my own lack of clear understanding at that time, Miss D experienced me as an absent mother and as a lost 'identical' twin, who had abandoned her to her lonely pain and unresolvable thoughts and feelings. She walked around the consulting room, unable to sit in the chair or lie on the couch. She was extremely agitated and in a fragmented state of mind. She spoke about her psychotic twin whom she believed to be very mad and beyond help. I interpreted that she was afraid that I would declare her as un-helpable as her twin, and that there would be no point in continuing analytic work; no hope for her to find a containing mother-analyst.

I was quite taken aback by the change in Miss D. It was evident that Miss D felt assailed by terrifying and unbearable anxieties of the kind associated with fragmentation, falling into a void, nameless dread. She had entered a psychotic mad-twin state of mind in the new consulting room (although by all accounts she continued to function adequately outside). However, unlike her twin, she was later able to recover her fragile sense of self as she re-established her relationship with me as a container. Gradually she began to recover her ego functions within her sessions and it became evident that an important psychic change had occurred.

I was later able to understand with greater clarity the significance of what Miss D was experiencing at the point of separation from a twin in a narcissistic twinship, a time of great vulnerability. In the preceding analytical work Miss D had partially separated from a twin who had previously

---
[4] This episode is explored in more detail in a previous publication (Lewin, 1994).

provided her with an identity, and whom she had regarded as a physical embodiment of herself. In emerging from the destructive narcissistic twin bonding she now encountered new emotional territory without the security of her own adequate individual psychic skin. Miss D's dream about the mermaid was linked with her sense of abandonment and loss of self as she relinquished an 'identical' twin-analyst, as well as the loss of a mother-analyst as the break approached. The additional circumstances of moving my rooms stimulated memories of past experiences of being separate, cast out and painfully alone. Did the move to a new consulting room occur just at that point of vulnerability in the emergence from the narcissistic twinship, or did it precipitate the crisis that led to her experience of fragmentation?

In offering her longer sessions at that particular time, perhaps I unconsciously colluded to try to protect Miss D from these anxieties. One aspect of this would be a wish not to be the twin-analyst who banished her into intense loneliness and nothingness. Another would be a wish not to be the mother-analyst who was unavailable to meet her at the station to help her into her new psychic home. In offering Miss D longer sessions, perhaps I colluded with an idea that I could be a mother who could take extra effort to tolerate her difficulties and help her through a process of change, not by analysis, but in a concrete manner. This was certainly not a conscious idea.

It is also interesting to note that after the session time had been increased, Miss D (like Lacombe's patient, Chapter 7) brought new and alive material previously not remembered in the analysis. Of course it was also directly linked with my move to another consulting room, but perhaps the memories were further 'loosened' by the change of session time. I think that unconsciously we both wished to avoid intolerable anxieties of a psychotic nature that threatened to destroy Miss D's fragile emergent self. However, the phantasies did emerge, Miss D did survive them, and further progress was possible.

Guilt, jealousy and reparation

Gradually Miss D began to discover herself anew and find her own boundaried identity. Not too surprisingly, this then led to a further intense and deathly struggle between her and her twin. As she started to see herself as more separate from her twin, Miss D felt guilty, torn apart. She felt both shocked and relieved at understanding the depth and complexity of her relationship with her twin. Her feelings of guilt, and a wish for reparation, meant she could now begin to mourn the loss of the narcissistic twinship. She became more aware of her jealousy of other patients (twins) and of her wish to have me to herself.

Her jealousy poisoned the good milk I offered her. It was as if she felt she always had to feed with her twin present, spoiling her pleasure. Miss D believed I would be intolerant of the sickly-baby-her who could not or would not use my milk (like her projectile vomiting). She thought I gave all my good milk to her twin while she got poisoned milk – my criticism and judgement –

like in a parasitic twinship (Athanassiou, 1986). This understanding paved the way for the emergence of a more positive transference mother who could help her, and Miss D began to emerge as a sexual woman for the first time.

Miss D had extricated herself from a frozen cocoon of twinship. She had severed the link with her enmeshed twin and felt that she had evacuated her twin from inside her. She felt empty, but she also felt relief. She became aware of the importance of her privacy and of her relationship with me as a separate person. She recognized changes in herself both here and in her external world. Her family, friends and colleagues also noticed these changes. She looked forward to her fortieth birthday as a turning point in her life, putting aside the past 40 years that were so dreadful for her. Her twin, in contrast, dreaded the event, as she became more ill under the relentless decline in her condition. So Miss D was able to separate from her twin psychically while also recognizing the existence of her ill twin sister.

As thoughts of ending emerged, many of the old anxieties resurfaced. Miss D became very angry with me about her separateness, and tried to regress into the twinship. She insisted on my using only her words and understanding things only her way, as an 'identical' transference twin. Miss D was almost deluded into believing that her twin was again present in the consulting room, that I embodied the twin's presence, and that she could get right inside her/me like a parasite and never have to leave. Likewise, she felt I would invade her. She felt there were things she could not talk about because her twin would hear, things she had never told Jane. She was disquieted by my separateness, envious, and angry with me. I became the transference father who pushed her off my lap, to accommodate the other twin.

Gradually, Miss D expelled the cruel 'God' (the persecuting internal parents who insisted on sameness) and found more loving external and internal parents. She resumed her pleasure in being her own person. She described how she had seen a video of herself and for the first time she could see that she was different from her twin. When her twin asked, 'are we the same?' she said 'no'. Her twin said she felt she was losing her. Then Miss D wondered whether I (as a clinging transference twin) would allow her to leave when she was ready.

Was it right to enable Miss D to emerge as a person in her own right when it appears to have been at the expense of her twin? Did she cause or just contribute to her twin's decline? Might her twin have been as ill as she was anyway, whatever happened to Miss D? These questions are important but unanswerable, and they do raise serious ethical issues about work to enable separation in twins, especially where the twinship is enmeshed. I will address these issues further in Chapter 9.

In a developmental move (like Mr P, Chapter 6), Miss D recovered her epistemophilic instincts. As her capacity for thinking developed, Miss D became more curious about me. She wondered if I was a twin, as she believed I had such insight into her. She alternated between retreating to the twinship to try to deal with the pain of separation and wanting to go forward.

She froze me out and ridiculed me, as she offered her 'Lewin's theory of freezing and unfreezing'. Alternatively, she mourned her loss of a separate twin-mother-analyst. She could understand that when her twin told her she was 'horrible', it had its roots in her new separateness. She felt she had been born into a world of opportunities, with her separation from her twin as the key.

At last, Miss D began to think of herself as 'me', not 'us'. She recognized that for much of the analytic work she had brought with her the burden of another, her twin. Now she was separate. She saw her twin as childlike in her vulnerability, fearsome in her anger. She felt able to stand up to her parents, to be different, and to say she was different. She also respected their difference and had a gentler view of them, as they were no longer such persecuting figures.

Miss D: in conclusion

Miss D was initially in a narcissistic twin state of mind that she used to protect herself and her 'identical' phantasy twin from external interference. At first she experienced my interventions as a sadistic attack on the twinship, but as she became more able to tolerate them, she began to distinguish me as a separate person, at that stage a 'non-identical' twin. As her anxieties about separation mounted, I enacted a protective mother-twin-analyst by increasing the session time. My move to another consulting room precipitated a dramatic change in Miss D and I think it represented a psychic move away from a thick-skinned narcissistic twin refuge. She experienced uncontained anxieties of a psychotic kind linked with fragmentation and the loss of a sense of self as she relinquished her 'identical' twin identity. In this thin-skinned state, she had difficulty in distinguishing inner and outer realities. Gradually Miss D was able to use the containment of the analytic work (as opposed to the false container of the narcissistic twinship) to develop a more reliable individual psychic skin. In this state of mind she felt free of the imprisoning, destructive narcissistic twinship and could become her own person while also recognizing her twin sister without eliminating her.

Chapter 9
Psychoanalytic fallout: the threat of separateness

The twin left out of treatment

I described in the last chapter the way in which the struggle for separateness within an enmeshed twinship may be experienced as a life and death issue. While the development of an individual identity within a twin relationship may be life-enhancing for the liberated twin, it may have serious consequences for the twin not in treatment. In certain circumstances development towards separateness in one twin may even be seriously damaging for the other twin, as I will describe below. This raises complex ethical issues that do not have any simple solutions.

The twin not in analysis may find it extremely threatening to see the changes in the twin patient as a result of the analysis. The extent of the entanglement of the twins and their relative levels of development will affect the degree of disturbance caused within the twinship by the processes of separation. The more narcissistic the twin relationship, the more challenging to the excluded twin will be the psychic movement out of the imprisoning twinship by the twin in analysis. In this situation, development in one twin seems to threaten the remaining twin with a sense of annihilation of the self. This echoes the experience of the twin in analysis emerging from the narcissistic twin envelope (see Chapter 8). But while the twin in analysis has the necessary help at hand, the excluded twin may not be so fortunate.

Several factors may make the development of separate identities for each twin more difficult than would be the case for singletons, including the idealization of the twinship and intense rivalry between the twins as a corollary to their dependence on each other. Even for twins who have achieved a greater level of maturity, the movement away from the twinship by either twin would affect them both – more so than would occur in an ordinary sibling relationship. As described in Chapter 3, the generational closeness of the twin pair may lead to a particular kind of entanglement leading to a lifelong narcissistic link between the twins.

The nature of the transference relationship with the analyst is complex and the patient's intentions regarding the projected transference object may vary. Henri Rey (1988) suggests that narcissistic patients may bring into analysis their damaged or dying internal objects because they need help in making reparation or in bringing them to life. The hope is that as long as the internal objects are still alive, there is a chance of repairing them. The patients keep their damaged objects alive as they wait for someone to help them do the reparative work that they are unable to do themselves. As described in Chapter 5, a twin patient may bring a damaged internal twin relationship into the analysis in the hope of repairing either the helpful internal parental objects or the limiting twinship.[1] Which object is selected for repair will depend on whether the patient is seeking either separation from the twin or the reinstatement of the twinship.

When the patient's intentions towards his/her objects are murderous rather than reparative, the effects that the analysis will have on the external object may need careful consideration. Analysis will be likely to affect the patient's relationships externally as well as internally in both conscious and unconscious ways. While analysis is a disturbing process for both patients and their relationships with those closest to them, the usual expectation is that the growth of the patient will have overall beneficial effects. However, this may not always be the case.

In Chapter 8, I described Miss D's hatred towards her twin sister and her twin's reported serious decline in health at various times as Miss D extracted herself from the crippling twinship and gained in individual strength. As Miss D's emotional health improved, Jane's declined. In that situation, it was not clear whether Miss D's personal development was actually detrimental to her ailing twin. It would certainly have caused a disturbance to Jane's sense of herself and this may have been too much for a fragile ego to manage. Miss D reported that it was apparent from an early age that Jane was emotionally fragile. Although she was not diagnosed as schizophrenic until her mid-thirties after suffering injuries in an accident, the ghost of the condition seems to have been there much earlier. However, Jane had previously had a successful career and had formerly used her capacities to achieve a satisfying life.

As Miss D developed an individual sense of self through the analytic work, she was enabled to move out of the imprisoning twinship without psychically killing off her twin. She was able to repair her parental objects sufficiently, using the processes of containment in the analytic work, to enable her development. He earlier murderous wishes towards her twin were modified by her own development so that she could acknowledge the twin relationship without feeling trapped within it. However, it appears that the separation was much more difficult for Jane to manage.

It is quite possible that Jane was heavily dependent on the twinship for maintaining what little ego strength she had in her current condition and that Miss D's separation from her narcissistic twin was damaging to Jane. If this were so, was it right to enable Miss D to achieve the separation from her twin sister that she so desperately wanted? It was evident that Miss D was seriously

---

[1] Kohut (1984) regards this wish to repair damaged internal objects as pathological twinning (see p.86).

hampered in her own development by the enmeshed twinship with Jane. It would not seem ethical to refuse Miss D treatment on the grounds that it might harm Jane, or her relationship with Jane. Perhaps it might have been possible to help Jane deal with the processes of separating from her twin in a way that was more helpful to her? The treatment Jane did receive appeared instead to reinforce her use of the twinship as an emotional crutch. Unfortunately, it is often not possible to intervene in a way that would deal with this situation more helpfully.

We often do not know what patients do with the analytic gains after the analysis has ended. I have been fortunate enough to learn from Miss D that in the years following the end of her treatment, she realized how important it was for both of them that she help her twin sister understand what it was that Miss D had gone through. She took positive steps to create a time and setting in which to talk to Jane about her own struggle to find her sense of individuality. She believes that this was helpful in strengthening Jane's sense of self and in helping Jane to deal with the difficulties of her situation. In a further important move, Miss D realized that this was pointless unless she also entered into a similar process with her parents, which she has now done.

Sheerin's (1991) account of psychotherapy with an 'identical' twin in an enmeshed twinship went through some similar processes but had a different outcome. He notes that in a narcissistic and intensely dependent twin relationship, the twin not in psychotherapy will be especially vulnerable to the proxy effects of the psychotherapy. The patient uses the twin transference according to his intentions regarding his twin. Thus, Miss D was gradually able to understand the ways in which she used the twinning in the transference and was able to develop individually, becoming less hate-filled and more compassionate towards her sister. This was not so for Sheerin's patient.

Sheerin's patient instead became lodged in a static twinned transference with the therapist at the expense of his actual twin. The transference twinning by the patient was based on interconnected dependency and hostility, echoing the actual twin relationship. The patient used the transference twin not only as a refuge from development. He also used the twinship with the therapist against the excluded twin, and the excluded twin seems to have been badly damaged by the psychotherapy of his twin brother. Despite exhaustive interpretation of the transference twin, the patient was unwilling to relinquish his position as a twin of the therapist because it achieved his wish to be separated from his actual twin, while providing him with an alternative twinship. He feared that if he relinquished twinship he would lose his sense of self.

Sheerin believes that the twins were so enmeshed that individual separation did not seem possible. The twin brothers were therefore offered joint psychotherapy sessions. In the joint session, each twin's murderous intent towards the other was obvious and, like Miss D, each felt that the only way to be free of the other twin was through death. Each twin projected their loathing for themselves into the other twin and they were bound together by the processes of splitting and fusion, like Lacombe's (1959) patient and his twin.[2] After one joint session, the second twin discontinued the joint twin psychotherapy and the patient continued individual psychotherapy on his own.

A significant point was reached when the patient became able to recognize the way in which the primitive twinship trapped the twins together in their need for each other. The therapist hoped that this might be a developmental move in the psychotherapy. However, at this point of transition the patient's ambivalence about separating from his twin emerged. The patient now informed his psychotherapist that he had been offering 'psychotherapy-by-proxy' (Sheerin, 1991: 20) to his twin even before the joint session. After each session, the patient would tell the excluded twin the content of sessions, as if to share the experience (the therapist-mother) with his twin. The patient believed he had been cheated of half his share of maternal attention[3] and I think that in sharing the contents of sessions, he was acting out this phantasy. Thus the patient was offering palliative care to his twin while at the same time wishing him dead, and it became increasingly apparent that the twins were inextricably bound together.

The entwined nature of the twinship was explored in the psychotherapy. This led the patient to stop sharing his psychotherapy with his twin. However, the result of this action was 'disastrous' (Sheerin, 1991: 20). Like Miss D (Chapter 8), the patient now began to feel stronger as his twin became weaker. As the patient began to establish a personal boundary around himself, his twin started to attack this move by trespassing, cheating and undermining the patient. The situation deteriorated even further when the excluded twin then began to self-mutilate. 'The destruction of the internal twin had now manifested itself in reality' (Sheerin, 1991: 20).

Sheerin notes that it seemed that the patient's covert agenda in the psychotherapy was 'the appropriation of shared [emotional] life-support structures by one twin at the expense of the other' (Sheerin, 1991: 20). It was therefore felt to be mandatory that both twins should attend psychotherapy together again, but the patient sabotaged this. The therapist believed it would be dangerous to continue the psychotherapy and terminated it. Sheerin warns that psychotherapy-by-proxy must be guarded against when underlying hatred and murderous phantasies exist in such an undifferentiated twin pair.

The question of what to do about the twin left out of treatment is problematic and may create insurmountable difficulties. The conflictual nature of the situation may put pressure on the analyst to offer solutions, including the enactment of the twin transference. Sheerin offered joint sessions to the twin pair, but this did not resolve the damaging situation – the twins scuppered it, thereby maintaining their twin refuge even though they had separated physically. Essentially it is the internal twinning that has to be addressed for there to be movement towards healthy separateness of the twin pair. The

---

[2] This case was discussed in Chapter 7.
[3] This again echoes Lacombe's (1959) patient.

solution offered by Sheerin might also be seen as one that perpetuated the position of the twins in having to share everything. As noted above, the patient acted out this phantasy in sharing his psychotherapy-mother with his twin by psychotherapy-by-proxy. Perhaps the offer of joint sessions was the therapist's enactment of this phantasy of a shared mother-therapist.

The account also raises a further query. The patient psychically murdered his twin in his total disregard for his twin's wellbeing, as he got on with his own life. He appropriated the emotional life support systems in a wish to leave his twin dead, in order to achieve separateness from his twin through the psychic death of the twin. Sheerin later terminated the individual psychotherapeutic treatment with the twin patient because of the insoluble difficulties. Was this an enactment that echoed the patient's psychic murder of his twin? In severing the twin transference relationship by ending the treatment, perhaps Sheerin (as the projected murderous transference twin) enacted the psychic murder of the adherent twin, like his twin patient.

What is apparent from these accounts is that in some cases the narcissistic twin transference can create an impasse that it seems cannot be resolved satisfactorily without enactment.[4] The analyst feels obliged to act in ways that overstep the analytic boundaries because of his concern either for the patient or for the excluded twin. The analyst may be left to carry the concern about the excluded twin whom the patient reports as being damaged by the analytic work, while being unable to mobilize the patient's capacities for thoughtfulness and compassion towards the excluded twin. It is also possible that the patient's claims about the harmful effects of the analysis on the excluded twin may represent the patient's own anxieties about separating from the twin and the fears that this engenders.[5] This is one of the factors that will need to be assessed within the analysis.

As can be seen in a number of cases described in this book,[6] it is sometimes possible to work through the difficulties of narcissistic twinning in the analysis of the transference twin. The patient can then be helped to establish an individual identity within the twinship in such a way that the needs of the twin left out of analysis can be accommodated. The hope is that if the twin patient can be helped in the analysis to separate from transference twin, he/she may be able to help the excluded twin through the impasse of resolving the enmeshed twinship not via analysis-by-proxy, but through personal growth and development.

On the other side of the coin, sometimes it appears that the twins collude in attacking the analysis. The following vignette bridges the two sections of this chapter – the damage to the excluded twin and the twin patient's resistance to interference in the twin relationship. In the case below, the excluded twin was adversely affected by the twin patient's analysis. In

---

[4] See Chapter 7.
[5] See Chapter 8.
[6] Bion, 1967; Joseph and Tabor, 1961; Ablon et al., 1986; Athanassiou, 1986; and Mr P, Chapter 6, Miss D, Chapter 8.

response the patient then terminated the analysis in order to nurse the twin and to reinstate the twinship.

Ms G, a female MZ twin in her mid-thirties, was referred to an analyst because of her depression and difficulties in relationships. She felt highly ambivalent about her relationship with both her mother and her twin sister, and this ambivalence was lived out in the analytic work. Ms G limited her sessions to twice weekly and would not increase the frequency of her sessions or use the couch. She narrated her experiences aggressively and wanted instant cures as she pressurized her analyst to come up with answers.

Initially, Ms G spoke little about her twin sister but as the work progressed she seemed to become less resistant and antagonistic towards her analyst. She noticeably snuggled down into the armchair, creating the impression that she and her analyst were becoming engaged in the work and that a greater trust was developing – the harmonious 'identical' twin transference. However, very soon after, and only a few months into the analysis, she reported that her twin sister was jealous of her being in analysis. Shortly after that, Miss G reported that her sister had become ill and that she had to go and look after her. As the sister lived in the North of England, this meant she would have to end her analysis. She decided to terminate the analysis immediately and left abruptly.

The primacy of the twinship: resistance to intervention in the twinship

Some patients do not feel able to negotiate the move from a narcissistic engrossment with a twin towards an individual sense of self within the twin relationship. In this situation, the patient feels that contact with a 'non-identical' transference twin and a productive mother is an interference in the twinship. As noted in Chapter 5, the twin patient may create a barrier to analytic intervention. In some situations, as described below, this interference in the twinship may be felt to be so threatening that the patient may leave treatment as soon as it occurs.

Miss T

Miss T is a small, robust, middle-aged woman who has a twin brother. She sought help because she had difficulties in her relationships with her parents, her partner, and her employer. It is notable that her twin brother was omitted from this list. In what seemed to be an insightful development that brought her to analysis, she believed that her relationship with her partner was becoming problematic. She had begun to feel that he was weak and dependent on her and her recognition that this was a regular and destructive pattern distressed her. However, she felt her relationship with her mother was her main problem. She experienced her mother as possessive, intrusive, dominating and demanding.

Mother was a powerful, well-educated woman with a successful career. The patient was much in awe of mother, but also felt extremely defensive in relation to her, which left her with a sense of being paralysed. Father, on the other hand, was felt to be ineffectual. He was not as clever as mother and Miss T found him to be more distant and unemotional than mother. Mother constantly denigrated father and both parents used their children in the battle between them, each trying to gain support against the other.

Miss T's twin brother was the physically weaker of the two at birth and remained so throughout his life. Although he had established a successful career as a hospital doctor, Miss T continued to feel that he was weak and helpless and that she had always had to look after him in one way or another.

Miss T was persistently late for her sessions for the first few months. She complained repeatedly of not being cared for and of being used by others for their benefit. While thus displaying her uncared-for needy self, she did not recognize the needy twin who had come to me for help. Instead, I was the needy transference twin who had nothing to offer her and whom she reluctantly came to sessions to take care of. She talked at me in a patronizing, know-it-all, controlling manner that created a sense of paralysis in me. In this manic overpowering state, I felt silenced, struggling and incompetent (like her incubator twin brother, see below).

Miss T's initial interest in coming for help seemed to have become deadened as she filled the space with her angry complaints and she appeared to feel that I had nothing to offer her. This echoed what happened in all her relationships. Miss T described how she initially felt as if she were diving into a pool, excited and exhilarated by the dive and the swim under water. Then she came to the surface and found that everything was ordinary and dull. She would then feel very let down. She reported that her partner had started out as a strong and caring man, but as the relationship progressed he became increasingly withdrawn and depressed. It was if he became the pathetic twin brother and she resented having to look after him. Miss T presciently described her fears that this would happen with me – that there would be premature excitement leading to flatness, and then she would feel that I was no good. The breakdown of this manic solution to her neediness was eventually played out and she felt I had indeed become 'no good' to her.

Initially, we seemed to be making progress. Gradually Miss T began to recognize the unconscious elements in her lateness and her defensive talking at me, and she said she found it difficult to trust me. She acknowledged that she secretly set me tasks to prove myself to her. However, when I said anything insightful she felt persecuted by my interpretations as they punctured the manic twinship in which she was always the powerful carer. Miss T had great difficulty recognizing a more vulnerable side of herself as she relegated all the weakness to her twin-brother-analyst.

Understanding this enabled us to see that the split-off 'bad' self tormented her with its presence, the needy self represented by her twin and projected into others, including me. Miss T recognized that owning this side of herself was very important and she began to talk about the buried turbulent feelings of which she was so afraid. She believed these intense feelings of both love and murderous hatred would destroy her and could not be modulated or integrated.

As the transference twin became more visible in the analysis, Miss T described how she felt rather guilty about her twin, as she had been the healthier baby. Her twin was substantially underweight at birth and she believed she had taken more sustenance than was her due. Soon after they were born her twin was put in an incubator, and as is common practice, Miss T was placed alongside him to help him in his struggle for survival. Throughout her life she felt she had to rescue him from difficult situations, and although she hated the forced intimacy and sharing that this created, she felt she could never rid herself of her brother, as they were never allowed to be separate.

Miss T noted that she and her twin competed for mother's love, but Miss T felt she always won, as if she took possession of mother. In identification with the possessed mother, the patient saw herself as the source of power and resources, and felt that those around her flocked to her for help. As a child, when she heard her asthmatic brother struggle for breath, she thought (wished and feared) that he would die. She felt painfully entangled with her twin as she nursed her feelings of both guilt and fierce resentment. It seemed as if only one of the twins could survive while the other was a half-dead twin.

Miss T's experience of being in the incubator with her twin would be an unconscious one enriched by parental comment, a birth narrative. Looking back on the work, it is possible to see that Miss T's birth narrative occupied a central role in her perception of her world. It represents both her relationship with mother – an incubator mother, hard, impenetrable and intrusive, a high-achiever mother making enormous demands on her – and her relationship with her twin. While she longed for a non-demanding, non-intrusive mother, she identified with the incubator-mother-twin and colluded with a high-achiever-mother to denigrate the warm, soft mothering that tolerates vulnerability. She was contemptuous of her weaker twin-brother-self.

Miss T felt that the analytic work echoed her experience that there was no one available to look after her, and that she had to be an incubator-mother-twin to care for her weak needy-twin-analyst. As I listened to her angry outpourings at the start of the analytic work, I felt dominated and rather helpless. It was as if I was encased in a struggling-incubator-twin transference relationship. Miss T offered her opinions and understanding of what was happening in her life and had little interest in anything I might have to say. As long as I remained the struggling transference twin in the incubator whom she (the incubator-mother-twin) had to look after, she was in control and safe. When I did intervene, she felt that the tables had been turned and that I was now the intrusive, dominating incubator-mother-twin. The incubator-mother-twin/struggling-incubator-twin relationship represents the enclosed narcissistic twinship in which one twin is all-powerful and all-providing in a non-reciprocal relationship, while the other twin is weak and helpless. It is an identification with a hard mother-twin, not a maternal container.

Miss T said that she felt that difficult things had been stirred up in the analytic work and she was reluctant to come to sessions. Her pale, needy split-off 'bad' twin-self was a constant presence that tormented her with all the buried feelings of which she was so afraid, torturing her with his existence. She complained of being a victim and of not valuing herself or being valued by others. Too much was demanded of her and she gave too much of herself. Yet she described how she was experienced by others as overwhelming and felt that she did not receive much in return. She started missing sessions, and became more and more angry and controlling. When I suggested that she felt she needed to fill all the space to ensure that she got enough for herself, she responded defensively, and complained about being criticized. As she felt more vulnerable and less powerful, she became increasingly angry and distressed.

Miss T became enraged with her mother and complained of never being in a rewarding relationship. When I interpreted that she felt I was a mother who expected too much of her, but gave her too little, she took this as confirmation that I was indeed behaving like her mother and was acknowledging it. Miss T found it intolerable that I might be able to provide insight that she lacked, all the while complaining that she never found any of her relationships, including that with me, rewarding. She felt unable to take anything from me, and she now felt she was filled with emptiness, an inner void. She had sought a mother but felt she could not find one. It seemed she felt I was giving all my attention to a needy twin-brother, not a needy-twin-her. It was as if the discovery of her twin in the transference resulted in her feeling that she had lost her mother-analyst to her twin. He had now taken possession of mother, as Miss T previously believed she had done.

At this point, Miss T left treatment precipitately without making any further contact with me, despite my repeated invitations to her to try to establish what had happened. It seems that as long as I accepted being the helpless-incubator-twin whom she could look after, she could tolerate the analytic work. But with evidence of my separateness, as a 'non-identical' twin-analyst or an insightful mother-analyst who could help her, she abandoned me, as she wished to do with her needy twin-self. I was the twin to be left high and dry while she made off with all the resources. It seems that Miss T was unable to tolerate owning a needy-twin aspect of herself who could be helped by a productive mother.

The significance of her birth story and her prescient expectation that after the first puff of excitement she would feel I was 'no good', became a fact of the analytic work. Initially, Miss T paralysed my thinking as I represented a weak twin in the incubator. When I mobilized my resources as a maternal container, she terminated the analysis. Miss T was unwilling to extricate herself from the narcissistic twinning both with her twin brother and the analytic transference twin. She would not allow my intervention in the twin relationship as this exposed her to a loss of power, a hard-edged incubator power with which she kept herself together. She was not ready to confront a needy side of herself that responded to warm mothering.

Abrupt endings just as a functioning maternal container challenges the twin relationship are not uncommon in the analysis of a twin. I will describe below another example of an analysis terminated as the patient found a containing transference object.

Miss V

Miss V, a 35-year-old MZ twin, came to see me because she suffered from panic attacks. She was a lawyer and believed her career was being adversely affected by her anxiety. Her twin sister had married an Indian and now lived in India with her husband and three children. Although the twin sisters had frequent contact, Miss V felt that her twin had betrayed her both by marrying and in moving so far away. In what might well have been a projection of her own feelings (since her twin had created a rift by marrying and establishing considerable distance between the twins), Miss V believed that her twin's husband was jealous of the twinship and felt excluded by the twin sisters. Miss V was the second-born twin, and considered herself to be a younger, passive partner in the twinship.

Miss V complained that she had difficulties in maintaining relationships as she found it difficult to allow anyone to get close to her – a portent of her experience of the analytic relationship. She had had several fairly long-term relationships with men but she had backed out of them the moment that there was any thought of marriage or commitment. She longed to have her own children, but she did not want their father to be a partner or husband. He was to provide the sperm and then leave. Miss V explained that she did not want to depend on anyone either financially or emotionally. Her twinship was her closest and most intimate relationship. She was also very close to her twin's children, whom she regarded as her own.

Miss V was extremely ambivalent about involving herself in analytic work and manifested this by her frequent lateness and missed sessions. She began to undermine the analytic work very early on, attacking the setting, messing about with session times, arriving so late for sessions it seemed pointless to begin. Although she acknowledged her ambivalence, she could not see that this might be connected with her lateness and resistance to coming to sessions. She never hesitated to put some other activity before her session, always blaming outside events rather than owning her reluctance. She seemed to operate on a very concrete level, and had little sense of having an internal world that affected her behaviour and mood. She preferred to regard all untoward events as having been caused externally.

Alongside this activity destructive to the analytic work, Miss V had a phantasy of her relationship with me as nice and cosy and she avoided any disturbance or conflict with me. I interpreted her wanting a twinship with me in which there would be no discord or distance, a twinship in which we would be as one. Her wish for a conflict-free state, for harmonious twinning, was echoed in her outside life where she always acted as the family mediator, smoothing any ruffled feathers. However, despite these difficult beginnings, Miss V began to move psychically from an 'identical' transference twinship with me, and through the hard work of establishing difference. As a result, Miss V became anxious about feeling involved in a relationship that lacked the harmony of the 'identical' twinship.

The shift from the harmonious twinship and the establishment of a little distance between us led to Miss V becoming angry about the connections I made as they stirred up uncomfortable thoughts. She felt resentful of my having my own thoughts and understanding. She became silent, resistant and withholding in her sessions. Then she believed that I would decide I did not want to work with her. She had projected her anger into me, so creating a transference twin who was to be angry about difference. As we worked through this, Miss V gradually began to own her anger and the sessions became more alive. She said she recognized herself as an angry person. Although she did not like this picture of herself, she feared letting go of her protective anger as it would expose her vulnerability. She used her anger as a protective shield and she was afraid that I would take advantage of her if she let go of it.

Miss V arrived for a session and found the outside door open (presumably left open by the last patient). She did not announce herself by ringing on the bell and I was unaware of her presence until I heard noises in the waiting room some minutes after her session was due to start. I interpreted her behaviour as reflecting her wish to get inside me without my knowing of her presence in order to re-establish the safe 'identical' twinship, as if we were 'identical' twins with no boundary between us. Miss V became silent in order to protect herself from her fear of any further exposure to her own thoughts and feelings. In her silence she withheld her thoughts from herself and from me. She felt that her actions in coming in unannounced had betrayed her feelings to me, and that this made her vulnerable as she had previously feared.

Miss V frequently remained silent in sessions or spoke in some sort of code. This often took the form of obscure psychoanalytic jargon or brief unintelligible references to something I knew nothing about. I suggested that she saw me as a twin who would automatically know her thoughts and therefore she believed that she did not need to communicate directly with me. Miss V responded, saying it was funny that I should say that about a twin, as she and her twin sister had always thought alike and each knew what the other was thinking.

In the next session Miss V reported a dream:

> She was at a party. A male colleague came and stood next to her and another stood on the other side. She took off her top and stood there half-naked but continued talking as if nothing had happened.

Miss V had no associations to her dream but said she thought the dream meant that she must be attracted to her colleague, though she was not aware of it. I suggested that in the last session she had shown me something of herself, i.e. her wish to twin with me by getting inside me. I thought that she now felt ambivalent about having exposed her wishes and she wanted to act as if nothing had happened or been seen. Miss V could not comprehend what I was on about, and said, in what I took to be confirmation of my interpretation, that she had now been made a partner at work (i.e. that she had established her position with me).

Miss V had difficulty allowing meaningful connections to be made and acknowledged, and she seemed to have little sense of internal space to play with ideas. She maintained a repetitive competition with a twin-analyst using her superficial mini-self-analysis. In response to my interpretation of the competitive-twin transference, she told me about nature–nurture issues in twins and how her twin sister was always busy and active, whereas she was always exhausted and closeted herself in her home in the evenings and weekends. So I was the busy active analyst-twin while she closeted herself behind a silent, impenetrable and exclusive twin barrier. Her concrete state of mind protected her from having to think about herself in relation to a twin-analyst who was not as she wished me to be (an 'identical' thought-sharing twin). She was at a point at which allowing herself to think about her use of me would expose her to painful feelings.

In a moving session, Miss V told me that at the weekend she had been walking along the banks of a river where she saw a water bird making a funny noise. She noticed that the bird kept swimming back to its dead mate floating in the water, pecking at it, maybe trying to wake it up, then making the noise again. I interpreted that she felt I was like a dead twin who did not respond in a twin-like manner to her call and her prodding. Miss V responded saying she had thought her twin was there for her, but then her twin had gone off and got married. After a long pause, Miss V said it was the first time she had ever felt depressed.

After this contact, Miss V withdrew again. She kept to herself, an outsider who felt she did not know or trust me. If I was not an identical twin to her, then I was too foreign and threatening to be recognized as someone with whom she could be connected. She felt that as someone different from her, I was not available to her; that I had abandoned and betrayed her as her twin had done in marrying and going abroad. She would offer me brief coded phrases and then wait for my response. If I did not respond knowingly, I was like her abandoning twin, dead to her.

Miss V could not contemplate an idea of a couple of any kind that was based on difference rather than sameness. Men were different, and while they were useful for producing babies, she did not want to be married to one. I took this to mean that she rejected me as a 'non-identical' twin analyst or a mother-analyst who could help her productively.

Following the summer break, Miss V complained about lack of progress in the analytic work. Again she wanted to change session times, to reduce the number of sessions, and to reduce her fees. If she had to miss a session because of her work commitments, she expected me to make it up to her either by offering her a telephone session at her convenience or by not charging for the missed session. It was as if she wanted magically to create a situation where nothing was lost. There was to be no absence, her twin was to be present always, and would never leave her. Despite these attacks, Miss V now increased the frequency of her sessions and she began to become aware that her inner world had an effect on what she thought and did. She softened, and became concerned about issues of sameness and difference.

Throughout the analytic work, there was a persistent sense of a lack of a parental couple, expressed in her wish to have a baby but eschewing the idea of a husband/partner or a father for the baby. It now emerged that there had been very little adequate parental involvement in her early life. After the twins were born, mother had had another two children in very quick succession, and there was not enough maternal emotional space for any of them. Mother had received little in the way of financial or emotional help from her husband and had felt burdened by motherhood. As a result, Miss V had turned to her twin for help and gratification.

In the transference I was now perceived as the unloving mother and Miss V felt that she was gaining nothing from me and that she failed to thrive in the analytic work. The analytic food I offered did not seem to satisfy her. She still missed sessions on a whim and almost invariably came late. It then emerged that her belief in a productive parental couple had been shattered when her father had embarked on an affair during her early childhood. Her mother had been devastated and began to drink, leading to her premature death. Miss V felt her parents had abandoned her by their lack of a true marriage. The story unfolded further. Miss V told me she and her twin sister were born two months premature and had been placed in an incubator. The parents lacked any positive belief in their twins. They were not expected to survive; when they went to school they were put in the lowest class, as they were not expected to develop and learn. Miss V thought that mother had no belief in them and their abilities, and she began to express her immense anger with her mother.

It was apparent that this lack of maternal containment and belief was connected with Miss V's panic attacks. She had not established a sufficiently good internal integrating object upon which she could rely for processing her experiences. As a result, she suffered high levels of anxiety. Her anxiety led to her grave difficulty in trying to get hold of and process her feelings. Miss V found this understanding helpful and she became more responsive to my interventions. She could see how she flared in anger when I made links that she had not expected, links that showed her something of her internal world.

Then there was a dramatic change. Miss V became entangled in a difficult situation at work but she was reluctant to investigate what lay behind it. She felt that she needed some help but was resistant to getting it, in a way echoing her ambivalent feelings about the analytic work. I helped Miss V think through her work difficulty, enabling her to engage a senior partner in a proper investigation and the source of the problem was discovered. She found she could deal with the difficulty and she experienced much relief. She began to feel very positive about her life. She was able to acknowledge the analogy with the analytic work where the internal investigation had exposed some of her difficulties and this understanding had been helpful to her in her view of herself and her life. She had found a helpful maternal transference object.

However, her appreciation was short-lived. Miss V missed several sessions, and when she did arrive halfway through the session, she was filled with bitterness about all the years lost and the time wasted in her life as a result of not having thought about herself differently. She no longer saw me as a helpful figure in any capacity. Her regrets about her past losses had become a grievance that poisoned any further work.

Miss V went to India to visit her twin sister, and on her return, it was clear that she had reverted to the twinship and no longer considered that she had any connection with me at all, either as a transference-twin or as a transference-mother. She had met a man on holiday and had become pregnant by him. She now planned to return to live with him, although she barely knew him. But she had achieved her aim. She would be reunited with her twin sister, and she was pregnant by a man who she did not really consider as a permanent partner. In fact, it was as if she and her twin sister were the couple that had produced this baby. In her mind the narcissistic twin couple had been reinstated at the expense of the parental couple, and she no longer needed me or my analytic interference in the twinship.

Thus, Miss V had sought analytic help in order to reinstate the twinship that was the source of her identity in the absence of a united parental couple with capacities to help their twins. Despite having felt helped by me, her persistent experience was of a mother who had no belief in her and in whom she could not believe.

It is not clear why some twin patients feel able to negotiate the struggle towards an individual identity while others back away from it. As can be seen from the two examples above, it is not just about the quality of the twin relationship – harmonious or rivalrous – nor just the degree of enmeshment *per se*. The fear generated about separateness from the twin may be immense, and the loss of the special twin relationship will also be a factor. But I think the individual personality of the twin patient will be a deciding factor enabling or preventing the move from an enmeshed twin relationship, through the use of the analyst as a transference object, towards a personal sense of self.

SECTION 3
ENDURING ISSUES

The internal twin relationship is an enduring one that would affect all other object relationships. In this section, I will discuss the psychobiological basis of the twin relationship and the effects of its lasting presence.

In Chapter 10, I will explore the nature of the affectional bond with the mother and the way in which this relationship would influence the development of the neurological structures in the brain upon which emotional relationships are based. The persistent presence of the other twin would alter the development of the relevant structures for a twin infant as compared with a singleton. I hope to show that the enduring nature of the twin relationship is neurologically as well as emotionally based.

The psychobiological nature of the ego and its links with the development of a sense of self raises issues for conjoined twins. I speculatively explore what these might be and the importance this might have for the development of conjoined twins and their sense of individuality.

The twin bond would be based on enduring psychobiological and emotional structures and would affect all intimate relationships in the life of a twin. The pull towards or away from the twinship relative to external relationships would affect the intimacy of marital relationships and those with children. The dynamics of the twinship would also be reflected in these relationships. I will describe this in Chapter 11.

Finally, in Chapter 12, the focus will be on the death of a twin – how would this affect the survivor? What would happen to the twinship? I believe that the life and death struggle for individuality that is encountered in some twins may become amplified by the death of one of the twins. I will explore this issue through both case studies and literature.

Chapter 10
The psyche-soma

The main focus of this book has been the effect of a twin relationship on the individual development of each twin and the manner in which this manifests in the transference. I believe that the enduring nature of the internal twin relationship is rooted in its psychobiological basis. In this chapter, I will explore the links between attachment behaviour in an infant–mother couple and the development of structures in the infant brain that are relevant to current and later affectional bonds and relationships. Within this context, I will also consider the position of conjoined twins.

Beginnings

The twin transference relationship that has been explored in this book originates in the earliest developmental experiences of the individual. As discussed in Section 2, the transference twin would be a powerful dynamic in analytic work with a twin, whether or not it is recognized. It is to the detriment of psychoanalytic work that twin (and other sibling) relationships have been neglected in both practice and analytic understanding. As a result of this neglect, one of the primary relationships that twins experience is not represented in the psychoanalytic theories about the structuring of the internal world of a twin.

In Chapter 3, I discussed the nature/nurture issue with regard to twins. Even MZ twins who are as close genetically as it is possible to be, perceive the world differently, uniquely to themselves, each constructing their own reality. Modell (1991) addresses the matter of brain development in response to the environment. He notes that 'even within the constraints of genetic instruction, the embryological development of the nervous system shows a remarkable degree of variability from the level of the cell to the level of global functioning' (Modell, 1991: 236).

The enduring tie to a twin is a bond on the level of early parental relationships. Anna Freud (1958) notes that breaking the tie to a twin is of the same libidinal order as breaking a tie with mother. The attachment to the twin is 'rooted in the same deep layer of the personality as the early attachment to the mother' (Freud, 1958: 266). Other sibling attachments, while of a lesser intensity than the twin relationship, will also affect development. Coles (2002) notes that 'sibling attachments have a passionate intensity of their own, and when they appear in the transference they have a powerful effect on the therapy' (Coles, 2002: 37). She argues that siblings are of primary importance and should not be regarded as just 'second editions' (p. 37) of the parents in the internal world. Coles believes that Freud was right in claiming that the important attachments children make to each other become 'ineradicably fixed' (Coles, 2002: 29) in the psyche, that they are never forgotten and have a lasting effect. The twin relationship would be even stronger in this regard.

This book started with an exploration of the origins of 'twinning', especially in the context of Melanie Klein's (1963) paper 'On the sense of loneliness', followed by an account of development in twins and case material relating to twins in psychoanalytic treatment. I am now coming full circle back to the mother and infant. Beginnings are crucial in this respect. Within the genetic endowment of any individual, singleton, twin or other multiple, there is a potential for development based both on what is offered to the infant and what the infant is able to make use of. I will explore the neuro-biological aspects of development. As no particular attention has been paid to twins in this respect, I will extrapolate from the established work in this area and speculate on the effects on the brain development in twins of the twin relationship and the relationship of each twin with mother.

Attachment theory

It is stating the obvious to say that the early mother–infant relationship is crucial to development. In Chapter 4, I described two observations of twin infants. In another study, Ainsworth (1967) observed infants with their mothers in Uganda, with specific attention to the development of attachment behaviour. Amongst the observations recorded were those from two sets of twins. Both were boy–girl twins, one pair observed from 14 months of age, the other from two weeks. Ainsworth notes that the older twins were competitive with each other and clamorous for mother's attention, and were regarded as insecurely attached to their mother. Unfortunately, there is virtually no mention of the relationship between the twins other than the observation of their rivalry with each other for mother. Thus, in some ways, this echoes Davison's (1992) observation of twin infants (see Chapter 4).

The younger twins in Ainsworth's study were non- (or not-yet-) attached to a mother who was exhausted by the twins' demands. She was not affectionate with her infants and largely ignored them. Neither twin indicated any attachment to mother or cried when she left the room. Instead they responded to mother as they did to any other carers, i.e. father and two school-age girls who lived with the family in order to attend school nearby, and earned their keep by looking after the otherwise neglected twin babies. The older girl appeared to be about 8 years old. Mother was judged to be inattentive to her babies' needs, not engaged with them, and generally rejecting of her twin babies.

Ainsworth notes that an insecure attachment to mother tends to prevent the development of attachments to other figures, and that the later development of an attachment to mother is of a different quality from early attachment.[1] She suggests that the amount of motherly care is the most significant factor in stimulating attachment behaviour in the infant, the most important aspect of this being the actual interaction between mother and baby. This would include the quality of mutual delight; mother's sensitivity to the infant's signals and the timing of her response; her enjoyment of breastfeeding; and whether mother is preoccupied with other matters, thoughts, anxieties or grief. Ainsworth notes that 'a baby's attachment to his mother is founded on and grows out of his own behaviour towards her, strengthened (or weakened) by the kind of response his mother makes to his behaviour' (Ainsworth, 1967: 412).

In exploring the nature of love and its origins in the attachment behaviour of the infant to its mother, Ainsworth raises an important point about the mother–infant relationship and its later effects on other relationships. She recognizes the psychobiological nature of attachment behaviour and makes the connection between the mother–infant relationship and the dynamic structural internalization of this bond. Ainsworth notes,

> Attachment is internal - built into the nervous system in the course of and as a result of the infant's experience of his transactions with mother and other people. This internalised something that we call attachment has aspects of feelings, memories, wishes, expectancies, and intentions, all of which constitute an inner program acquired through experience and somehow built into a flexible yet retentive inner mechanism (which we identify with central nervous system functions) which serve as some kind of filter for the reception and interpretation of interpersonal experience and as a kind of template shaping the nature of outwardly observable response (Ainsworth, 1967: 42–43).

In the foreword to Ainsworth's book, Bowlby states, 'When a baby is born he cannot tell one person from another and indeed can hardly tell person from thing' (Ainsworth, 1967: v). Our current understanding would no longer support Bowlby's view and it has been observed that just seven hours after

---

[1] This would be an important factor in infants who spend a prolonged period in an incubator. Cohen (2003) observed twin infants from their birth at 27 weeks' gestation. They were placed in incubators where they were attached to all manner of life-saving equipment. This made it difficult for the parents to feel close to their infants. There was too little eye contact with, and intimate handling of, the infants, and not enough opportunity for the mother to process the infants' experiences. As Cohen notes, 'the baby in the incubator is not having ... a story woven around him' (p. 47). As time went by, mother appeared to feel more involved with the weaker male infant, but the carers noted and became concerned about mother's lack of attachment to the female twin. On their return home, mother cared for the male twin while grandmother fed the baby girl. Although mother later began to relate to the female twin more closely, she found it more difficult to love her. It seemed that the girl twin missed out on the 'special' relationship with mother and this showed in her indiscriminate smile for everyone.

birth an infant responds to and specifically searches out its mother (Proner, 2000 - see below). Furthermore, far from being an undiscriminating blob, each infant responds uniquely to its environment and its impact upon it even in utero (Piontelli, 2002). Piontelli also records infant twins responding to the presence of each other by three months of age. Initially, each twin responded primarily to the gaze of the caregiver and they each struggled to be pre-eminent in gaining this attention. When the twins were interacting with each other, the sound of mother's voice would prompt both immediately to turn to look for mother. Piontelli notes that this changed by 12 and 15 months when the twins become more preoccupied with each other than with mother. She observed that the MZ twins did not cry or rejoice when mother left the room or reappeared, but only when separated or reunited with each other. They had developed a 'strong and prevailing horizontal attachment' (Piontelli, 2002: 90).

While the timing for the development of an attachment bond between twins has not really been explored, a great deal of work has been done on singleton attachment. Attunement behaviour in the mother–infant couple is a central element for the infant in developing a sense of self (Stern, 1985). Reporting on an infant observation study, Proner (2000) explores the synchronized protomental engagement between the mother–infant couple. She documents the way in which a seven-hour-old infant searches out its mother and is able to distinguish her from the observer. The mother's response and her receptivity to her infant shape the infant's next move towards or away from her. And this process is not one-way. The mother also seeks out her infant, wanting to find out who he is, thus creating a 'synchronised "dance" between mother and infant' (Proner, 2000: 58).

Proner suggests that the interactional synchrony between mother and infant brings them into juxtaposition for further identification to develop; i.e. the observed protomental synchrony precedes projective identification that in turn leads to mentation. (She links these observations with Schore's exploration (see below) of the interactive regulation between mother and infant.) The idea that the infant is born with an expectation of finding a mother originates in the infant's being neurologically wired to make a specific relationship that would lead to its being fed, cleaned and cared for. Proner suggests that the infant is actively seeking a purposeful relationship, acting with perseverance, specificity and discrimination.

The primitive synchronous response between mother and infant is the first form of communication between them. It is this early contact that creates the sense of oneness,[2] bringing 'the mother and baby together into an orchestrated attunement that is the prerequisite to being in a position of projective receptivity' (Proner, 2000: 58). The instinctual synchrony stimulates mother's reverie, rather than mother's reverie creating the

---

[2] Klein (1963) describes the sense of oneness between mother and infant, the understanding without words that later engenders a sense of loneliness, as being based in the infant's earliest relationship with mother (see Chapter 1).

grounds for the attunement. The synchrony is a preface to mother's falling 'in love' with her infant, and for the infant to feel it 'fits'.

Proner conceptualizes the developmental process using Bick's (1968) framework of a psychic 'skin' that holds together parts of the personality. This emotional 'skin' may be 'provided by qualities of the mother's presence, such as her voice, her face (particularly her eyes), her smell, her rhythm, the way in which she holds the baby, etc.' (Proner, 2000: 58). The infant in the above observation responded bodily to mother's voice, communication and emotionality. Thus the synchrony between mother and infant is crucially important in the infant's development. A repeated sense of 'fitting' creates the psychic 'skin'. In contrast, a lack of receptivity in the mother may lead the infant to project the charged bodily sensations into its own body where they will be either evacuated as faeces, or become the focus of psychosomatic ailments.

The psychobiological basis of attachment behaviour and development of a sense of self

Attachment theory forms the framework within which Schore (1994, 1996, 2001a and b) understands neuro-biological development in the infant. He believes that interactive affect regulation is at the centre of early development and stresses the psychobiological rather than the purely psychological nature of development. He defines psychopathology in terms of the dysregulation of affect. I will attempt to summarize Schore's theories about early infantile development in relation to mother–infant attachment and its effects on the development of brain function. I will then extrapolate from this to explore the significance of this theory for twins.

The cortico-limbic system

The infant's early experiences with the mother or primary caregiver shape the development of the self-regulatory system in the brain. This system comprises a particular area of the right hemisphere of the infant's developing brain called the orbitofrontal lobe of the cerebral cortex – 'the "senior executive" of the social-emotional brain' (Schore, 2001a: 309), and the limbic system in the deeper substrata of the brain – involved in unconscious processing of facial expressions. This self-regulatory system is called the cortico-limbic system. The self-regulating system is the repository of elements of the attachment relationship with the primary object and it mediates the functioning of the unconscious mind. The cortico-limbic system is thus the neurological substrate of the unconscious.

The infant's experience of the primary caregiver is internalized first pre-symbolically and later (at the end of the second year) symbolically, and stored representationally. The internalized representations serve intra-psychically as internal affect regulators (a good internal integrating object, the core of a developing ego). Thus, the primary object relationships of the infant are internalized and transformed into a psychic structure on a neurological base.

The internal object relationships are visually imprinted self- and object-images that are encoded in implicit (i.e. unconscious) procedural memory and are stored as right-hemispheric nonverbal internal working models.

Schore (2001a) notes the coherence and functionality of the unconscious neural substrate: 'Rather than being a cauldron of untamed passions and destructive wishes, I propose that the unconscious is a cohesive, continually active, mental structure that takes note of life's experiences and reacts according to its scheme of interpretations' (Winson, 1990; quoted by Schore, 2001a: 301).

The maturation of the cortico-limbic system is dependent on the nature of the experience with the primary caregiver. Both the type and quality of early experiences will influence the structural maturation of the brain in infancy. A socio-emotional environment that facilitates growth would offer a modulated and varied experience to the infant. This would lead to the ontogenetic emergence of more complex auto-regulatory functional systems in the infant's brain. In contrast, mis-attuned experiences with the primary caregiver would lead to a high level of infantile affect that would inhibit the development of cortico-limbic system.

Attachment and the promotion of the mother–infant interaction

The essential task of the first year is to develop a secure attachment bond between the infant and the primary caregiver. Initially, the olfactory-gustatory and thermal-tactile sensory modalities predominate in the communication between the mother–infant pair. Later (at about two months) the myelination of the occipital areas of the cerebral cortex increases. As a result, visual information, particularly that conveying mother's affective responses to the infant, would play an important role that leads to the development of synchronous changes in the internal states of both mother and infant. At two months, mother's face as a visual stimulus would promote an intense mutual gaze.

Mother regulates her infant's state of arousal through a bond of unconscious communication that leads to rapid matching responses in the mother–infant pair. This interactive matrix promotes the outward expression of internal affects between the pair. In this way mother modulates the level of affect experienced by the infant. However, the interaction between mother and infant may also induce stress states in the infant. Mother repairs these in the process of interaction with her infant by regulating the infant's levels of affect. There would be alternating periods of engagement and disengagement. Where the infant's affect has been modulated by mother, the infant's arousal levels during periods of disengagement become manageable. However, when the arousal has been left at a high level, periods of disengagement are more difficult for the infant to tolerate.

The key to mother's capacity to repair the infant's overly aroused state is her ability to monitor and regulate her own affective state, particularly her negative feelings, and this would lead to 'good enough' mothering (containment). Negative affects in the infant will be minimized and the opportunities for the development of positive feelings will be maximized, as is found in play states. This would lead the infant to a sense of safety and a positively charged curiosity about life.

Schore (1996) describes the developmental process:

> During the first year of life visual experiences play a paramount role in social and emotional development. In particular, the mother's emotionally expressive face is, by far, the most potent visual stimulus in the infant's environment, and the child's intense interest in her face, especially in her eyes leads him/ her to track it in space and to engage in periods of intense mutual gaze. The infant's gaze, in turn, reliably evokes mother's gaze, and this dyadic system forms an efficient interpersonal channel for the transmission of reciprocal mutual influences. These mutual gaze interactions represent the most intense form of interpersonal communication, and to enter into this affective communication, the mother must be psychobiologically attuned not so much to the child's overt behaviour as to the reflections of his internal state. She initially attunes to and resonates with the infant's resting state, but as this state is dynamically activated (or deactivated or hyperactivated) she contingently fine tunes and corrects the intensity and duration of her affective stimulation to maintain the child's positive affect state (Schore, 1996: 61).

Attachment behaviour is stimulated by the affective state that is promoted by the mother–infant synchronous attunement and communication, as described above. Schore (1996) notes that the mother not only modulates the child's affective state, 'she is also regulating the infant's production of neuro-hormones and hormones that influence the activation of gene-action systems that program the structural growth of the brain regions essential to future socioemotional development of the child' (Schore, 1996: 63). Thus an emotionally responsive mother would create a secure base for her developing infant, and later for the toddler to return to, to re-engage with her and rebalance his levels of emotional arousal.

Psychopathological states

The organization and stability of the emergent core self would be dependent on the smoothness of transition between affective states. The infant's early experiences would shape the bias of the affective core towards certain emotional responses. 'The mother's participation in interactive regulation during episodes of psychobiological attunement, misattunement, and reattunement not only modulates the infant's internal state, but also indelibly and permanently shapes the emerging self's capacity for self-organisation' (Schore, 1996: 75).

During the period that the brain grows most rapidly, the infant would be most vulnerable to non-optimal or growth-inhibitory environmental events. The resultant disturbance of personality formation would lead to attachment or empathy disorders. In these situations, the infant would suffer a deficit in social cognition, in self-regulation and in its capacity to modulate the intensity and duration of its affects, especially the primitive states of mind such as shame, rage, excitement, elation, disgust, panic-terror, or hopeless despair. Therefore, for such an individual stress would produce diffuse, undifferentiated, chaotic states (as experienced in narcissistic and borderline disorders). There would also be a deficit in mentalization (Schore, 2001a). Schore suggests that the basis of empathy is nonverbal psychobiological attunement. Defence mechanisms are the strategies for emotional self-regulation that are used to avoid or minimize affects that are too difficult to tolerate, to prevent the emergence of dreaded states that are charged with intense unmanageable negative affect.

As Schore (2001b) notes, the infant's attachment status depends on both its genetically encoded psychobiological predisposition and its experience of the primary caregiver. Maternal dissociation blocks infantile attachment. The consequences are long-term as regards social relationships and the developing infant's capacity to deal with new and stressful experiences. Schore further notes that there is an intergenerational transmission of adaptive and maladaptive styles of parenting and responsiveness to the infant.[3] The early experiences of female patients with their own mothers would influence how they are with their infants when they become mothers.

The application of Schore's theories to twins

For twins, the picture must be more complex. It seems clear that each twin would have unique experiences in its relationships both with mother and with the other twin. The synchronous interaction between mother and each infant would stimulate the neuro-hormones that activate the genes for programming the development of structural systems within the cortex that are linked with the socio-emotional development of each child. The relationship with the other twin would have a different effect (see below) but would again be unique to each twin and to the perception each twin has of its own and its twin's relationship with mother. Each twin would therefore develop differentially according to its unique experience with mother and with its twin, whatever its zygocity. So I come back again to the fact that the notion that any twins are 'identical' is a phantasy.

I will consider the two aspects of mother–twin–twin interaction and the creation of an affectional bond that would be affected by the presence of a twin. Firstly, neither twin can ever be solely in mother's focus, as she would always have another baby in mind even if it were not visually present. The excluded baby would be an absent baby in mother's divided mind. Thus, even when mother has the capacity to function as a mature container, well attuned to her infants, the fact of the presence of the second baby would affect the nature of the attention she pays to each infant. The quality of attunement to the infant at the breast and the mutual gaze would be interfered with by existence of the other twin. Given that these experiences

---

[3] This would be an important factor in twins and their parenting of their own children - see Chapter 11.

are formative in the infant's current and future capacities to develop intimate relationships, the effects of this situation would be long lasting. As noted in Davison's (1992) observation of twin infants,[4] a degree of interactive repair can be exercised in the mother-infant coupling. Davison observed that the mother apologized with understanding and empathy to one twin whom she had had to leave aside in order to attend to the other, more distressed, twin.

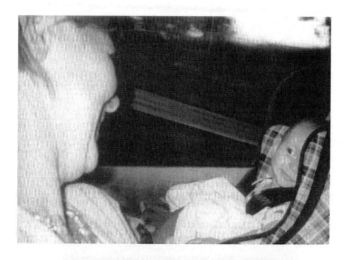

---

[4] See Chapter 4.

Secondly, where a twin rather than the mother serves as the primary object, the immaturity of each would affect the development of the structures in the brain in which the capacity for affectional bonds reside. This would be similar to the effects of a mis-attuned mother–infant couple. The twins would be too immature to modulate each other's states of arousal, and would be likely instead to elevate the degree of affect arousal in each other to unmanageable levels. Disengagement from the primary object would then leave the infant twin in a disturbed state and would not be accompanied by restfulness as it would with a mature container. The infant's ability to make affectional bonds, the development of sense of self and emotional maturity would be interfered with.

Where twins use each other as primary objects, their mutual immaturity might lead to a state of hyper-arousal rather than affect modulation, as observed in Bill and Bert (Burlingham, 1963).[5] These twins were observed to stimulate each other into ever-increasing states of excitation that the nursery staff seemed powerless to prevent or to end. The permanent effects of the experience of poor modulation of affect, hyper-arousal and its effects on the development of the cortico-limbic system would account for the considerable difficulty some twins have in establishing a degree of separation from each other that would allow them to lead independent lives. They will not have developed an internal integrated self-modulating system (a good internal integrating object) upon which they can rely to help them deal with the external world.

Schore (2001 – personal communication) suggests that MZ twins would share a biological synchronicity due to the unique genetic make-up that encodes the programming of their central and autonomic nervous systems. They would share similar brain and body rhythms, to an extent greater than most other individuals. Both in utero and after birth, the twins would act as interactive regulators for each other. Where the mother is either not able to or is excluded from performing this function, this would result in one immature system regulating another equally immature one with consequent developmental difficulties. MZ twins in particular would resonate psychobiologically – the state of arousal they experience would be amplified because the frequency of the external sensory stimulation would coincide with their genetically encoded endogenous rhythms. Schore concludes that ultimately this would have an impact on attachment–separation dynamics and the balance of auto-regulation and interactive regulation.

The effects of psychoanalytic work on brain development

Schore (2001a) describes the neurological background to the reparative effects of analytic attunement in psychoanalytic work. Neuro-biological changes occur as a result of both the analyst's empathy and interpretations (Schore, 2001b). The interactive communication between patient and analyst would provide an affect regulatory system, using the analyst's nonverbal attunement to the patient. One might conclude from this that the brain

---

[5] See Chapter 4.

remains relatively plastic, and that new and more functional pathways could be created in an adequately attuned psychoanalytic environment. This would also need to include the recognition and analysis of the transference twin by a maternal container/affect regulator.

The analyst who recognizes and attunes to the state of mind of the patient, and analyses rather than enacts the projected transference relationship,[6] will facilitate this development. In contrast, enactment of the twin relationship would perpetuate the maladaptive interaction between analyst and patient, reinforcing the pathological internal structures. Enacting the twin in the transference does not enable the patient to develop new ways of relating, but reinforces old patterns that have not served the patient well. However, it is clear that the development of new patterns of relating is not infinite. There would always be a twin 'scar' as an enduring aspect of the twin relationship.

The plasticity of areas of the brain would make psychoanalytic work effective in particular ways. Using research on functional-imaging studies of the effects of psychotherapy on brain functioning, Solms and Turnbull (2002) note that the functional activity of the brain is altered by psychotherapy. These changes are specific to the therapeutic outcome and are essentially located in the pre-frontal lobes. They suggest that these changes are achieved via two processes: firstly, the use of language in psychotherapy 'establishes connections ... between the concrete elements of perception and memory' (Solms and Turnbull, 2002: 288). The second process is that of internalization. They note that the mutative power of internalization is normally confined to critical periods of frontal-lobe development within the first few years of life. However, they suggest that the regressive nature of the transference relationship would rekindle the developmental plasticity of these areas of the brain.

My own experience and that of the cases and the scientific work I have referred to in this book indicate that the twin relationship is internalized, forms a permanent dynamic structure within the brain, and is enduring. As it is based on the early experiences with the mother and the other twin, the zygocity of the twins may affect the degree of twinning, but not the enduring nature of the internal twinship. I therefore cannot agree with Burlingham (1952) when she writes that in fraternal twins, the 'interest à deux' (p. 16) gradually fades. Glenn (1966) also disagrees with Burlingham's view. He explores the long-term effects of twinning through his analytic work with MZ and DZ twin patients. In addition, he has published two papers exploring the writings of the 'fraternal' twins Anthony and Peter Shaffer (Glenn, 1974a and b). He suggests that the Shaffer twins project their own twin characteristics and relationships on to the characters they create in their writing, and he maintains that these clearly demonstrate the persistent influence of twinning. As I described in more detail in Chapter 4, Engel (1975) also describes the persistence of the twinship in his account of a self-analysis in relation to his twin.

---

6 See Chapter 6.

Conjoined twins

'To begin with, the "self" is not a topology of mind like ego, id and superego, but a perspective on awareness and an interpersonal one, at that. The self is the way an individual personifies himself as he stands outside of himself. It is an act of hallucinatory self-consciousness' (Levenson, 1978: 571).

Much attention has been paid to conjoined twins in recent years, particularly as the development of better surgical techniques and increasing expertise in separating conjoined twins, have led to a greater chance of one or both twins surviving the separation. Nothing appears to have been written in the psychoanalytic literature about the psychological consequences of being a conjoined twin or the surgical separation of the twins. However, given the difficulty twins face ordinarily in establishing a separate identity, I believe the task for separated conjoined twins must be even greater as they share, to various degrees, some of the parts of their body or organs.

Schore (2001a) notes that the sense of both a corporeal and an emotional self resides in the right hemisphere of the brain. The right hemisphere is connected with both the sympathetic and parasympathetic nervous systems that are responsible for the expression of somatic states, and therefore the visceral and somatic states and the processing of 'self-related material' are represented in the right hemisphere. This must have implications for the emotional development of conjoined twins, both in relation to each other and to their mother.

The shared bodily experience of conjoined twins (i.e. not just the emotional and physical presence of another infant, as in ordinary twins) will interfere with the internalization of the early infant–mother relationship and the development of a relational psychic structure. Mother can never bodily hold one twin separately from the other, so she is not just holding the other twin in mind, but in physical presence too. This must profoundly affect the infant–mother relationship. Depending on how the twins are joined, they may both face the mother though she can only make actual eye contact with them one at a time. Some conjoined twins are not able to face the same direction (e.g. those joined at the back or head) and it may be that eye contact with mother can only be achieved for one of the twins at a time by turning the other away.

Historical records (see below) note that the mother and others sometimes regard conjoined twins as one person with some duplication of body parts. So the mother's mindset will be powerfully affected by having two babies joined at some part of their body. Some mothers of ordinary twin infants might feed both simultaneously, one at each breast. But they are bodily two separate babies and she will have times of being physically alone with one baby or the other. This is not possible with conjoined twins and I believe it makes it much more difficult for mother to bond with each baby individually.

And what confusion might develop between the twins about their body boundaries? Given that 'the ego is first and foremost a bodily ego' (Freud, 1923: 26), this must have profound implications for conjoined twins. Freud added, 'the ego is ultimately derived from bodily sensations, chiefly from those springing from the surface of the body. It may thus be regarded as a mental projection of the surface of the body, besides ... representing the superficies of the mental apparatus' (Freud, 1923: 26, footnote). Thus, even when conjoined twins are attached only superficially, there would be a confusion of bodily image between them. How much more profound this must be when they share internal organs.

The importance to the infant of its experience of its own body in developing a sense of self is highlighted by Fenichel (1946: 35–36):

> In the development of reality, the conception of one's own body plays a very special role. At first there is only the perception of tension, that is, of an 'inside something'. Later, with the awareness that an object exists to quiet this tension, we have an 'outside something'. One's own body is both at the same time. Due to the simultaneous occurrence of both outer tactile and inner sensory data, one's own body becomes something apart from the rest of the world and thus the discerning of self from nonself becomes possible. The sum of mental representations of the body and its organs, the so-called body image constitutes the idea of I and is of basic importance for the further formation of the ego.

Yet studies of conjoined twins have established that they have separate personalities and regard themselves at least as separate as are ordinary twins. Stern (1985) describes an experiment on conjoined twins connected on the ventral surface between umbilicus and sternum, but sharing no organs. They had separate nervous systems, and essentially shared no blood supply. Before surgical separation of the conjoined twins at four months, Stern explored the twins' individual volition in order to achieve something, and its relation to the sense of self. He reports:

> Twin A (Alice) was sucking on her **own** fingers, one of us placed one hand on her head and the other hand on the arm that she was sucking. We gently pulled the sucking arm away from her mouth and registered (in our own hands) whether her arm put up resistance to being moved from her mouth and/or whether her head strained forward to go after the retreating hand. In this situation, Alice's arm resisted the interruption of sucking, but she did not give evidence of straining forward with her head. The same procedure was followed when Alice was sucking on her sister Betty's fingers rather than her own. When Betty's hand was gently pulled from Alice's mouth, Alice's arms showed no resistance or movement, and Betty's arm showed no resistance, but Alice's head did strain forward. Thus when her own hand was removed, the plan to maintain sucking was put into execution by the attempt to bring her arm back to the mouth, while when another person's hand was removed the plan to maintain sucking was put into execution with the movement of her head forward. Alice seemed, in this case, to have no confusion as to whose fingers belonged to whom and which motor plan would best re-establish sucking (Stern, 1985: 78) ... The results indicated that each twin "knew" that one's own mouth sucking a finger and one's own finger being sucked do not make a coherent self.

Thus each twin knew which finger belonged to them and how to organize its movements to get the finger back to suck.

There are historical records of conjoined twins from the time of ancient cave drawings and carvings ('Joined', 2001). Smith (1988) researched the lives of a number of well-known conjoined twins from written records about them. Of those that survived after birth, many of the conjoined twins earned their living in 'freak show' venues, and were regarded as curiosities to both the public and the medical world. Smith undertook a psychological study as he sought to understand more about their personalities, how they functioned as a conjoined pair, and about their individuality. Overall, he notes that there were marked differences in the personalities, abilities and interests of each twin, and that the perception that conjoined twins are one person with some duplication of body parts is erroneous (see below).

Conjoined twins are MZ twins for whom the physical separation from each other is incomplete and as a result two people remain bound together. Burn and Goodship (2001) note that conjoined twins are always joined together at an identical area in each twin. They suggest that if the division of the fertilized egg into two embryos occurs early (before 12 days), two separate embryos would develop – MZ twins. If division of the fertilized egg is later, there may be incomplete division, or migration or crossover of cells from one twin embryo to another, and conjoined twins would develop. Each set of twins is unique in the way that they are joined, though experts define six basic categories of conjoined twins. (I will not detail these here.)

The picture that emerges from Smith's 1988 study is that despite the fact that the conjoined twins were markedly different in personality and abilities, they preferred to remain conjoined. Together they functioned as a unit and had ways of finding privacy for and from each other. (I think they must use the processes of splitting and dissociation to achieve such privacy.) I will briefly discuss some of the conjoined twins Smith studied.

The famous 'Siamese twins', Chang and Eng (1811–1874), led successful lives and had individual families and family homes, dividing their time between the two homes. They did enquire about separation, but were apparently discouraged on medical grounds. It seems that the main reason was that they were extremely successful as a conjoined pair, and the doctors were afraid that one or both might not survive the operation. (It now appears that surgical separation would have been a simple matter.) They both married and had 21 children between them. After decades exhibiting themselves in freak shows, they became successful farmers. They died within hours of each other. Chang died first, and Eng became weaker and weaker as his blood was pumped into the dead Chang without being returned to him. Effectively, Eng bled to death after Chang died.

The Biddenhead Maids (1100–1134) were joined at the hip and shoulder. They too died within a short time of each other. The possible survivor was offered separation when her twin died, but she refused, saying, 'As we came together, we will also go together' (Smith, 1988: 58). Like Chang and Eng they had also become wealthy through exhibiting themselves.

Millie and Christine McCoy (1851-1912), were joined at the trunk, and shared part of a common nervous system (but each also had an individual nervous system). They were known as the Two-headed Nightingale as they earned a living as vaudeville stars. They were nevertheless distinct individuals with independent minds. As Smith notes, 'the ways they found for existing with each other as individual beings must have been complex and difficult to comprehend' (Smith, 1988: 63). Christine died 17 hours after Millie, and the inscription on their tombstone was 'A soul with two thoughts. Two hearts that beat as one.'

The Tocci twins (1877-1940s) had separate upper bodies but shared the lower half of their body from the sixth rib downwards, thus almost approximating a two-headed person. They were reported as having 'regions of common sensibility and of purely individual sensation' (Smith, 1988: 64). Although they made a considerable amount of money exhibiting themselves, they were most unhappy about their condition as conjoined twins.

Daisy and Violet Hilton (1909-1969) were joined at their backs and made their living dancing and playing the saxophone. They both eventually married after initially being refused a licence in many states in America because of their conjoined condition. Neither marriage lasted long. They claimed to be able to 'get rid of each other mentally' (Smith, 1988: 74), as they either stopped paying attention to the other, or one slept while the other was awake. They 'learned how not to know what the other was doing unless it was our business to know' (p. 74).

Most of the twins described by Smith refused to be surgically separated even in the face of the death of one of them. However, Simplico and Lucio Godino (1908-1936), who were joined at the buttocks, did agree to separation when one had died of pneumonia. The survivor seemed to be recovering well and regaining his strength, but he died a few days later. It seemed that he was so weakened by the separation he could not survive.

Smith (1988) explains that he investigated conjoined twins because he was interested in the nature–nurture issue. He had found the arguments on both sides shallow and unconvincing. He understood from his study of conjoined twins that 'Heredity not only creates our physiology, it creates a physiology which allows us to be creative and flexible individuals. The environment not only molds us but also offer us a continually changing spectrum of opportunities' (Smith, 1988: 129). His main thesis is that we are not only the results of, but also the creators of, our environment to a significant degree. 'At every junction the developing mind, which is partially the consequence of past events and biological conditions is also engaged in an active re-creation of the world in which it exists' (Smith, 1988: 136).

Smith's understanding of the nature–nurture debate from his study of the most entwined of human beings is confirmation not only of the unique individuality of each person, but also of the centrality of the interactions between twins. Conjoined twins actually embody the twin dilemma - to

separate and lose something of oneself, perhaps with a disabling consequence; or to remain entwined with the consequent disfigurement of
individuality that might have been achieved through separation. In the past,
the financial aspect was a major factor. Conjoined twins were able to make a
lot of money by exhibiting themselves, and to separate them would have
deprived them of this possibility. Nowadays, this situation would not usually
arise.

With the much improved surgical techniques and knowledge, it is usual
these days to separate conjoined twins where it is possible to do so. However,
this does not mean that there is no controversy about it. Dreger and Briggs
(2001) argue that difference, such as that in the case of conjoined twins, is
treated as if it were a medical problem. Therefore attempts are made to erase the
difference in the fact of the twins being conjoined and thus solve the 'problem'.
They note that frequently the previously able-bodied conjoined twins are left
disabled after surgery, and the view that they are 'born to be separated' (Dreger
and Briggs, 2001: 180) is the view of singletons, not of the conjoined twins
themselves. This seems to confirm Smith's findings, above, but a longitudinal
study of separated conjoined twins would be necessary to reach such a
conclusion.

Dreger, who is a medical historian at the University of Michigan, also
addresses the issue of 'sacrifice surgery', i.e. sacrificing one twin to save the
life of the other, which she regards as euthanasia. She points out ('Conjoined
Twins', Horizon: 2000) that nowhere else in medical practice would
surgeons use a 'brain-live person and essentially asphyxiate them, to
effectively use them as an organ donor'. She believes that it is unlikely that
both conjoined twins would be viable when separated, and that they should
be allowed to live as they are and for their lives to run their natural course.

The case of 'Jodie' and 'Mary' in Manchester, UK (2000) highlighted the
dilemma. These conjoined twins shared a heart and other vital organs, and
one had only primitive levels of brain function. The separation of the twins to
save one twin would inevitably mean the death of the other, but to leave
them conjoined would have led to the death of both twins. The parents
wanted to leave the twins as they were, while the medical personnel felt
obliged to try to save the one viable baby. Finally, the Court of Appeal judged
that the twins should be separated, and as expected, one died. The other
survived apparently healthily, but will need repeated surgery to correct
defects as a result of being conjoined.

The other major area of ethical uncertainty is the surgical intervention on
conjoined twins who may otherwise be healthy. O'Neill (2001: 200) states
that 'long-term follow-up data on separated conjoined twins supports a
reasonable approach to separation of conjoined twins wherever feasible as
the preferred approach.' He insists that such surgery is functional, not just
cosmetic, and careful consideration must be given to the long-term side
effects of separation versus not-separation. Both quality of life and survival
are important issues in the decision to separate or leave conjoined. The

decision has to take into consideration whether the benefits outweigh the losses. For some conjoined twins, separation is medically impossible. Levenson (1978) reflects this dilemma when he suggests that 'Siamese twins [are] simultaneously irreconcilable and inseparable' (p. 577).

Professor Lewis Spitz and Edward Kiely at the Institute of Child Health, London, have performed 17 operations to separate conjoined twins. They necessarily work extremely closely, 'almost like twins themselves' (The Times, 22 June 2002). In a discussion with Professor Spitz, he told me that several of the surviving separated twins keep in contact with him, and he sees some of them regularly. He feels like a 'daddy' to the children that he has separated, as if he has been father to the birth of their individual sense of self, though he stresses that each is an individual from the start. Professor Spitz believes that life together for un-separated conjoined twins would be intolerable – they are regarded as freaks and they are indeed freaks of nature. If one twin dies as a result of surgery, his view is that a life has been saved rather than that one has been sacrificed.

Professor Spitz was involved in separating Eilish and Katy at three years of age. He described them as conjoined but healthy, with two upper torsos and a shared pair of legs. Katy died after the separation and Eilish was devastated that her twin had disappeared. She refused to speak to Professor Spitz for a year, but does now have regular contact with him. The moment of awakening after surgery is an ordeal for separated twins, even if the other twin has not died. It is common practice to place a mirror next to the separated children, so that they can see a mirror image to ease the passage of their separation. The babies or children are also prepared for the separation by encouraging them to play with dolls that are joined together with Velcro and can be pulled apart.

Professor Spitz described two conjoined twin boys he had separated as 'very close' and said that they had to be separated at school. These twins featured in a TV programme about conjoined twins ('Joined: The World of Siamese Twins', Channel 4: 3/10/01). Hussein and Hassan Abdulrehman (born 1986) were described at birth as joined at the chest and sharing a liver, and they had one leg each. The twins were separated at eight months and now, age 15 years, they believe their mother made the right decision in doing so. They don't like to be apart. They dress alike and frequently sit as if still conjoined. Their mother says that although each has his own bed, they often sleep together in one bed in their joined birth position.

In the above TV interview, Hussein and Hassan say that they feel they belong to a family tree of Siamese twins, and that having been conjoined is a 'weakness point'. Hussein said 'they' sometimes dream that Chang and Eng come back and join them together again – since Chang and Eng did not separate, why should Hussein and Hassan be allowed to do so? Hassan is now the more outgoing of the twins, although he was the weaker infant at birth. It was feared that Hassan would not survive after separation and it is of interest that in the video he clings to his mother's side as they sit on a couch, almost sucking at her shoulder. Hussein said that if Hassan had died when the twins were separated, he would not have forgiven his mother, as they are so close. However, they both believe it would not have been possible to live a normal life if they had remained joined. With their very different interests, they feel they would have had to make too many unacceptable compromises. Hassan and Hussein have a desire to assert their individuality and have different interests, but they also do things together, like riding a bicycle, in an extraordinarily well coordinated manner – as if they were one. They both suffered an extreme sense of dislocation and loss when they were separated, and when young they used to play with dolls, and break their legs off, to make the dolls like them.

Lori and Reba Schappell ('Conjoined Twins', Horizon: 2000) believe they live separate lives despite always being together. They are conjoined at the head and share brain tissue and a significant part of their frontal lobes. Dr John Templeton ('Conjoined Twins', Horizon: 2000) found 'a dense flow of nerve tissue that all comes together. There's not a dotted line there.' He notes that the frontal lobes are connected with personality and higher intellect,[7] but Lori and Reba have distinctly different personalities and interests. They feel that being conjoined is an integral part of their being, and they never want to be separated, even if they could. However, they are 'not solely conjoined twins ... just conjoined to another human being'.

Abigail and Brittany Hensel, born in 1990 in the USA, are a very rare pair of conjoined twins who are inseparable but appear to live happy, healthy lives. They share a torso and one pair of legs, but have two heads, hearts and stomach. They each 'own' one side of their body and feel sensation in that side. Mentally they are independent and have different abilities and interests.

Conjoined twins, being so literally stuck together, must find it imperative to emphasize their individuality in order to have any sense of personal as opposed to communal being. But the intense wish either not to be separated, or if separated, not to be apart, is an indication of the extent of sharing of a communal identity between them. As Masha and Dasha, the tragic Russian conjoined twins said, they are like 'a small collective'. They share their grief and their tears and would never agree to an operation to separate them. When Dasha fell in love in her teens, it was intolerable to Masha, who insisted the love relationship end. She felt she could not live with Dasha's beloved all her life and put a stop to the romantic relationship of her twin sister.

I believe that conjoined twins illustrate in an extreme form the essential dilemma faced by all twins in finding a sense of self that is separate from the twinship, but without annihilating the other twin or the twin relationship. They demonstrate the courage and resourcefulness needed to find an individual sense of self while remaining embodied in the twinship, even after a surgical separation that will invariably leave the twinship scars on their body as well as their psyche. Where twins are less enmeshed in the twinship, the difficulty will be less stark. Certainly the greatest and most poignant dilemma is that faced by conjoined twins and their carers.

---

[7] See earlier discussion about the work of Schore on the affectional bond and development of the cortico-limbic structures incorporating the orbitofrontal cortex.

Chapter 11
Intimate relations

In this chapter, I will explore the nature of incestuous phantasies and activity in twins; the ways in which the twin relationship may affect marital relationships; and the transgenerational effect of twinning that becomes evident in parent–child relationships.

Twin infants may use each other for gratification and the resultant libidinal attachment formed between them may be long lasting. It is not uncommon for the libidinal elements of the close twinship to lead to an incestuous relationship between the twins. The phantasies underlying the incestuous activity in children would shape the nature of the sexual encounter, and this will include phantasies relating to the libidinal twinship as well as to the parental objects and their sexual relationship. The nature of the incestuous phantasies in childhood sexuality will affect the development of the children. Childhood sexuality would be linked with oedipal passions and may also be an attempt to emulate the parental sexual intercourse or the child's misconception of it (Klein, 1932). Twins, like singletons with their siblings, may use their incestuous activity to ward off oedipal fears, or to delay the resolution of the oedipal conflict (Coles, 2002; Engel, 1975). For twins, however, there is an additional powerful component of their incestuous activity: some twins entertain the phantasy that they are two parts of one whole. This phantasy may be enacted in the incestuous relationship between them as they endeavour to re-unite with their 'other half' in their yearning to be one, like the Platonic beings (see Chapter 2).

Twinning, as a projected internal relationship, would be manifest in all the intimate relationships of a twin, and to this effect may influence the marital/partner relationships and parents' relationships with their children. The essential elements of the twin relationship may be transferred to the marital and parental relationships in the same way as would any individual's relationships with his/her parents. As in the analytic encounter, the twinship projected into a marital or parental relationship will reflect the nature and range of the twin's experience of the twin relationship on a spectrum from narcissistic to a more mature object relationship. The incestuous nature of the twin relationship may also be reflected in an adult twin's later sexual relationships with a partner. The formative internal object relationships remain alive and active to shape later object relationships. However, the closest relationship for many twins may be with their twin brother or sister, and any other relationship may be seen as a threat to the twinship and may be relegated to second position.

Incestuous relationships in twins

Reading the reports of incestuous relationships between twins in both psychoanalytic case studies and general literature has led me to conclude that, in many instances, the incestuous twin relationship is *the ultimate physical enactment of the entwined twin relationship*. Incestuous relationships in children are common (Klein, 1932), but twin incest has a unique quality that arises out of the interlocking nature of the identities of the twin pair. The relationship between twins may be intensely intimate, libidinally loaded and long lasting. As Glenn (1966) notes, a 'twin may be a potent satisfier of libidinal needs' (Glenn, 1966: 737). The profound intimacy between twins starts with their closeness in the first six months of life, when they 'learn that they can gratify each other sensually, through the tactile, visual, vocal and auditory modes' (Ortmeyer, 1970: 138). The libidinal attachment between twins may be enacted in both heterosexual and homosexual activity.

Incest in twins is essentially a narcissistic affair. Twins who lack a clear sense of self as a result of diffuse ego boundaries between the twin pair may seek wholeness through the intimacy between them in a phantasied coming together of two halves that emphasizes the oneness of the pair. The narcissistic gratification twins seek in each other through their incestuous sexual activity would thus have a masturbatory quality, a phantasy of the other twin as part of self. The libidinal loading in the twin relationship is a central element of the twinship and it creates a powerful temptation towards an incestuous relationship (Jacobson, 1965). Homosexuality in twins would also be based on narcissistic needs that lead to a wish for reunion with the twin (Joseph, 1961).

The closeness of the twin relationship and its incestuous core may lead some twins to feel that any sexual activity external to the twinship is a betrayal of the other twin and is only second best to the twin incest. Laufer (1968) reports on the analysis of a female MZ twin who believed that her sexual feelings during intercourse with a man interfered with her phantasy of oneness with her twin sister. To overcome the disturbance this created she would dissociate herself from her body during sexual intercourse with a man. In contrast with heterosexual intercourse, she found that when she masturbated she felt happier with herself. This indicated the narcissistic basis of her sexual preference for herself/twin-sister rather than a male partner.

Several elements may be operative in incestuous relationships between twins. In common with other siblings, sexual activity between twins may represent sexual exploration and curiosity. Phantasies of incest between twins and the enactment of these phantasies may contain some elements of identification with the parental intercourse, as the immature twin couple equate themselves with the generationally older and mature parental couple. The sexual activity between the twins may provide a refuge from the phantasied threat of the parent–child incestuous relationship of the oedipal constellation (Klein, 1932; Parens, 1988). In this way twins may use the gratification of the twinship to delay or avoid the resolution of the oedipal conflict (Engel, 1975). However, the more narcissistic aspects of the twin relationship are a major factor in the sexual phantasies and enactment in twins. In this respect it is interesting to note that the psychoanalytic literature reports more same-sex than opposite-sex phantasies and enactment of the incest phantasies.

Heterosexual and homosexual investigation of siblings based on sexual curiosity is a common childhood experience and it is difficult to distinguish it from brother–sister or same-sex incestuous relationships. I will follow Luzes (1990) in using the term 'incest' to cover 'coital relations or imitations of coitus, orogenital contacts, mutual masturbation, etc.' (p. 99), on the basis that whatever the sexual activity enacted, the underlying phantasy is an incestuous one. Unlike parent–child incest, a degree of childhood sexual exploration and experimentation is variably tolerated or even permitted in different families and cultures. However, actual sexual relationships between siblings are usually regarded as taboo.

Incestuous phantasies and the enactment of these phantasies between children in either homo- or heterosexual mode may begin early in life with mutual autoerotic stimulation (as described in Bill and Bert, below). Although sexual activity between siblings as children is widespread (Klein, 1932), it generally receives scant attention in the psychoanalytic literature or is noted only in passing. Accounts of actual adult sibling incest are rarely reported in psychoanalytic case material although sibling incest in adults is a common theme in mythology and general literature. Sibling incest is not generally regarded as a significant factor in the same way as parent–child incest is, or with the same horror, even where vaginal and anal penetration has occurred. This suggests that the sibling incest taboo is not applied to younger children but is activated as they approach adulthood, and the incestuous phantasies would remain repressed. However, this does not mean that sibling incest may not be as damaging as parent–child incest, as Klein (1932) notes.

Sexual touching and activity in children may be a normal form of exploratory behaviour and may not be symptomatic of difficulties. Klein (1932) notes that children are concerned with touching and being touched, and sexual activities between children are therefore important in the child's development towards its sexual life and personality. However, childhood sexual activity may become compulsive where it is linked with anxiety and feelings of guilt. The associated phantasies would shape the nature of the sexual activity engaged in by a child. Klein suggests that childhood sexual activity is based on sadistic masturbation phantasies and that these phantasies not only shape the sexual activity, but they also generate intense guilt. The associated guilt is reduced as the child's capacity for sublimation develops when the sexual impulses advance to the genital level.

Klein suggests that sexual relations between children are the rule in early childhood and are more common in latency and puberty than is commonly supposed. Sexual relations are only prolonged into the latency period and puberty where the child's sense of guilt is excessive and has not been sufficiently worked over. Ordinarily, sexual activities with other children including siblings are too realistic an enactment of the child's incestuous and sadistic desires to be continued through the latency period. During puberty, we move away from these incestuous sibling relationships as we detach ourselves from our incestuous objects and develop relationships with new objects.

The effect of incestuous childhood sexual activity on the development of children involved will depend on the nature of the impulses that underlie the phantasies. If positive and libidinal factors predominate, the childhood sexual relationship will have a favourable influence on the development of the child's object relationships and capacity for love. But the whole development of the child may be gravely impaired where destructive impulses and acts of coercion by one child in relation to the other predominate (Klein, 1932).

Mythical stories about incestuous relationships between twins abound (see Graves, 1992; Lash, 1993; Larousse Encyclopedia of Mythology, 1959). Luzes (1990) recounts a Melanesian story about brother–sister incest in which the incestuous siblings are overcome with shame and remorse at what they have done and retire to a grotto where they die of starvation and thirst. An aromatic herb grows out of their entwined skeletons and extracts of this herb form the basis of the magic of love.

Using this myth as central to his argument, Luzes suggests that it is incestuous love between siblings that is at the heart of sexual attraction, rather than the oedipal drama. Sibling incestuous phantasies are retained as a potent memory like the aromatic drug in the myth. Brother–sister incest, which is more common than oedipal themes in mythology and literature, would represent the central incest relationship in the unconscious world. The sibling-incest phantasy is not dependent on the actual experience of sexual contact between siblings of different sexes. It is based instead on narcissistic phantasies in relationships in which there is a blurring of boundaries between self and other, and on phantasies in which there is a similarity between self and other. The phantasy underlying sibling incest may represent a wish either for fusion of the sexes, or to possess the attributes of both sexes (echoing the Platonic myth). The wish for a twin and the phantasy of an imaginary companion would also be included. Mitchell (2000) echoes Luzes's idea that brother–sister incest is pre-oedipal or proto-oedipal and therefore dyadic in nature.

The place that sibling incest phantasies occupy in the internal world is thus variably allocated in different theories. Klein (1932) links children's masturbatory and inter-sibling sexual experiences with oedipal phantasies and sadistic impulses, and suggests that under normal conditions these activities diminish or cease with the waning of the oedipal conflict. They would persist only where excessive anxiety and guilt prevents their resolution. Luzes (1990) suggests instead that inter-sibling incestuous phantasies persist and are the basis of later love relationships. Parens (1988) suggests that inter-sibling erotic activity is an avoidance of the 'greater threat of fantasied *parental* incestuous gratifications' (Parens, 1988: 38) and that erotic attachments between siblings would usually dissipate. Normally they would be displaced by and transformed into peer sexual phantasies. However, sibling incestuous activity may persist where intrapsychic conflicts hamper such development.

What is common to all these views about sibling and twin incestuous phantasies and behaviour is the fact that siblings occupy an important place in the internal world of object relationships and would affect the development of later sexual relationships, particularly the intimate relationships of adult pairing in marital and other partnerships.

Sexual behaviour in children might also serve a protective function. Burlingham (1963) notes that normal autoerotic activity in children limits the extent to which environmental objects impinge on the child and would give the child a sense of independence. However, observations on Bill and Bert, the twins described in Chapter 4 that were so closely studied and followed from the nursery through school and later life (Burlingham, 1952, 1963), highlight the destructiveness of the 'autoerotism in partnership' (Burlingham, 1963: 406) that the twin pair created. As infants, activity to excite the other twin and be excited by him replaced normal autoerotic activity for both twins and led to a higher than usual degree of stimulation. In addition to the excitement of each twin, the excitement of the twin partner was a further seduction and it incited each twin to increasing abandonment to the autoerotic activity between them. Eventually, both twins would become intensely agitated to an overwhelming degree. Later, as adolescents, they showed openly homosexual elements in their behaviour towards each other. It was observed that when they were physically close, they always touched each other, either in a friendly or a hostile manner.

Case studies of twin incest

Several psychoanalytic accounts uncover the sadistic phantasies associated with sexual activity in twins and the way in which it echoes the narcissistic relationship between them.

In the simultaneous analysis of twin brothers, Joseph (1959) and Joseph and Tabor (1961; see Chapter 5) describe a twin relationship in which the twins engaged in overt homosexual activity including anal penetration and fellatio. The analysis revealed the sadistic phantasies of the parental intercourse that were associated with this sexual activity. I will use aspects of the analysis of one of these twin brothers to explore the phantasies underlying their sadistic incestuous activity.

Joseph (1959) reports that the patient had a phantasy that intercourse with a woman was dangerous because his penis would be nipped off and she would keep it inside her until her next period. Her bleeding would then be both from her own body and from the bloody stump of his penis, so that by bleeding she would lose the stolen penis. This phantasy emerged in the analysis at a time when the patient's mother had been robbed of her jewels in a burglary. The patient reported feeling sympathy with father rather than with mother – he felt that it was father's loss, not mother's. He believed mother had squeezed and extorted the jewels out of father, 'out of his life's blood' (Joseph, 1959: 191) over the years, and that father had been helpless to resist mother's demands. Thus it seems the patient believed that mother had robbed father of his penis – his jewels.

The twins were described as 'inseparable' (Joseph, 1959: 191), having been born 3.5 minutes apart. Joseph's patient was more submissive than his twin and more feminine in orientation, identifying with mother. His twin was identified with father and was regarded by the twins as superior. The homosexual activity between the twins represented the confusion of identities between them as they sought to be united. The phantasy of the *vagina dentata* described above is an indication of the sadistic nature of the incestuous phantasies of the patient, and of the mutual feelings of hostility and guilt between the twins. In their urge to re-unite, Joseph's patient referred to his twin as his 'cock and balls' (Joseph, 1959: 193), which he could acquire by taking them inside himself. On the other hand, the closeness and the lack of perceived difference between the twins also generated intense hostility between them, which they enacted in their incestuous activity.

In another description of incestuous activity between twins, Lacombe (1959) reports on the analysis of an MZ twin male (described in Chapter 7). He and his twin practised mutual masturbation, with one twin playing the male, the other the female part in the sexual encounter. The patient believed that a twin was half-man, half-woman. The twin brothers would sometimes double date and exchange girls in the dark, thus expressing their inter-changeability, the primary closeness of the twin bond as compared with attachments to others, and a homosexual longing for each other. The analysis also uncovered the fact that the patient had stolen his twin's girlfriend and married her.

A common phantasy in twins is that of sexual activity in utero. Glenn (1966) reports an analysis of a male twin who described his phantasy of having an incestuous relationship with his twin sister in the womb. The sadistic nature of the phantasies underlying this belief was exposed in his belief that his sister had robbed him, leaving him incomplete with only half a penis. The patient wished to recapture the half-penis he believed his twin sister had stolen from him. He confused his wife and his twin sister and often called his wife by his sister's name. Like the *vagina dentata* phantasies described by Joseph (1959) above, Glenn's patient believed his sister/wife had a tooth-like structure inside her vagina that would clip off his penis. His sexual life was affected by this phantasy. He could only offset the imagined dangers of this twin-intercourse phantasy if during intercourse with his wife, he imagined having sex with an older post-menopausal woman who 'no longer had clippers' (Glenn, 1966: 740) in her vagina. Another mechanism that he believed enabled him to avoid this danger was to tell his wife a story – as if the story added to the size of his penis so that he need no longer envy his wife/twin her half-penis. The patient had masturbated from the age of 13, sometimes looking in the mirror while doing so, so as to be able to see his own anus. Seeing his mirror image in this way reflected his wish to see his twin sister whose presence so aroused him sexually.

Commenting on the above material, Jacobson (1965) suggests that Glenn's patient protected himself from the temptation of a heterosexual incestuous phantasy by believing that his twin sister had a penis. If she possessed a penis, she would be converted into a homosexual object. Evident in this material is the patient's experience of a confusion of identity with his twin sister and a wish to be intimately reunited with her, but also a terror of their mutual intimacy which is phantasized as a mutilating experience. His phantasies of a sadistic intercourse with his twin sister indicate the damage he anticipates in a union, whether with his wife or twin sister, and indicate the damage he feels he has suffered in being a twin. This case material also demonstrates that it is not only MZ twins or even same-sex twins who form so close an identity and who may serve as homosexual or narcissistic love objects for each other.

The pre-oedipal nature of the twin incest and its enduring nature in adult life are described by Abraham (1953). In her record of an analysis with a woman who had phantasies of an incestuous relationship with her twin brother, Abraham notes that the twin may be the primary object, with mother occupying a secondary position. Abraham suggests that when they were children, the patient and her twin brother enacted a narcissistic, pre-oedipal encounter in their predominantly anal and phallic sex play. The incestuous activity was an expression of the girl's wish for a penis rather than representing a genital object relationship. As an adult, the patient tended to act in such a way as to provoke men to the point of danger of forceful penetration. Abraham suggests that in so doing the patient was enacting a phantasy of an incestuous relationship in utero with her twin brother. The patient frequently dreamed of an incestuous relationship with her twin brother.

For a time the patient lived with her twin brother and his wife. In her sister-in-law's absence, the patient and her twin would use the bathroom together, naked, 'as they were naked and together inside her mother'

(Abraham, 1953: 225). She moved out of her twin brother's home only when his wife became pregnant (one year after her analysis began), i.e. when her rival twin had presented proof that the patient's desired union with her twin was not an exclusive relationship. Abraham draws attention to the fact that the incestuous phantasies of her patient were based on a pre-oedipal phantasy of gaining a penis through intercourse with her twin, and in so doing, of being made whole. The narcissistic nature of this phantasy is indicative of the narcissistic involvement of the twin pair, whether same- or opposite-sex.

As noted above, although sibling incest is generally regarded as less damaging than parent–child incest, where twins have become enmeshed in an exciting mutually autoerotic relationship, like Bert and Bill (see p.189), they will have great difficulty moving on to more socially appropriate, non-incestuous relationships. This is especially so given the narcissistic nature of the phantasies and sexual encounters of incestuous twin couples.

Literature sometimes provides us with the clearest examples of the internal dynamics of particular states of mind. In this vein, Mann (1905), in 'The Blood of the Volsungs', describes with depth and clarity the intensity and exclusivity of the twin relationship, leading to an incestuous encounter. I will summarize the story below. Although there are many levels to understanding this story, including racial issues, I will focus only on the aspects of the entwined twinship.

In an echo of Wagner's twin brother and sister in *The Valkyrie*, Mann tells the story of Siegmund and Sieglind, childlike 19-year-old twins who had been largely sheltered from the outside world. Despite the presence of Sieglind's fiancée, the twins are exquisitely wrapped up in each other, touching and fondling each other in persistent sensuous play. They are very much alike in appearance. Siegmund feels Sieglind has been 'at his side since the dawn of memory' (Mann, 1905: 165), while she regards him as her lord and master. All their activity is evocative of a deep twinship separated from a hostile external world, but united in 'loving each other for the sake of their exquisite futility' (Mann, 1905: 165). Their lives are empty and incomplete.

A week before Sieglind is due to marry the twins go together to see Wagner's *Valkyrie* at the opera. On their return from the opera, Siegmund retires petulantly to his room. He gazes at himself in the mirror and then at Sieglind who has just entered the room, and he is comforted by the feeling that she is just like him. They both felt that they had reached new depths with each other. Then,

> She kissed him on his closed eyes; he kissed her on her throat under the lace of her bodice. They kissed each other's hands. Each loved the other with sweet sensuality for their pampered and precious elegance and their good fragrance. They breathed in the sweet scent with voluptuous and careless self-abandonment, coddling themselves with it like egoistic individuals, seeking intoxication as people do who have lost all hope, lost in caresses that exceeded their bounds and turned into a hurried turmoil and finally no more than a sobbing (Mann, 1905: 178).

The incestuous encounter is an act of revenge, not only on the fiancée who is about to separate the twins, but also on the hostile outside world. It is an enactment of the incestuous bond between these twins in an attempt to realize to the full their twin relationship before it is ruptured by Sieglind's marriage a week later.

Twins in marital and parental relationships

The tendency for twins to form twinships with other people in their lives (including their analysts) has been recognized by many psychoanalysts, including Arlow (1960); Glenn (1966); Joseph (1959); and Joseph and Tabor (1961), amongst others. This 'twinning' reaction has been observed to be endemic in twins and it is based on the internalized twin relationship in addition to the ubiquitous twinning between infant and breast (Chapter 1). As I have argued, the relationship with a twin may be a primary develomental relationship and it will certainly have profound effects on the development of each individual twin. The enduring nature of the internal twin relationship and the effects that twinship has on individual development would affect all object relational bonds, and most especially those that are most intimate. As Ablon et al. (1986: 243) note,

> Every twin, except those separated at birth, grows up with an object tie with his twin, auxiliary in addition to the primary object tie with his mother and father. For both identical and fraternal pairs, this strong object relationship between the two is likely to affect ego and superego development.

Thus, even where the twin relationship is regarded as auxiliary or secondary to the primary relationships with the parental objects, the effects on development of being a twin are acknowledged.

In psychoanalytic case material, the effect on a marriage where one spouse is a twin is usually mentioned only in passing. It seems that whereas psychoanalytic theory places maternal and paternal transference relationships centrally in marital and other partnerships, the twin transference relationship is regarded as more peripheral. Given the importance of the twin relationship to the twin, this seems to me to be an important oversight. This would be especially so where the twins retain a strong narcissistic link. I have come across a number of situations in which the twin relationship has profoundly affected the marital relationship.

It is not uncommon for the marital couple to adjust the marital partnership to include a third member - the excluded twin. One example of this, recorded by Abraham (1953), has been described above. In some situations the twinship is felt to be a closer and more important relationship to the twin than the marriage, and this may lead to a breakdown of the marriage. As I will outline below, the nature of marital relationships is always complex, and for twins, alongside the oedipal components, the twin relationship may play a major role.

The following vignette is an example of both the marital difficulties that twins may encounter and a trans-generational twin entanglement: Mrs R is a DZ twin, the 'younger' of the pair. At birth Mrs R's twin sister was small and undernourished and was therefore breast-fed, while Mrs R, the stronger baby, was bottle-fed. Mrs R believed her mother loved the smaller twin more than her and this had always been a source of considerable pain to her. The twins' mother died when they were in their mid-twenties. They were both devastated and it seems they were unable to mourn their mother and instead turned to each other for comfort.

Both twin sisters married unhappily and kept in close contact with each other. Mrs R and her husband were in persistent conflict in the marriage over her attachment to her twin sister. Her husband felt he was excluded from a close relationship with his wife by her relationship with her twin. He loathed the twin sister, not because of her personality, but because he felt that she interfered in their marriage. He had always to fight to separate the twins so as to secure a place for himself in his wife's orbit.

The twin sisters were like a couple, neither of whom could have a successful relationship with a man from which the other twin was excluded. Mrs R's twin sister married unhappily and moved abroad, where she lived for many years. The twin sisters always took their holidays together despite living quite some distance apart. Mrs R and her husband repeatedly separated and then reunited, seemingly unable to be happy either apart or together. Throughout her marriage, Mrs R had a long-term affair, tolerated by her husband who in turn also had affairs. Mrs R's twin sister eventually divorced her husband.

When Mrs R's children had left home, her twin sister moved into the marital home, where the husband, wife and wife's twin live as a threesome. There has been both marital harmony and twin reunion ever since. Mrs R's marriage improved continuously with the establishment of her twin sister in the marital home, and Mrs R believes her twin has stabilized her marriage. Her husband is calmer and more secure and as a result has become a happy and generous person. In their reunion, the twin sisters bicker all the time but are inseparable. They read the same books, have the same friends and carry out the same activities. They have, in the words of one of their daughters, reverted to their primary relationship.

The developmental effects on the children of having a parent who is a twin may also be profound. Where the twin parent is still developmentally attached to and preoccupied with the twin, the attention paid to the child would be reduced. As described in Chapter 10, a reduced capacity for parental containment for whatever reason would affect the child developmentally, particularly as regards affectional relationships. The nature of the child's internal parental couple will be shaped in a marriage where the actual parental couple is interfered with by the twin relationship. In some situations where the twin couple, not the marital couple, is foremost, this interferes with the ordinary boundaried development of the child. Glenn (1986) notes that having a parent who is a twin creates a situation conducive to the child developing a phantasy of being a twin.

Miss N is the 38-year-old daughter of Mrs R (above). She expressed her feeling that her mother is married to her twin sister rather than to her father. Thus the mother–twin sister couple have supplanted the parental couple in both her external and her internal world. Mother's twin sister is exciting and imaginative but flighty, and is dependent on Miss N's mother for her stability. Mother in contrast is depressed and needy, and lives through her twin sister's vitality. As a young child, when mother's twin moved abroad, Miss N became mother's confidante, replacing mother's twin.

As an adult, Miss N is a lively engaging woman with a great interest and commitment to her work in a creative sphere. However, she is unable to sustain an intimate, loving, long-term relationship. After her marriage to a distant, unavailable man ended, Miss N moved from one intense but unsuitable relationship to another, sometimes with married men. She seems unable to find a stable partner who could satisfy her emotional needs.

Miss N feels extremely close to her mother and she describes the relationship with her mother as the most successful and intense relationship in her life. No other relationship matches it and she believes that the intensity and dependency of this entwined mother–daughter relationship has adversely affected her relationships with men. Mother lives vicariously through her daughter's affairs, as she had previously lived vicariously through her twin sister. It is as if Miss N has become mother's exciting twin sister. Miss N is so harmoniously twinned with her mother that she feels profoundly grateful to her mother and does not feel the need to seek a dependent relationship anywhere else. Miss N believes that if she were seriously involved in a relationship with a man, mother would feel excluded – like an excluded twin.

The trans-generational effects of being a twin are evident in this material, as is the effect of the twin relationship on the marital relationship.

Comparative research on parenting by twins raises some interesting ideas. Sandbank and Sandbank (2001) report their findings into research on parenting patterns in twins. They note that an MZ twin parent tended to respond positively towards a child who was helpful and affectionate, and the researchers suggest that this may mirror the twin relationship. They also found that twin parents did not regard self-sufficiency in their children as an attractive attribute. The control group, in contrast, did not uniquely favour any attribute in a child. The authors suggest that twins frequently regard the relationship with their twin as their closest relationship. This was most prominent in MZ twins, and the authors suggest that MZ twin parents do not have a sufficiently developed sense of identity to cope with confident children. They also found that an MZ twin parent was more competitive with their children than a DZ twin parent. They conclude rather obviously that being a twin affects parenting.

Several authors elucidate the way an emotionally incestuous relationship between the twins becomes enacted in the marital relationships, and also in parent–child relationships. In the simultaneous analysis of a pair of twins, Joseph and Tabor (1961) note that the twin patients were engaged in an extremely enmeshed twinship with a diffuseness of ego boundaries between the pair (see Chapter 5). When one twin married, recognizing 'his need to be joined with someone else' (Joseph and Tabor, 1961: 280), his expectation was that his wife would be a twin. However he was disappointed to find that she was different, and that she refused to twin with him. This did not affect his own phantasies of being twinned with his wife. He identified with her pregnancy, and experienced birth phantasies accompanied by bodily sensations.

The patient likewise identified with his newborn infant. As an example of how the twinship affected his personal development, at one point he had a phantasy that all people were twins, 'mother and father were a twin pair, and the older brother was a twin who had incorporated his twin. This, he felt, accounted for the brother being larger than either he or his twin' (Joseph and Tabor, 1961: 282). The second twin analysed used his secretary as a replacement twin and although he did not marry her, he felt guilty when he went out with other girls. He was bitterly opposed to his twin brother's marriage, and in his intense jealousy, he tried to win him back into the twinship.

In another case in which a twin patient was twinned with his son, Lacombe (1959) reports that the patient treated his son as brutally as he wished to treat his twin brother. I have described in Chapter 7 the way in which the patient psychically annihilated his twin brother. He also 'stole' his twin brother's girlfriend and married her. Orr (1941) reports on Cronin's (1933) analysis of young male adult twins who started analysis because their shared love object, the wife of one and the mistress of the other, threatened to leave them. They lived in a triangular relationship, with the wife/lover deciding each night which twin she would sleep with. Orr continues cryptically 'but she also came to analysis, and after about two years all three were much better adjusted' (Orr, 1941: 286). Orr attributes the triangular relationship to homosexual phantasies in the twins that they satisfied through sharing a common love object.

Looking at the trans-generational issues related to being a twin, Coen and Bradlow (1982) describe the analysis of a single male patient whose mother had a twin brother. Mother and her twin brother were left in an orphanage at the age of two after their father had died. The authors assume that intense twinning occurred between the young twins at this time. The patient experienced his mother as craving for him to fill and complete her, to replace her lost love objects (a dead father, dead sister), but most especially her twin brother who was no longer close to her. The patient was afraid that his mother would not survive his separation from her.

This twinning was reflected in the analysis and the patient was extremely upset at his analyst's separateness. In an attempt to deny this separateness, the patient so identified with his analyst that he began to impersonate him. He had phantasies of making a complete complementary fit with his analyst as if together they would make one unit. This reflected his wish to become an enmeshed twin with his mother-analyst, to replace all her needed objects by totally occupying her womb.

Coen and Bradlow locate the root of the patient's phantasies of having a twin in the fact that mother was a twin who, in a depressed state about her lost objects, had used her son in a twin-like role. In the authors' view, the major mode of relating to mother is one that is learned, in this case the learning of a twin role. As previously noted (Chapter 1), they explore the role of an imaginary twin in fending off the loneliness and depression of oedipal encounters. Importantly they differentiate the common phantasy of having a twin from a stable, persistent, central twinship paradigm as a model of intrapsychic relations between self and object.

Thus the twin-like relationship with mother became a permanent feature of the patient's mode of relating to others, in the same way as does an actual twinship. I would add that perhaps the patient not only learned to relate to his mother as a twin, but that the development of his internal object relationships was based on a rather narcissistic mother who as a twin felt incomplete and preoccupied with her twin rather than her infant. She engaged her infant son in a narcissistic twin relationship to compensate herself for her missing objects, particularly her twin brother. This profoundly affected the development of the patient's capacities. In common with the presence of an actual twin, the stable central twinship paradigm described in this case would be embedded in the nature of the patient's early affectional bond with his mother, and hence in the development of the cortico-limbic structures of his brain (see Chapter 10).

In a tragic account, Kogan (1995) describes the analysis of a woman whose mother, a twin, was a survivor of Auschwitz. Grandmother, mother and mother's twin sister were all transported to the camp, but the twins were rescued by nuns while mother perished in the camp. The twins were separated and brought up in different homes. Eventually mother and her twin were taken to Israel and grew up in an orphanage for children who had survived the Holocaust. The mother's twin sister became an invalid following an operation many years later, and it seemed that the cause of her invalidity was emotional rather than physical, perhaps representing the severely damaging traumata of her life.

The analysis of the daughter of the twin mother exposed the phantasy that she was her mother's twin sister, in a pathological twinship in which it seemed that one twin could only survive by killing the other. The patient identified with the battered, abused Holocaust child-mother and felt unable to separate herself from this phantasy, to mourn and develop, because she believed that to do so would repeat mother's history and result in a dead mother. The life and death struggle with the mother-twin was thus based on a lack of separateness and a difficulty in mourning, as a result of which the patient was unable to sustain loving relationships with men. The patient also twinned with the analyst-mother, and this was recognized and interpreted.

The twinning with mother was thus partly based on identification with mother's traumatic experiences that also left the patient damaged as a mother to her own child. It is noteworthy that in this record of an apparently successful analysis, although the daughter regarded herself as taking the place of mother's damaged twin, little attention was paid to the fact that mother was an actual twin. The terrible experiences and damage in the mother's history would of course be a central focus of the developmental difficulties in the children. However, mother would also have been affected developmentally by the fact that she was a twin, that she and her twin survived while their mother perished, and that her twin sister was obviously damaged by her experiences. This would also have influenced her relationship with her daughter, as was evidenced in the report of the analysis. This is another example where the issues relating to twinship are often given little attention.

Twins face difficulties, as do borderline patients (Steiner, 1990a), in mourning their lost objects. They are reluctant to relinquish control over their objects and, consequently, they fail to experience true separateness. The projected parts of the self are bound with the object containing them in a complex structure, creating a rigid organization. This enmeshed structure will have to be gradually dismantled before the twin object can be recognized as separate, and relinquished and mourned. Guilt and mental pain would be experienced as disowned parts of the self are regained and the ego is enriched.

The inability to mourn and separate from primary objects would affect the individual's development of a capacity to form mature love objects (Kogan, 1995). Where a twin has been used as a primary object, it creates an enduring alliance between the two, whether the pairing is twin–twin or twin parent–child. The capacity to love another outside the twinship would be variously impaired depending on the degree of entanglement in the twinship and hence of the developmental difficulties in the twin pair.

Siblings of twins

Twins may create jealousy and anxiety in their siblings, particularly as the twins tend to generate a greater than usual fuss around them (Burlingham, 1952). The twins may be exclusive of their other siblings in their twin relationship, creating difficulties for siblings of twins. Joseph (1975) reports on a patient who had twin siblings and who believed that she was the only one in the family who was alone. The patient longed to be united with someone, to be a pair, like all the others in the family.

The significance of the twin relationship for the siblings of twins is another area that has been largely neglected. Bernstein (1980) notes that twins stir in their singleton siblings an intensified longing for a twin, a longing to be a united couple, as the twins appear to be. The twins would represent for a single sibling a concretization of the universal longing for a twin (discussed in Chapter 1). The siblings of twins are greatly affected by the 'impenetrable mystery' (Bernstein, 1980: 143) of the twins' intimacy. Bernstein describes her findings that in the analysis of siblings of twins, the singleton siblings searched incessantly for a twin. The universal difficulties of separating and the complex feelings around the oedipal conflict were intensified in the siblings of twins. She concludes, 'The actual experience of having twin siblings is for the most part, painful and fateful for the nature of future object choices' (Bernstein, 1980: 136).

The difficulties siblings of twins encounter are reflected in the transference. Bernstein noted that these patients created a twinship with their analyst. She suggests they are so identified with the twins and so wish to be a twin that they relate to others as if a twin. While twins envy their singleton siblings for their individual completeness and sense of clear identity, singletons envy their twin siblings for having an actual longed-for imaginary twin. For siblings of twins, ordinary sibling rivalry is intensified and singleton siblings may have an urgent wish to replace the twins.

Chapter 12
Till death us do part

The death of a twin

The death of one twin would be a considerable loss not only to the parents, but especially to the surviving twin, whatever the age of the twins or the nature of the twin relationship. When one twin has died at or near birth, the surviving twin has a particularly difficult developmental task. Although a twin relationship creates additional developmental obstacles for an infant, the death of the other twin would not have freed the surviving twin from a possibly difficult twinship. It would instead have added an additional developmental burden in that the dead twin may carry powerful projections linked with life and death, survival and revenge in the phantasies of the survivor. These phantasies would be omnipotently controlled by the surviving twin and could not be tested against the external reality of a present twin. In analytic work, the dead-twin phantasies would become active in the transference.

The infant has been together with its twin from the beginning and the twins interact from early on in the pregnancy (Piontelli 1989, 2002). It is unclear when the foetus becomes conscious of the other twin. However, the pattern of relating between twins has been observed by Piontelli to persist after birth, and as discussed in Chapter 10, the experience would be laid down in the neural substrate along with the affectional bond to the mother. Where both twins survive the birth, the infants face separation from both mother and twin. Where one of the twins dies, the surviving newborn baby will experience not just separation from, but an absence of, the other twin, as well as a grieving mother and father. Both the survivor guilt of the live twin and its confusion of identity with the dead twin would be likely to affect the personality development of the infant (Lewis and Bryan, 1988).

The parental reaction to the surviving baby is likely to be mixed. Lewis and Bryan (1988) note, 'Death at birth or in the womb, though natural events, seem contradictory and against the natural order of life. When birth and death are fused not only hurt and bitter disappointment but confusion and unreality are felt' (Lewis and Bryan, 1988: 1321). This complexity is especially acute when a twin dies during pregnancy or soon after birth. The birth is an event not only to be celebrated; it is also laden with mourning and loss. There may be an increasing polarization of feelings. The surviving baby may seem more precious to the parents, but there is also ample scope for idealization of the dead baby with the consequent difficulty in fully accepting the survivor. Even where the surviving twin is welcomed, the parents will also be preoccupied with the dead baby and with their loss. Their attention is divided by contradictory feelings. The painful emptiness of the stillbirth contrasts with the mother's increasing emotional commitment to the live baby. The missing twin is always present in the reflection of the surviving twin.

'Birth myths', i.e. the stories that are woven around the births of all babies, are also very important to the surviving twin's sense of acceptance or rejection by the parents, and to the infant's tolerance of feelings of guilt and anxiety in relation to the death of the twin. The surviving baby does not yet have the capacity to deal with the traumatic event of the death of its twin and its grieving parents. It is not able to resolve the conflict created by the triumph of its survival and the death of its twin, nor can it mourn its loss. The surviving twin can only deal in a very rudimentary way with these issues. The infant is greatly dependent on the parents to enable it to emerge from this complex situation without feeling extremely persecuted and perhaps fragmented. But the parents have such conflicting feelings themselves at this time, that the situation is inherently fraught with difficulty.

It is common for each twin to be referred to as 'the twin', whether or not they have both survived, and surviving twins may well resent being regarded as a singleton (Case, 1993). The enduring twinship exists not only in the twins themselves, but also in the perception of others, most notably their parents. After the death of one twin, parents have described feeling upset and angry if the surviving twin is referred to as a singleton (Swanson, 2001). In response to the question, 'When is a twin not a twin?', Swanson states categorically, 'NEVER'. Thus it is important for the surviving twin's development of a sense of self that both the birth stories and the parental attitude in talking to the surviving child reflect the fact that the other twin has died.

It is common for a surviving twin to create and maintain a phantasy twin to replace the lost twin. While other conscious childhood phantasy twins tend to disappear,[1] the phantasy of the dead twin would remain a potent object relationship for the survivor. It may be used either as a developmental refuge to protect the surviving twin from its painful experience of loss and the perhaps unmanageable anxiety about the loss, or it may be employed as an aid to mourning and further development. Frequently such phantasy twins may be felt to be, and are spoken to as if they are, actually present (Arlow, 1960; Case, 1993; Engel, 1975).

The dead-twin phantasy would be expressed in the transference, in common with any other internal twin relationship. I have found that the

---

[1] See Chapter 1.

resistance by the surviving twin patient to interference in this internal twinning with a dead phantasied twin may be even more powerful than when the other twin is still alive. The surviving twin may regard the dead-twin phantasy as part of their survival structure in a psychic retreat against fears of annihilation, of non-being like the twin who has died. Relinquishing the dead-twin phantasy and mourning the lost twin involves the survivor in facing feelings of guilt in relation to the dead twin, and demands an ability to tolerate what must be a terrifying sense of aloneness. Where one twin feels that it has survived only at the expense of the other twin, the analytic twin may be rigidly controlled and not allowed to live or think independently.

The creation of a phantasy twin in a dead-twin refuge

In the following excerpt from my own work with a surviving twin, the patient sought an uninterrupted analytic twinship that would eliminate all the pain of loss of his twin, while living out the life and death relationship with his transference twin. As a transference twin, I was to him the embodiment of his phantasy dead twin.

Mr McD was a 38-year-old man whose twin sister had died at birth. He came from a wealthy upper class family in Scotland and was largely brought up by nannies. He had a brother five years older but they were never close as both boys were sent away to school at an early age. The parents were emotionally distant from their children and seem to have had little awareness or understanding of their needs.

Mother had felt unwell throughout her pregnancy with the twins. When the twins were born and his twin sister died, mother withdrew from her surviving baby boy and seemed to become a rather shadowy figure. The 'birth myth' was that Mr McD had 'taken too much', although it became apparent that his twin sister had a congenital heart defect as a result of which she was small, had failed to develop adequately, and was unable to survive. He believed he had taken more sustenance than he needed thus depriving his twin sister of her life. He phantasized that had he taken less, she would have had more, would have developed properly, and hence would have survived. He thus felt himself to be responsible for her death, and he lived in constant fear of discovery of his crime and the retribution it would draw.

This central life and death dynamic was acted out in the transference. Mr McD felt that he had to sacrifice himself for a dead-twin-analyst to try to assuage his guilt. He felt that there was nothing he could safely take for himself without consequent punishment. He dared not allow himself to feel he was benefiting from the analytic work, and he negated any gains in understanding by blanking them out. He idealized the death of his twin: Mr McD believed that in dying, his twin sister had rid herself of him and of life's burdens, and lived a blissful life. In the breaks he felt that I was doing likewise. I was experienced as the twin who had died, and I consequently became the envied trouble-free twin who had abandoned him to intolerable pain. He also believed that I was in an idealized twinship with my husband who protected me and cared for me, and that we formed an ideal twin couple, as he wanted his twin-analyst to do with him.

When this phantasy had been uncovered and understood, Mr McD felt sad and he became more thoughtful in sessions. Like Bion's (1967) patient A,[2] recognition of the twinning in the transference allowed Mr McD to feel better understood and contained by my interpretations, rather than persecuted by the recognition of his intra-psychic state. The dead twin then became personified as a potent force in the transference. It seemed to Mr McD that he and I were in a struggle as to which twin would survive. He watched me closely and took every opportunity to retreat into a cold dissociated state to try to eliminate his rivalrous transference twin. But the rivalry was for life itself. This struggle was not just about abandonment or possible death, but about which of us would take the life-giving sustenance away from the other,[3] as if we were parasites feeding off each other. He felt desperate to have enough to survive each break, but unable to take what he needed because of the shadow of the twin that he had 'killed' by 'taking too much'. So he felt trapped in a paradoxical situation where he demanded a great deal of me but took in too little.[4] In this form of parasitic twin transference, it was as if the twins had to feed off each other in the absence of a mother.

As this life–death battle with his dead transference-twin was gradually better understood Mr McD began to find a maternal transference object that was not withdrawn and distant. This allowed him to become more in touch with his feelings about the loss of his twin. He became acutely aware of his loneliness without his twin and spoke of how he never felt complete, as if he had lost a part of himself. He constantly searched for his twin sister in other people, thinking that he would eventually find her in a crowd of people – at a party or on the underground.

Mr McD had romanticized the idea of twinship but was disturbed by any closeness with a dead-twin-analyst or an absent-mother-analyst. He felt that closeness would subject him to the experience of a twin who took up the space that he wanted, like a twin in utero squashing and suffocating him (a projection of his phantasy about what he did to his twin). He believed that he had to deny that his analyst had any needs because he himself was so needy that he was afraid he would take too much and thus kill me. This reflected Mr McD's wish to avoid his feelings of guilt about his dead twin and to deny her neediness. Mr McD also believed that he had killed his twin sister by the exposure of the phantasy that he wanted to get rid of his twin-analyst, and this was deeply upsetting to him. After a prolonged struggle to gain analytic understanding about these transference issues, Mr McD began to recognize

---

[2] See Chapter 5.

[3] Like Sheerin's (1991) patient, Chapter 9.

[4] Although I have not discussed here much of the detail of the dynamics of the maternal transference, it was apparent that at this time Mr McD also experienced me as the distant withdrawn mother who withheld her affection from him.

more of his internal and projected twinning and, as a result, his guilt about the death of his twin gradually lessened.

With a decrease in his feelings of guilt, Mr McD was able to acknowledge that he had created an imaginary twin to take the place of his dead twin sister. This phantasy twin was a constant presence, and when he spoke to her he both knew and did not know that she was not really present. She was a conscious construction on a base of unconscious twinning with his dead twin. Mr McD's twinship with his phantasied dead twin had acted as a refuge from contact with a maternal container. He was resistant to analytic interference in this internal twinship that protected him from pain and loss. In working towards recognizing that his twin had actually died, he felt that I was taking his phantasied twin away from him and that he now had to face the unbearable pain of loss. For the first time he became overtly angry with me for exposing him to this painful truth, instead of dissociating himself from his feelings by blanking me out.

As he gradually relinquished his dead-twin phantasy Mr McD became aware of his aggressive and angry feelings towards his dead twin sister. In his immaturity, he had been unable to mourn the loss of his twin and his guilt about 'killing her' had made this even more intolerable. To avoid these feelings, he had created a phantasy twin whom he idealized – a constant companion, under his absolute control, a twin who in his mind replaced his need for a mature container that would be separate but could also have helped him develop.

Mr McD's development towards separateness from his twin-analyst and mother-analyst evoked poignant feelings about the death of his twin. He felt he had been torn apart from his twin sister and he was extremely upset as he recognized that this was an irrecoverable loss. However, he was also aware that unlike his twin sister, both he and his twin-analyst went on living and he was able to recognize that his twin sister had died even though, and not because, he had lived. Gradually he was able to experience his profound sense of loss at the death of his twin. He also became consciously aware that his mother had been unable to help him deal with the loss of his twin, in part because of her difficulties in coping with her own grief.

Lone twins

Conscious memories of the death of a twin are not the only source of knowledge about this tragic event. As I have described in the case of Mr McD, the 'birth story' which the child learns will influence his view of himself. Joseph (1975) reports on the analysis of a patient whose twin had been born dead. He notes that although the patient had no conscious memory of her twin, the death of the twin had a developmental impact on the surviving twin. The stories the family told her about this event played an important role, 'adding to a burden of guilt derived from both the actual and psychic reality of her fantasies' (Joseph, 1975: 26).

Twins frequently deny that the other twin has died, either by creating a phantasy twin as Mr McD above did, or by simply not acknowledging the death. In either case, the surviving twin uses a process of disavowal, so the fact that the twin has died is both known and not known.[5] The loss of the twin may be profoundly painful for the surviving twin in a way that is felt to threaten their belief in their own survival. Barens (2001) describes her breakdown six months after the death of her twin sister as a young adult. She developed severe agoraphobia from which she took four years to recover. During this time, she felt that she had to face the psychic death of herself as a twin, and that she had to grow another half (representing her lost twin-self). It was as if she had to take on the characteristics of her dead twin, and felt taken over or inhabited by her. She describes feeling unsafe in a very primitive way, saying that she had panic attacks in which she could not breathe and feared that she, like her twin, would die. She had felt protected when her twin was alive. Now she felt that part of her body had been hacked off.

The primitive nature of these feelings echoes the experience that I described in Chapter 8, when a twin patient faces psychic separation from the other twin. This leads to a fear of fragmentation or annihilation as the narcissistic twin membrane is ruptured. In this respect, Woodward (2001) believes that the loss of a twin is unique, and is different from the loss of another sibling. She describes a dream relating to the death of her twin (aged three and a half), that is indicative of the loss of known boundaries, a sense of loss of identity. In her dream she was hovering around a trellis, unable to get back to a safe place. Like Barens above, she too suffered from agoraphobia that she believes was a direct reaction to her terrible separation anxiety after her twin died.

Some lone twins resort to a phantasied idealized reunion with the lost twin to deny the death. Glenn (1966, 1986) takes up this idealized reunion with the dead twin in two papers. In the analysis of a woman patient whose twin brother had died two years earlier, Glenn (1966) notes that the patient was in denial about her brother's death. She had not cried at his funeral, and the day after the burial she had asked whether her brother would visit her. The patient felt that she and her twin were inseparable and that she had died with him. She believed she shared thoughts with her twin telepathically. In this fusion after death with her twin, no jealousy and hatred between them was apparent. It was as if they were now one.

In a later paper, Glenn (1986) traces the influence on the writer Thornton Wilder of the death at birth of his twin brother. Glenn uses Wilder's writings to explore the enduring nature of the twin relationship, even after the death of one twin. He describes the story of *The Bridge of San Luis Rey*, in which Wilder writes about twin brothers, one of whom dies at birth. Later, the Bridge of San Luis Rey collapses, killing the surviving adult twin – as a result of which the brothers are reunited in death.

---

[5] This process is described by Steiner (1985), as 'turning a blind eye' to the truth.

In the analysis of an MZ male twin whose twin died at the age of 18 years, Arlow (1960) explores the subjective experience of having and losing a twin. The twin brothers were so alike as infants that their mother had difficulty telling them apart. They apparently developed an enmeshed twin relationship in which their personal identities were blurred. The twins operated as a unit and behaved in a complementary manner towards each other, competing as a pair with others rather than with each other. In their teens, just at the point when the patient wished to be more separate from his brother, his twin died.

Initially, the patient denied his twin brother's death, averting his gaze from any possible proof of the fact. He talked to his twin as if he were still alive. Arlow describes how he also introjected his lost twin and incorporated his twin's initial into his own name. The patient began to suffer psychosomatic symptoms that clearly represented his phantasied incorporation of his deadly twin into his body. However, this compromise allowed him to continue to deny the death of his twin.

When an uncle died in his arms some time later, the patient suffered an emotional crisis. In his analysis it was revealed that he felt guilty about his twin's death because of his hostile wishes towards his brother and to the twinship. Thus he believed that the phantasized introjected twin was a hated and injured rival that had made him ill by his incorporation into the patient's body. Through this incorporation, the patient phantasized that his twin still lived within him and that he need not feel any guilt about him. He was afraid to relinquish his introjected dead twin because 'Expelling the introject was unconsciously equated with killing the brother again' (Arlow, 1960: 188).

In a later paper, Arlow (1976) notes that the above patient's parents were deaf-mutes. It is hardly conceivable that this factor would not have caused additional difficulties for the twins in communicating with the parents, and would have contributed to this patient's enmeshment with his twin. It is interesting that Arlow does not comment on this in the 1960 paper, although he stresses that the twins were in utero together and born together. The greater facility of communication through spoken and heard language with the twin would surely have been a significant factor in the development of the twinned relationship.

I have already written of Engel's (1975) experiences following his twin's death (Chapter 4), noting his narcissistic unconscious identification with his twin. Engel writes of his continuing identification with his twin, who died of a heart attack at the age of 49. He explores the unique aspects of the object relationship in twins, the enduring nature of the twinship, and the process of mourning after his twin had died. Engel and his brother were MZ twins, with a close, intensive but extremely rivalrous relationship, very alike in appearance and as children, 'constant and exclusive companions' (Engel, 1975: 24). They moderated their mutual aggression towards each other and operated in a highly complementary way.

On hearing of his twin's death, Engel's initial disbelief was followed by a profound confusion between himself and his twin. Almost 11 months later, Engel also suffered a coronary attack. His initial reaction was one of relief – 'the other shoe had fallen' (Engel, 1975: 25). He identified with his dead twin and even responded when called by his twin's name. In this way, he avoided his feelings of guilt about his brother's death – he had survived and his brother had not. He dreamed of their fusion of identities and his longing for a reunion with his dead twin.

Engel notes the persistence of the unconscious identity confusion in twins, even after the death of one. He suggests that attachment needs and behaviour are powerful positive forces that intensify the inter-twin relationship, solidifying the twinship. Engel sums up the effect on relationships of being and losing a twin:

> Death of a twin, even after the degree of separation and independence usually achieved by mid-life, nonetheless has special implications because of the unique developmental features of twinning. Three features in particular may influence the character of the grief response: the enduring diffuseness of the ego boundaries between self and object representations, the narcissistic gains of twinship, and the delicate balance of the defences against aggression. While many other variables undoubtedly operate these three factors must differentiate the grief experienced upon loss of a twin from that upon loss of a sibling. Siblings typically begin social relations with peers early and hence move more easily into less interdependent and more overtly rivalrous relationships than do twins. Their bonds are further loosened when they marry and raise their own families. Twin bonds are more lasting; some even make marriages based on twin object choice, even marrying twins (Engel, 1975: 34-35).

Narcissistic loss and the difficulty in mourning a lost twin

The death of a twin, especially for enmeshed twins, represents a narcissistic injury as aspects of the self are felt to be lost and the gratifications associated with the twinship are brought to an end. The process of mourning is therefore much more difficult than the loss of an object that is felt to be more separate and may perhaps be relinquished more readily. The difficulty in mourning a lost twin is an underlying theme in the following excerpts.

Both Case (1993) and Woodward (1998) have written books about the experience of the loss of a twin. While these accounts are not analytic material that can be 'tested' through exploration and interpretation, they are nevertheless illuminating about the effects of losing a twin both early and later in life.

Case (1993) quotes from a number of letters about the feelings generated by the death of a twin. I have selected some as they indicate particular aspects of the twinship and its enduring nature. The enmeshed nature of a narcissistic twinship is evident in the following:

Karrie writes,

A major part of my life and of me was laid to rest when Kathy died. For 23 years one-half of me was her, and I think it always will be. Just as a part of me is gone, a part of Kathy lives on through me (Case 1993: 18).

So, even when one twin has died, the survivor feels that the twins have not separated, indeed are not separable. Together they will always form a unit. Like Castor and Polydeuces, the twins remain forever united.

Where separation from the dead twin feels intolerable, some may seek to maintain the twinship through spiritual union with the dead twin, in denial of loss. One year after the death of her twin, Caroline describes a Narcissus-like dream in which she sees her dead twin in the flowing river. She writes:

Since Mary's death my whole world has become clouded. I have become overwhelmed with fears of isolation and abandonment. In a sense, I search for her. I surround myself with pictures, talk about her constantly, relive memories, and share every thought and prayer with her. Despite my efforts to survive, I feel that it is not natural to be physically separated from her. In fact it seems terribly wrong. I keep thinking, 'I am going to die because Mary and I must always be together'. I feel a separation from Mary that causes physical pains in my chest. On the other hand, I have never felt closer to her, as we are now joined by a spiritual bond which is unique to us (Case, 1993: 50).

Sarah's twin died in utero, four months into the pregnancy. I suspect that her experience of the loss of her twin is based mainly on her 'birth story' and the attitude of her parents. Nevertheless, she suffers intense survivor guilt, and a sense of having to live for her lost twin as well as herself. Aged 22 years, she writes:

One moment, I can feel devastatingly lonely and not be able to wait for the day when I can die to go meet him in heaven. Just to hug him and tell him how much I love him. Yet at the same time I feel so incredibly guilty for being alive, like I don't deserve it ... (Case, 1993: 63).

Like Mr McD above, it seems that Sarah has created a phantasy twin to replace the lost twin and to try and cope with her guilt and loneliness.

The denial of the loss of the twin will be at great cost to personal identity. However, mourning may enable the enrichment of the life of the surviving twin. Sandy writes:

Seventeen years have passed. As long without Karen as with her. I now realise that I've been running instead of dealing with the pain of the loss. I stopped denying the loss and I'm able to be aware of my body, opinions and thoughts. I'm now developing a life that includes Karen as a fond memory. I'm not forsaking Karen, instead I'm honoring myself and the life I have to live (Case, 1993: 28).

In a further development, Paula discovers the value of separateness after the death of her twin:

And now? Finding oneself. Knowing one's capabilities. Finding sudden joy in knowing that I could attempt something: an assignment at work, writing poems, accomplishing a new weight-loss program, all without the twin-oriented dependence. Laughter coming easily (it never did before). A new person discovering capabilities and potential never known before (Case, 1993: 42).

Both these accounts show that it is possible to achieve separation from a twin and therefore to mourn the death of the twin. There will no doubt still be a residue of the twinship, but it is possible to have a separate and continuing life after a twin has died.

Live twins have been neglected in the analysis of the transference, but twins who have died have been even more sidelined. Woodward (1998) notes that throughout her two Freudian analyses, the death of her twin sister when she was three years old was not considered as a particularly significant factor in her life. In a survey of lone twins, Woodward notes that the loss of a twin is a profound experience, having a marked effect on the life of the surviving twin. In her view, this is greatest in same-sex twins, whether MZ or DZ. She also found a significant correlation between the death of a twin before the age of six months and the experience of this loss as being 'marked' or 'severe'. Woodward attributes this finding to two factors. Firstly, when a preverbal child experiences the death of a twin, the child's ability to share the loss and make sense of it through verbal understanding is severely limited. This will affect the child's ability to grieve. 'They have no knowledge of themselves with which to understand such a loss and are engulfed with feelings' (Woodward, 1998: 3). The second factor is the child's closeness to its parents and dependence upon them. Their grief will affect how the child is received and responded to.

Woodward suggests that the surviving twin may become particularly anxious because its dependence on the parents is shaken by their inability to prevent the death of the twin. Parents may be over-protective of the surviving twin. If the parents are overwhelmed by grief for the dead twin, the survivor may feel devalued, and may indeed be neglected. Woodward explains (as in the case of Mr McD, above) that the surviving twin may feel like a 'murderer', and may also be seen as such by the mother. Those twins whose twin died later in life may seek to replace the lost twin, often seeking this within marriage. In this way they do not differ from twins where both survive, where twinship is sought with the marital partner.

It is also noteworthy that several of Woodward's accounts of the therapeutic treatment of lone twins include obvious enactments by the therapist of the transference twin. A woman whose twin sister died at birth writes:

Even when I have not talked directly about my sister with my counsellors, I am sure that being a lone twin has drastically influenced my attitude to therapy. I believe that my need for communication at a deep level is to do with me missing the opportunity that I would have had for that type of relationship with my twin (Woodward, 1998: 149).

And the enactment of this twinship:

> Occasionally during a session ... our feelings seem to merge. She feels moved to
> tears, I feel moved by her tears and it seems difficult to separate out whose
> feelings are whose. There is no need for words and we just end up hugging
> each other. I love those moments. They feel so safe and natural to me, as if that
> is how communication with other people 'should be' and I am sure I feel that
> way because I am a lone twin. I would have had shared moments of inter-
> mingled feelings with my sister in the womb and throughout my life, had she
> lived (Woodward, 1998: 150).

Obviously this woman is not referring to psychoanalytic work, but the
insistence that her counsellors become her twin comes through strongly
throughout the account. She then feels relieved when her counsellor does
enact the twinship, even though the counsellor later reasserts her individuality.

All the issues that affect twins are encountered in lone twins, regardless of
the age at which their twin dies. However, the capacity of the survivor to
separate from the dead twin and mourn the loss varies. Unconscious factors
relating to the twinship play a major part, and are an enduring factor in the
surviving twin's ability to establish a life without their twin. The lost twin
always casts a shadow on the survivor, even if the death was in utero or in the
first few months of life, before any conscious memory of the event. To what
extent this is a function of unconscious memory traces or parental input is
difficult to discern.

An adolescent lone twin

I want to end this section with a description of an analysis in which many of the
main themes of this book are evident. The presentation of this case uncovers
the developmental effects of being a twin based on both life events and birth
narratives. It is clear that the internal twinship is enduring and is used as a
psychic retreat. It takes time for the twin to emerge into the transference, and
when it does, there is a pressure on the analyst to enact rather than analyse the
transference twin in order to try and avoid primitive/psychotic anxieties.
Although the core phantasy for the patient (described below) at that point in
the analysis was the twinship, it seems that it was difficult for the analyst to give
primary position to the twinship and its effects on the analyst. While
recognizing the transference twin, he treats it rather tentatively and places
primary importance on the maternal transference.

I will describe aspects of the case material in some detail. It is a rich and
informative account of an analysis and of the difficulties encountered. I
believe the material provided by the analyst affords a possibility to make
interpretations other than those offered by the analyst. I will take the liberty
of suggesting an additional understanding of the material and I think that the
patient's responses would support this view. I think that the analyst has

recognized the central issues relating to the twin transference, but his emphasis on a maternal transference relegates this to a sub-heading.

Kennedy (1990) describes the analysis of an adolescent whose twin aborted while he continued to develop until term (we don't know at what stage the twin miscarried). Kennedy notes that the significance of this fact did not become apparent until there had been a breakdown in communication in the analysis. At the start of the analysis, the patient at times cut his skin, and this was linked with a sense that his skin was too thin to act as a barrier between himself and the world. Although the analysis started smoothly and was a lively encounter, it soon ran into difficulties. The patient found interpretations intrusive and felt they were robbing him of his individuality. Any sense of separateness and dependence was defended against by the creation of a mindless state through drug use.

As the more florid aspects of the patient's behaviour diminished, the analysis became bogged down in silence, boredom and meaninglessness. At this time the patient was aware of a wish to submerge himself in his analyst, to lose his individuality in a leech-like dependency on the analyst. Kennedy began to sense not being able to hold the thread of communications, and he felt deadened by the patient. 'It was as if Simon felt that he could not live without deadening or even destroying the other' (Kennedy, 1990: 313). Initially this was taken up in terms of the patient leaving home and fearing his parents would not survive this emotionally.

Kennedy notes, 'I began to realize that I had often experienced a fight to stay alive in the sessions, while all my "nourishment" was being taken away by some sadistic process' (Kennedy, 1990: 313), and that the patient felt he was 'living at a price' (p. 313). Kennedy then realized that the patient's 'core' disturbance was emerging and being repeated in the transference. This 'core' disturbance was centred on having survived the death of his twin in utero. In the transference Kennedy had become the dead twin or the mother preoccupied with the dead twin. This interpretation was immediately recognizable to the patient, who was relieved, and his analyst felt he had again become alive to both the patient's communications and his belief in his own understanding.

Kennedy points out that he 'had to experience the deadness for it to be a clinical phenomenon pressing to be understood' (Kennedy, 1990: 313), and that it is likely that the patient would not have made sense of the inter-pretation and reconstruction without having gone through the experience of the 'core' breakdown. He had not previously understood the significance of the dead twin material. Thus, as discussed in Chapter 5, the dead twin had to emerge into the transference before it could become a 'live' presence to be worked with. Kennedy adds that he is not suggesting that the patient actually remembered the death of the twin, but that the aborted twin was part of the patient's 'birth story' that informed and affected his emotional development.

With the experience of the 'core' phantasy (the dead twin) in the transference, recognized and interpreted by the analyst, and acknowledged by the patient, Kennedy then presents the following dream.

> He [the patient] was standing outside his parents' house, talking to a three-foot tall dwarf with incredibly well-developed muscles. As he talked to him, the dwarf shrank, becoming smaller and smaller, until he was six to seven inches high, like some sort of plastic doll, but still with incredible muscles, which the dwarf wanted Simon to inspect. The dwarf kept on talking and all his flesh disappeared, and ended up as just a few bones which were not human but the remains of someone's dinner, the bones from a lamb chop.

> He thought that the dwarf was a parody of himself – weight-lifting muscles on a small body. I took up how he felt dwarfed by me and belittled. This led on to him saying that I was the dwarf of the dream. He admired my superiority, but I was made smaller and smaller into a plastic doll, and then I was just like the remains of the dinner, nothing much left at all. I took up his (oral) devouring quality, how he stripped the food he had from me, leaving him feeling empty and only left with the scraps. This uncovered his horrifying wish to devour me, as he put it, in order to get close to me; as well as his fear that I would want to keep him with me and not let him go and get jobs and separate from me; as if I wanted him for me, so that he remain a dwarfed man with a small penis, 'an adult trapped in a child-size body', as he put it.

> In this frightening world, his fantasy was that I could only survive because of my 'good muscles'; but he then ate me up, which made him feel disgust and horror. If he took nourishment from me, it was only at the cost of survival. The more he took from the analytic feed, the smaller I became. The plastic doll may have been a reference to the dead girl twin, with whom he was identified in his presenting symptom of self-mutilation. There was also the fear of having a live communication with me. The moment he felt alive in the session, or that I was alive, he tended to cut off the discourse (Kennedy, 1990: 314).

It is important to acknowledge that the analyst, in the consulting room with his patient, is in touch with myriad clues as to the temperature and atmosphere of the transference relationship. However, it seems to me that the most obvious understanding of this dream and the patient's associations to it was relegated to an afterthought. This is an example of the twin transference being placed second to the maternal transference in the face of much evidence that at *that* time it was the 'core' transference, representing the 'core' disturbance, and that much evidence was produced by the patient to this effect. I wish to take up some aspects of the material to illustrate this.

The patient thought the dwarf in his dream was a parody of himself. I suggest he is saying that the dwarf is his twin. The analyst interpreted that the patient felt dwarfed by him, but the patient said that the analyst *was* the dwarf. Thus, taking this alternative line of thinking, the analyst would be his twin. The dwarf shrinks until he is just bones, a skeleton, a dead twin. But the analyst interprets this as the patient devouring mother in order to remain close to her, not to have to separate from her. He also suggests that the patient fears that the analyst would not let him leave and develop into an adult (a very adolescent preoccupation, but is it the dominant phantasy at the moment?). The emphasis is on the nourishing analyst/mother who will be devoured by her baby 'at the cost of his survival' (Kennedy, 1990: 314).

Then, as if an afterthought, Kennedy adds, 'The plastic doll may have been a reference to the dead girl twin with whom he was identified in his presenting symptom of self-mutilation' (Kennedy, 1990: 314). The plastic doll is described in the dream as being a stage in the disintegration of the muscular dwarf. I suggest that the muscular dwarf represents the twin who has been such a powerful influence in the patient's psychic life, and whom the patient feels he has robbed of his strength and his life in the patient's own need for survival. The dwarf-twin was then left as bones, 'not human' (Kennedy, 1990: 314), i.e. not to be born alive.

The dream seems to me to indicate a sense of competition for survival between the twins - a common twin phantasy where one has died - and this would account in part for the patient's feelings of guilt in the next dream. In the second dream the patient felt he was being blamed for something he did not do, feeling guilty, and expressing his fears about being seen to be eating. Kennedy took this up as the patient's fear of being seen to be eating because it symbolized for him taking too much from his twin, or from his mother, so that twin would not survive, making him responsible for the death of his twin. The patient then acknowledged he had a phantasy of eating up his twin. Here, Kennedy recognizes the twin transference, but he is tentative about exploring the extent and centrality of it.

The patient felt freer and became more 'alive' in his communications, with the recognition of these phantasies. I wonder about referring to the deadness created in the analyst as a breakdown in communication between patient and analyst. As Kennedy says, 'I had to experience the deadness for it to be a clinical phenomenon pressing to be understood' (Kennedy, 1990: 313). The 'live' issue that was recognized through this deadness was the dead twin. The communication was a powerful one and led to the analyst feeling deadened - a vital communication of the current 'core' transference. The 'dead transference' represented the patient's phantasy of his dead twin, as well as his relationship with a mother deadened to his needs.

Kennedy is very clear about the need to understand and interpret the transference phenomena related to early childhood, in this case the dead twin, rather than enact them. He stresses that the 'breakdown in communication' (Kennedy, 1990: 309) needs to be tolerated by the analyst and that we should not be tempted to turn to 'false' solutions such as

alterations in analytic technique or non-analytic interventions. The difficulty
needs to be worked through to give a fuller understanding of its origins and
significance. Kennedy (1990: 317) suggests that at times

> the patient communicates a quality of despair and hopelessness that appears to
> demand action by someone. The analyst may then feel that his presence in itself is
> not enough. But it is possible that he may then, if unusual interventions are
> attempted, miss an opportunity really to grasp the significance of this moment in
> the analysis and this may then merely repeat some 'basic' fault in the patient's early
> history.

I am grateful to Kennedy for providing such a full, thoughtful and clear
description of case material about a transference twin. I believe that despite
his close attention to transference issues and his adherence to the analytic
setting, he demonstrates not only the difficulty in recognizing the (dead)
twin in the transference, but also the difficulty in seeing its centrality in the
material at that time in the analysis. The tendency to take up the parental
transference rather than the twin transference is an issue that I have
addressed earlier (Chapter 5), and I believe it is an important subject that has
been much neglected. I hope this book will bring the centrality of the twin
transference to the attention of all who work psychoanalytically with twins.

References

Ablon S. L., Harrison A. M., Valenstein A. F., Gifford S. (1986) 'Special solutions to phallic-aggressive conflicts in male twins.' Psychoanalytic Study of the Child 41: 239–57.

Abraham H. (1953) 'Twin relationship and womb fantasies in a case of anxiety hysteria.' International Journal of Psycho-Analysis 34: 219–27.

Abrams S. (1980) 'Therapeutic action and ways of knowing.' Journal of the American Psychoanalytic Association 28: 291–307.

Abrams S. (1986) 'Disposition and the environment.' Psychoanalytic Study of the Child 41: 41–60.

Abrams S. and Neubauer P. (1994) 'Hartmann's vision.' Psychoanalytic Study of the Child 49: 49–59.

Agger E. (1988) 'Psychoanalytic perspectives on sibling relationships.' Psychoanalytic Inquiry 8: 3–30.

Ainsworth C. (2001) 'And then there was one.' New Scientist, 20 October.

Ainsworth M. D. S. (1967) Infancy in Uganda. Baltimore, MD: The Johns Hopkins Press.

Akhmatova A. (1959) 'The Summer Garden'. In: The Complete Poems of Anna Akhmatova. Boston, MA: Zephyr Press and London: Canongate Books Ltd, 2000.

Allen D. W. (1967) 'Exhibitionistic and voyeuristic conflicts in learning and functioning.' Psychoanalytic Quarterly 36: 546–70.

Andreas-Salomé L. (1962) 'The dual orientation of narcissism.' Psychoanalytic Quarterly 31: 1–30.

Anzieu D. (1979) 'The sound image of the self.' International Review of Psycho-Analysis 6: 23–36.

Arlow J. A. (1960) 'Fantasy systems in twins.' Psychoanalytic Quarterly 29: 175–99.

Arlow J. A. (1976) 'Communication and character – a clinical study of a man raised by deaf-mute parents.' Psychoanalytic Study of the Child 31: 139–63.

Athanassiou C. (1986) 'A study of the vicissitudes of identification in twins.' International Journal of Psycho-Analysis 67: 329–34.

Athanassiou C. (1991) 'Construction of a transitional space in an infant twin girl.' International Review of Psycho-Analysis 18: 53–63.

Bach S. (1971) 'Notes on some imaginary companions.' Psychoanalytic Study of the Child 26: 159–71.

Bandstra B. L. (1999) 'Reading the Old Testament. An introduction to the Hebrew Bible.' Wadsworth Publishing Company. www.hop.edu/academic/religion. bandstra/RTOT/RTOT/htm [3/4/02]

Barens K. (2001) 'The twin ourselves.' Olivia O'Leary interviewing Kate Barens and Joan Woodward, BBC Radio 4, 7/6/01.

Bateman A.W. (1998) 'Thick- and thin-skinned organisations and enactment in borderline and narcissistic disorders.' International Journal of Psycho-Analysis 79: 13–25.

Benjamin J. (1961) 'Interim report on a twin research.' Quoted in A. Pfeffer (1961) 'Research in psychoanalysis.' Journal of the American Psychoanalytic Association 9: 562–70.

Bernstein B. (1980) 'Siblings of twins.' Psychoanalytic Study of the Child 35: 135–54.

Bick E. (1968) 'The experience of the skin in early object-relations.' International Journal of Psycho-Analysis 49: 484–6.

Bion W. R. (1959) 'Attacks on linking.' International Journal of Psycho-Analysis 40: 308–15.

Bion W. R. (1962a) Learning from Experience. New York: Jason Aronson.

Bion W. R. (1962b) 'The psycho-analytic study of thinking.' International Journal of Psycho-Analysis 43: 306–10.

Bion W. R. (1965) Transformations. New York: Jason Aronson.

Bion W. R. (1967) 'The imaginary twin.' In: W.R. Bion (1967) Second Thoughts. Selected Papers on Psycho-analysis. New York: Jason Aronson, pp. 3–22.

Birksted-Breen D. (1996) 'Phallus, penis and mental space.' International Journal of Psycho-Analysis 77: 649–57.

Biven B. (1982) 'The role of skin in normal and abnormal development with a note on the poet Sylvia Plath.' International Review of Psycho-Analysis 9: 205–29.

Blum H. (1981) 'The forbidden quest and the analytic ideal: the superego and insight.' Psychoanalytic Quarterly 50: 535–56.

Bollas C. (1987) The Shadow of the Object: Psychoanalysis of the Unthought Known. London: Free Association Books.

Brenman E. (1993) 'Freud's "On Narcissism: An Introduction".' International Journal of Psycho-Analysis 74: 627–30.

Brett J. (1981) 'Self and other in the child's experience of language: Hofmannsthal's "Letter of Lord Chandos".' International Review of Psycho-Analysis 8: 191–201.

Britton R. (1989) 'The missing link: parental sexuality in the Oedipus Complex.' In: The Oedipus Complex Today. London: Karnac Books, pp. 83–101.

Britton R. (1998) Belief and Imagination. Explorations in Psychoanalysis. London and New York: Routledge.

Britton R. (2000) 'What part does narcissism play in narcissistic disorders?' Paper presented at the Rosenfeld Conference, Brunei Centre, London, 18 April.

Britton R. (2002). Comments. Conference on 'Second thoughts on narcissism', Tavistock Centre, London, April 20.

Brody M. (1952) 'The symbolic significance of twins in dreams.' Psychoanalytic Quarterly 21: 172–80.

Burlingham D. T. (1945) 'The fantasy of having a twin.' Psychoanalytic Study of the Child 1: 205–10.

Burlingham D. T. (1946) 'Twins – observations of environmental influences on their development.' Psychoanalytic Study of the Child 2: 61–73.

Burlingham D. T. (1949) 'The Relationship of Twins to Each Other.' Psychoanalytic Study of the Child 3: 57–72.

Burlingham D. T. (1952) Twins: A Study of Three Pairs of Identical Twins. London: Imago.

Burlingham D. T. (1963) 'A study of identical twins – their analytic material compared with existing observation data of their early childhood.' Psychoanalytic Study of the Child 18: 367–423.

Burn J. and Goodship J. (2001) 'Human clones: which side are you on?' 10th International Congress on Twin Studies, London, July.

Case B. J. (1993) Living Without Your Twin. Portland, OR: Tibbutt Publishing.

Cassorla R. M. S. (2001) 'Acute enactment as a "resource" in disclosing a collusion between the analytical dyad.' International Journal of Psychoanalysis 82: 1155–70.

Coen S. J. and Bradlow P. A. (1982) 'Twin transference as a compromise formation.' Journal of the American Psychoanalytic Association 30: 599–620.

Cohen M. (2003) Sent before My Time. A Child Psychotherapist's View of Life on a Neonatal Intensive Care Unit. London and New York: Karnac Books.

Coles P. (2002) 'The children in the apple tree: some thoughts on sibling attachment.' In Ideas in Practice. Practice of Psychotherapy Series: Book 2. Ed. B. Bishop, A. Foster, J. Klein and V. O'Connell. London and New York: Karnac Books, pp. 25–38.

Conjoined Twins (2000) www.bbc.co.uk/science/horizon/2000/conjoined.twins.transcript.shtml [10/10/02].

Corner L. (2001) 'A family affair. Music is as close as we get to ESP.' Independent, 2 July.

Cronin H. (1933). 'An analysis of the neurosis of identical twins.' Psychoanalytic Review 20: 375–87 (quoted in Lacombe, 1959).

Damasio A. (2000) The Feeling of What Happens. London: Vintage.

Davison S. (1992) 'Mother, other and self – love and rivalry for twins in their first year of life.' International Review of Psycho-Analysis 19: 359–74.

Demarest E. and Winestine M. (1955) 'The initial phase of concomitant treatment of twins.' Psychoanalytic Study of the Child 10: 336–52.

Dibble E. and Cohen D. (1981) 'Personality development in identical twins – the first decade of life.' Psychoanalytic Study of the Child 36: 45–70.

Dreger A. D. and Briggs L. (2001) 'What would it mean to think of conjoined twins as individuals? Ethical problems in the management of conjoined twinning.' 10th International Congress on Twin Studies, London, July.

Elazar D. J. (2002) 'Jacob and Esau and the emergence of the Jewish people.' www.jcpa.org/dje/articles/jacob-esau.htm [3/4/02]

Emanuel R. (2001) 'A-void – an exploration of defences against sensing nothingness.' International Journal of Psycho-Analysis 82: 1069–84.

Engel G. (1975) 'The death of a twin: mourning and anniversary reactions. Fragments of 10 years of self-analysis.' International Journal of Psycho-Analysis 56: 23–40.

Fanthorpe U. A. (2000) 'Sightings.' In: Consequences. Calstock: Peterloo Poets.

Fayek A. (1981) 'Narcissism and the death instinct.' International Journal of Psycho-Analysis 62: 309–22.

Feldman M. (1989) 'The Oedipus complex: manifestations in the inner world and the therapeutic situation.' In: The Oedipus Complex Today. Clinical Implications. London: Karnac Books, pp. 103–28.

Feldman M. (1993) 'Aspects of reality, and the focus of interpretation.' Psychoanalytic Inquiry 13: 274–95.

Feldman M. (1997) 'Projective identification: the analyst's involvement.' International Journal of Psycho-Analysis 78: 227–41.

Feldman S. (1956) 'Crying at the happy ending.' Journal of the American Psychoanalytic Association 4: 477–85.

Fenichel O. (1946) The Psychoanalytic Theory of Neurosis. London: Routledge and Kegan Paul.

Fonagy P. (1991) 'Thinking about thinking: some clinical and theoretical considerations in the treatment of a borderline patient.' International Journal of Psycho-Analysis 72: 639–56.

Freud A. (1958) 'Adolescence.' Psychoanalytic Study of the Child 13: 255–78.

Freud A. and Dann S. (1951) 'An experiment in group upbringing.' Psychoanalytic Study of the Child 6: 127–68.

Freud S. (1900) The Interpretation of Dreams. S.E. 4, 1–338 and S.E. 5, 339–626.

Freud S. (1913) 'Totem and taboo.' In Totem and Taboo and Other Works. S.E.13, 1–162.

Freud S. (1920) 'Beyond the pleasure principle'. In Beyond the Pleasure Principle, Group Psychology and other works. S E 18, 7–64.

Freud S. (1923) 'The ego and the super-ego.' In the Ego and the Id and Other Works. S.E. 19, 28–39.

Freud S. (1924) 'The economic problem of masochism in The Ego and the Id and Other Works. S.E.19, 157–70.

Friedman P. (1955) 'Journal of the Hillside Hospital. III, 1954.' Psychoanalytic Quarterly 24: 473–4.

Gabbard G.O. (1995) 'Countertransference: the emerging common ground.' International Journal of Psycho-Analysis 76: 475–85.

Garma A. (1962) 'The theory of the parent–infant relationship – contributions to discussion.' International Journal of Psycho-Analysis 43: 252–3.

Gifford S., Murawski B., Brazelton T. and Young G. (1966) 'Differences in individual development within a pair of identical twins.' International Journal of Psycho-Analysis 47: 261–8.

Girard R. (1988) Violence and the Sacred. London: The Athlone Press.

Glenn J. (1966) 'Opposite-sex twins.' Journal of the American Psychoanalytic Association 14: 736–59.

Glenn J. (1974a) 'Twins in disguise. II. Content, form and style in plays by Anthony and Peter Shaffer.' International Review of Psycho-Analysis 1: 373–81.

Glenn J. (1974b) 'Twins in disguise – a psychoanalytic essay on Sleuth and the Royal Hunt of the Sun.' Psychoanalytic Quarterly 43: 288–302.

Glenn J. (1986) 'Twinship themes and fantasies in the work of Thornton Wilder.' Psychoanalytic Study of the Child 41: 627–51.

Goldman H. (1988) 'Paradise destroyed: the crime of being born – a psychoanalytic study of the experience of evil.' Contemporary Psychoanalysis 24: 420–50.

Graves R. (1992) The Greek Myths. Combined Edition. Harmondsworth: Penguin Books.

Graves R. and Patai R. (1992) Hebrew Myths. Detroit, MI: Wayne State University Press.

Gringras P. and Chen W. (2001) 'Mechanisms for differences in monozygous twins.' Early Human Development 64: 105–17.

Grotstein J. (1979) 'Who is the dreamer who dreams the dream and who is the dreamer who understands it? – a psychoanalytic inquiry into the ultimate nature of being.' Contemporary Psychoanalysis 15: 110–69.

Hartmann H. (1964) 'Psychiatric studies of twins.' In: Essays on Ego Psychology. New York: International Universities Press, 1964, pp. 419–45 (quoted in Ortmeyer 1970).

Heimann P. (1942) 'A contribution to the problem of sublimation and its relation to processes of internalization.' International Journal of Psycho-Analysis 23: 8–17.

Hinshelwood R. D. (1989) A Dictionary of Kleinian Thought. London: Free Association Books.

Howell E. (1996) 'Dissociation in masochism and psychopathic sadism.' Contemporary Psychoanalysis 32: 427–53.

Jacobs E. G. and Mesnikoff A. M. (1962) 'Alternating psychoses in twins: report of four cases.' American Journal of Psychiatry. CXVII, 1961, abstract in Psychoanalytic Quarterly 31: 134.

Jacobson E. (1965) Meetings of the New York Psychoanalytic Society. Ed. J. Shorr. Psychoanalytic Quarterly 34: 637–8.

Joined: the World of Siamese Twins (2001) www.channel4. com/health/microsites/H/ health/magazine/conjoined/cases [3/10/01]

Joseph B. (1978) 'Different types of anxiety and their handling in the analytic situation.' International Journal of Psycho-Analysis 59: 223–7.

Joseph B. (1981) 'Towards the experiencing of psychic pain.' In: Psychic Equilibrium and Psychic Change. Selected papers of Betty Joseph. Ed. M. Feldman and E. Bott Spillius. London and New York: Tavistock/Routledge (1989), pp. 88–97.

Joseph B. (1983) 'On understanding and not understanding: some technical issues.' International Journal of Psycho-Analysis 64: 291–8.

Joseph B. (1985) 'Transference: the total situation.' International Journal of Psycho-Analysis 66: 447–54.

Joseph B. (1987) 'Projective identification: some clinical aspects.' In: Psychic Equilibrium and Psychic Change. Selected Papers of Betty Joseph. Ed. M. Feldman and E. Bott Spillius. London and New York: Tavistock/Routledge (1989), pp. 168–80.

Joseph E. D. (1959) 'An unusual fantasy in a twin with an inquiry into the nature of fantasy.' Psychoanalytic Quarterly 28: 189–206.

Joseph E. D. (1961) 'The psychology of twins.' Journal of the American Psychoanalytic Association 9: 158–66.

Joseph E. D. (1975) 'Psychoanalysis – science and research: twin studies as a paradigm.' Journal of the American Psychoanalytic Association 23: 3–31.

Joseph E. D. and Tabor J. H. (1961) 'The simultaneous analysis of a pair of identical twins and the twinning reaction.' Psychoanalytic Study of the Child 16: 275–99.

Kellaway K. (1997) 'Two little boys...' The Observer Review, 16 November.

Kennedy R. (1990) 'A severe form of breakdown in communication in the psychoanalysis of an ill adolescent.' International Journal of Psycho-Analysis 71: 309–19.

Klein G. (1962) 'Blindness and isolation.' Psychoanalytic Study of the Child 17: 82–93.

Klein M. (1932) The Psycho-analysis of Children. London: The Hogarth Press (1980).

Klein M. (1946) 'Notes on some schizoid mechanisms.' International Journal of Psycho-Analysis 27: 99–110.

Klein M. (1963) 'On the sense of loneliness.' In: Envy and Gratitude and Other Works. London: The Hogarth Press (1980), pp. 300–13.

Klotz H. P., Balier C and Javal I. (1962) 'Presentation of a Case of Mental Anorexia Which Required Hospitalization in a Female Identical Twin.' In: Revue De Médecine Psychosomatique. III, 1961, Psychoanalytic Quarterly 31: 436.

Kogan I. (1995) 'Love and the heritage of the past.' International Journal of Psycho-Analysis 76: 805–24.

Kohut H. (1957) 'The Arrow and the Lyre. A study of the role of love in the works of Thomas Mann.' Psychoanalytic Quarterly 26: 273–5.

Kohut H. (1971) The Analysis of the Self – a Systematic Approach to the Psychoanalytic Treatment of Narcissistic Personality Disorders. New York: International Universities Press.

Kohut H. (1984) How Does Analysis Cure? Chicago: University of Chicago Press.

Lacombe P. (1959) 'The problem of the identical twin as reflected in a masochistic compulsion to cheat.' International Journal of Psycho-Analysis 40: 6–12.

Laplanche J. and Pontalis J.-B. (1973) The Language of Psychoanalysis. London: Hogarth Press.

Larousse Encyclopedia of Mythology (1959). London: Paul Hamlyn.

Lash J. (1993) Twins and the Double. London: Thames and Hudson.

Laufer M. (1968) 'The body image, the function of masturbation, and adolescence – problems of the ownership of the body.' Psychoanalytic Study of the Child 23: 114–37.

Leonard M. (1953) Review of 'Twins: a study of three pairs of identical twins'. By Dorothy Burlingham. New York: International Universities Press, Inc.; London: Imago Publishing Co., Ltd. Psychoanalytic Quarterly 22: 577–80.

Leonard M. (1961) 'Problems in identification and ego development in twins.' Psychoanalytic Study of the Child 16: 300–320.

Levenson E. (1978) 'A perspective on responsibility.' Contemporary Psychoanalysis 14: 571–8.

Levi-Strauss C. (1955) 'The structural study of myth.' Journal of American Folklore 68: 113–44.

Lewin V. (1994) 'Working with a twin: implications for the transference.' British Journal of Psychotherapy 10: 499–510.

Lewin V. (2002) 'The twin in the transference.' In: On Ideas in Practice. Practice of Psychotherapy Series: Book 2. Eds B. Bishop, A. Klein, V O'Connell. London and New York: Karnac Books, pp. 3–24.

Lewis E. and Bryan E.M. (1988) 'Management of Perinatal Loss of a Twin.' British Medical Journal 297: 1321–3.

Lidz T. (1961) Quoted in Panel report by E. D. Joseph (1961): 'The psychology of twins.' Journal of the American Psychoanalytic Association 9: 158–66.

Lorand S. (1957) 'Dream interpretation in the Talmud (Babylonian and Graeco-Roman Period).' International Journal of Psycho-Analysis 38: 92–7.

Luzes P. (1990) 'Fact and fantasy in brother–sister incest.' International Review of Psycho-Analysis 17: 97–113.

Mack J. (1971) 'L'homme et sa psychose [Man and his psychosis].' Psychoanalytic Quarterly 40: 159–61.

Maenchen A. (1968) 'Object cathexis in a borderline twin.' Psychoanalytic Study of the Child 23: 438–56.

Major R. (1980) 'The voice behind the mirror.' International Review of Psycho-Analysis 7: 459–68.

Mann T. (1905) 'The blood of the Volsungs.' In: The German-Jewish Dialogue. An Anthology of Literary Texts, 1749–1993. Ed. R. Robertson. Oxford: Oxford University Press (1999), pp. 150–78.

Mann T. (1956) 'Freud and the future.' International Journal of Psycho-Analysis 37: 106–15.

Meissner W. (1994a) 'Psychoanalysis and ethics: beyond the pleasure principle.' Contemporary Psychoanalysis 30: 453–72.

Meissner W. (1994b) 'The theme of the double and creativity in Vincent Van Gogh.' Contemporary Psychoanalysis 30: 323–47.

Meltzer D. (1966) 'The relation of anal masturbation to projective identification.' International Journal of Psycho-Analysis 47: 335–42.

Meltzer D. (1967) The Psycho-analytical Process. Strath Tay, Perthshire: Clunie Press.

Meltzer D. (1968) 'Terror, persecution, dread – a dissection of paranoid anxieties.' International Journal of Psycho-Analysis 49: 396–400.

Meltzer D. (1974) 'Narcissistic foundation of the erotic transference.' Contemporary Psychoanalysis 10: 311–16.

Meltzer D. (1975) 'Adhesive identification.' Contemporary Psychoanalysis 11: 289–310.

Meltzer D. (1984) 'The conceptual distinction between projective identification (Klein) and container–contained (Bion).' In: Studies in Extended Metapsychology. Clinical Applications of Bion's Ideas. Strath Tay, Perthshire: Clunie Press, pp. 50–69.

Meltzer D. and Harris Williams M. (1988) The Apprehension of Beauty: The Role of Aesthetic Conflict in Development, Art and Violence. Strath Tay, Perthshire: Clunie Press.

Miller I. (1994) 'Psychoanalysis at the boundary of self and other.' Contemporary Psychoanalysis 30: 169–81.

Milton J. (1644) 'Areopagitica.' In: Areopagitica and Other Prose Works. London: J. M. Dent and Sons Ltd. Everyman's Library No. 795.

Mitchell J. (2000) Mad Men and Medusas. Reclaiming Hysteria and the Effect of Sibling Relationships on the Human Condition. London: Allen Lane/Penguin Press.

Mitrani J. (1994) 'On adhesive pseudo-object relations – part I: theory.' Contemporary Psychoanalysis 30: 348–66.

Modell A. (1991) 'A confusion of tongues or whose reality is it?' Psychoanalytic Quarterly 60: 227–44.

Money-Kyrle R. (1945) Review of: The Origin and Function of Culture by Géza Róheim. International Journal of Psycho-Analysis 26: 79–81.

Money-Kyrle R. E. (1968) 'Cognitive development.' International Journal of Psycho-Analysis 49: 691–8.

Money-Kyrle R. E. (1971) 'The aim of psycho-analysis.' In: The Collected Papers of Roger Money-Kyrle. Strath Tay, Perthshire: Clunie Press, pp. 442–49.

Moulton R. (1977) 'Women with double lives.' Contemporary Psychoanalysis 13: 64–84.

Myers W. A. (1976) 'Imaginary companions, fantasy twins, mirror dreams and depersonalization.' Psychoanalytic Quarterly 45: 503–24.

Myers W. A. (1979) 'Imaginary companions in childhood and adult creativity.' Psychoanalytic Quarterly 48: 292–307.

Nachmani G. (1979) Discussion. Contemporary Psychoanalysis 15: 446–53.

Nagera H. (1969) 'The imaginary companion – its significance for ego development and conflict solution.' Psychoanalytic Study of the Child 24: 165–96.

O'Neill J. A. (2001) 'Conjoined twins – whether to separate.' 10th International Congress on Twin Studies, London, July.

Omwake E. and Solnit A. (1961) '"It isn't fair" – the treatment of a blind child.' Psychoanalytic Study of the Child 16: 352–404.

Orr D.W. (1941) 'A psychoanalytic study of a fraternal twin.' Psychoanalytic Quarterly 10: 284–96.

Ortmeyer D. H. (1970) 'The we-self of identical twins.' Contemporary Psychoanalysis 6: 125–42.

Ortmeyer D. H. (1975) 'Comments and criticisms.' Contemporary Psychoanalysis 11: 511–12.

Parens H. (1988) 'Siblings in early childhood: some direct observational findings.' Psychoanalytic Inquiry 8: 31–50.

Pausanias. (1979) Guide to Greece. Volume 1: Central Greece. Harmondsworth: Penguin Books.

Petö E. (1946) 'The psycho-analysis of identical twins – with reference to inheritance.' International Journal of Psycho-Analysis 27: 126–9.

Pines M. (1984) 'Reflections on mirroring.' International Review of Psycho-Analysis 11: 27–42.

Piontelli A. (1989) 'A study on twins before and after birth.' International Review of Psycho-Analysis 16: 413–26.

Piontelli A. (2002) Twins: From Foetus to Child. London and New York: Routledge.

Plato (360 BCE) 'The Symposium.' In: The Essential Plato. Translated by Benjamin Jowett (1871). London: The Softback Preview, 1999: Book-of-the-Month Club Inc.

Priel B. (2002) 'Who killed Laius: on Sophocles' enigmatic message.' International Journal of Psycho-Analysis 83: 433–43.

Proner, K. (2000) 'Protomental synchrony: some thoughts on the earliest identification processes in a neonate.' International Journal of Infant Observation 3: 55–63.

Quinodoz J.-M. (1993) The Taming of Solitude. Separation Anxiety in Psychoanalysis. London and New York: Routledge.

Rank O. (1971) The Double. A Psychoanalytic Study. Translated and edited by H. Tucker. Chapel Hill, NC: The University of North Carolina Press.

Raphael-Leff J. (1990) 'If Oedipus was an Egyptian.' International Review of Psycho-Analysis 17: 309–35.

Rey H. J. (1988) 'That which patients bring to analysis.' International Journal of Psycho-Analysis 69: 457–70.

Rhode E. (1994) Psychotic Metaphysics. London: Karnac Books/The Clunie Press.

Roberts M. (1996) 'That makes two of us.' Observer, 5 May.

Rosenfeld H. (1964) 'On the psychopathology of narcissism: a clinical approach.' International Journal of Psycho-Analysis 45: 332–7.

Rosenfeld H. (1971a) 'A clinical approach to the psychoanalytic theory of the life and death instincts: an investigation into the aggressive aspects of narcissism.' International Journal of Psycho-Analysis 52: 169–78.

Rosenfeld H. (1971b) 'Contribution to the psychopathology of psychotic states: the importance of projective identification in the ego structure and the object relations of the psychotic patient.' In: Problems of Psychosis. The Hague: Excerpta Medica, pp. 115–28. Reprinted in: Melanie Klein Today. Developments in Theory and Practice. Volume 1: Mainly Theory (1988), ed. E. Bott Spillius, pp. 117-37.

Rosenfeld H. (1983) 'Primitive object relations and mechanisms.' International Journal of Psycho-Analysis 64: 261–7.

Rosenfeld, H. (1987) Impasse and Interpretation. London and New York: Tavistock.

Roth S. (1992) 'Discussion: a psychoanalyst's perspective on multiple personality disorder.' Psychoanalytic Inquiry 12: 112–23.

Rycroft C. (1990) 'On selfhood and self-awareness.' In Viewpoints, London: The Hogarth Press, pp. 147–62.

Sandbank A., Sandbank B. M. (2001) 'Twin parenting patterns.' 10th International Congress on twin Studies, London, July.

Sandler J. (1976) 'Countertransference and role-responsiveness.' International Review of Psycho-Analysis 3: 43–7.

Sandler J. (1993) 'On communication from patient to analyst: not everything is projective identification.' International Journal of Psycho-Analysis 74: 1097–1107.

Schore A. N. (1994) Affect Regulation and the Origin of the Self: The Neurobiology of Emotional Development. Hillsdale, NJ: Erlbaum.

Schore A. N. (1996) 'The experience dependent maturation of a regulatory system in the orbital prefrontal cortex and the origin of developmental psychopathology.' Development and Psychopathology 8: 59–87.

Schore A. N. (2001a) 'Minds in the making: attachment, the self-organising brain, and developmentally-oriented psychoanalytic psychotherapy.' British Journal of Psychotherapy 17: 299–328.

Schore A. N. (2001b) 'The effects of early relational trauma on right brain development, affect regulation, and infant mental health.' Infant Mental Health Journal 22: 201–69.

Segal H. (1957) 'Notes on symbol formation.' International Journal of Psycho-Analysis 38: 39–44.

Segal H. (1981) 'Contribution to the memorial meeting for Dr Wilfred Bion.' International Review of Psycho-Analysis 8: 3–14.

Segal H. and Britton R. (1981) 'Interpretation and primitive psychic processes: a Kleinian view.' Psychoanalytic Inquiry 1: 267–77.

Segal N. L. (1999) Entwined Lives, Twins and What They Tell Us about Human Behaviour. New York: Plume.

Segal N. L. (2001) 'When twins lose twins: implications for theory and practice.' 10th International Congress on Twin Studies, London, July.

Sheerin D. F. (1991) 'Fundamental considerations in the psychotherapy of an identical twin.' British Journal of Psychotherapy 8: 13–25.

Shengold L. (1974) 'The metaphor of the mirror.' Journal of the American Psychoanalytic Association 22: 97–115.

Shorr J. (1965) 'Meetings of the New York Psychoanalytic Society.' Psychoanalytic Quarterly 34: 637–8.

Singer E. (1978) 'Kaiserschmarn.' Contemporary Psychoanalysis 14: 579–84.

Smith J. (2002) 'Lilit, Malkah ha-Shadim.' www.lilitu.com/lilith/lilit.html [1/4/02].

Smith J. D. (1988) Psychological Profiles of Conjoined Twins: Heredity, Environment and Identity. Connecticut and London: Praeger.

Solms M. and Turnbull O. (2002) The Brain and the Inner World. An Introduction to the Neuroscience of Subjective Experience. London and New York: Karnac Books.

Spillius E. B. (1983) 'Some developments from the work of Melanie Klein.' International Journal of Psycho-Analysis 64: 321–32.

Spillius E. B. (1995) 'Introduction to the topic of projective identification.' Paper presented at Conference on Understanding Projective Identification, London, UCL, 28–29 October.

Spitz R. (1966) 'Comment on Dr Gifford's paper.' International Journal of Psycho-Analysis 47: 269–73.

Stainer B. (2002) 'We do have very similar tastes.' Independent, 18 February.

Steiner J. (1982) 'Perverse relationships between parts of the self: a clinical illustration.' International Journal of Psycho-Analysis 63: 241–51.

Steiner J. (1985) 'Turning a blind eye: the cover up for Oedipus.' International Review of Psycho-Analysis 12: 161–72.

Steiner J. (1987) 'The interplay between pathological organizations and the paranoid-schizoid and depressive positions.' International Journal of Psycho-Analysis 68: 69–80.

Steiner J. (1990a) 'Pathological organizations as obstacles to mourning: the role of unbearable guilt.' International Journal of Psycho-Analysis 71: 87–94.

Steiner J. (1990b) 'The retreat from truth to omnipotence in Sophocles' Oedipus at Colonus.' International Review of Psycho-Analysis 17: 227–37.

Steiner J. (1993) Psychic Retreats. Pathological Organisations in Psychotic, Neurotic and Borderline Patients. London and New York: Routledge.

Steiner J. (2002) Comments at Conference on Uncertainty (Melanie Klein Trust), Brunei Gallery of the School of Oriental Studies, London, June 15.

Stern D. N. (1971) 'A micro-analysis of mother–infant interaction: behaviors regulating social contact between a mother and her 3.5 month-old twins.' Journal of the Academy of Child Psychiatry 10: 501–17.

Stern D. N. (1985) The Interpersonal World of the Infant. A View from Psychoanalysis and Developmental Psychology. New York: Basic Books, Inc.

Swanson P. B. (2001) 'When is a twin not a twin?' 10th International Congress on Twin Studies, London, July.

Ulrich G. (1996) 'Thunderchildren: Yoruba twin figure carvings from Nigeria.' Lore Magazine, Milwaukee Public Museum, Inc.

Wallace M. (1996) The Silent Twins. London: Vintage.

Whitehead, C. (1986) 'The Horus–Osiris cycle: A psychoanalytic investigation.' International Review of Psycho-Analysis 13: 77–87.

Winnicott D. W. (1945) 'Primitive emotional development.' International Journal of Psycho-Analysis 26: 137–43.

Winnicott D.W. (1954) 'Metapsychological and clinical aspects of regression within the psycho-analytic set-up', In: Through Paediatrics to Psycho-Analysis. London: Hogarth Press (1987), pp. 278–94.

Wittels F. (1932) 'Reports of proceedings of societies.' Bulletin of the International Psychoanalytic Association 13: 389–99.

Wittels F. (1934) 'Mona Lisa and feminine beauty: a study in bisexuality.' International Journal of Psycho-Analysis 15: 25–40.

Wolf E. (1991) 'Advances in self psychology: the evolution of psychoanalytic treatment.' Psychoanalytic Inquiry 11: 123–46.

Wolff W. (1996) 'I am a twin.' Manna, Autumn, p. 6.

Woodward J. (1998) The Lone Twin. A Study in Bereavement and Loss. London and New York: Free Association Books.

Woodward J. (2001) 'The twin ourselves.' Olivia O'Leary interviewing Kate Barens and Joan Woodward, BBC Radio 4, 7/6/01.

Wright L. (1997) Twins. Genes, Environment and the Mystery of Human Identity. London: Phoenix.

Author Index

Subject Index